ENVIRONMENTAL TQM

Second Edition

John T. Willig, Editor

McGraw-Hill, Inc.

New York San Francisco Washington, D.C. Auckland Bogotá
Caracas Lisbon London Madrid Mexico City Milan
Montreal New Delhi San Juan Singapore
Sydney Tokyo Toronto

Executive Enterprises Publications Co., Inc.

New York

Library of Congress Cataloging-in-Publication Data

Willig, John T.
  Environmental TQM / John T. Willig—2nd ed.
    p. cm.
  ISBN 0-07-019844-6
  1. Environmental policy. 2. Total quality management. I. Title
  GE170.W55 1994
  363.7—dc20   93-26684
                                                               CIP

1 2 3 4 5 6 7 8 9 0   DOC/DOC   9 9 8 7 6 5 4 3

ISBN 0-07-019844-6

The sponsoring editor for this book was Gail F. Nalven and the
production supervisor was Donald F. Schmidt.

Printed and bound by R. R. Donnelley & Sons Company.

Table of Contents

INTRODUCTION

John T. Willig

In today's business world changes in consumer demands, technology, and global competition are forcing most companies to rethink their strategies in order to ensure survival. Managers are compelled to experiment and implement innovative ideas in running their operations.

Total Quality Management (TQM) has been embraced as a new approach for its wide applicability to management systems, the work environment, and manufacturing processes. As companies awake to the fact that good environmental practices are consistent with the short- and long-term goals of a well-integrated company, TQM's principles are being integrated into their environmental and pollution prevention programs.

Environmental TQM brings together for the first time first-hand reports on how leading companies are applying TQM practices to their operations. These firms are going beyond meeting regulatory compliance to gaining competitive advantage and improved profitability from these initiatives.

The practical tools and techniques covered in this timely, comprehensive work include how companies are

- Benchmarking towards environmental excellence
- Measuring environmental results
- Creating cross-functional teams
- Designing new products for the environment
- Reducing costs
- Improving employee involvement and morale
- Developing effective auditing practices and communicating with all their stakeholders

These topics are illustrated by recent case studies that will be of interest to environmental health and safety professionals and managers in many other functional areas. Contributors from leading companies share their experiences, ideas, and successful techniques that have increased the efficiency and effectiveness of their environmental performance. The industry's top consultants present their seminal findings and recommendations, which give companies better strategies and practical tools to compete in today's global marketplace.

Pollution prevention, sustainable development, and environmental responsibility have become key corporate goals for the nineties. *Environmental TQM* demonstrates how environmental improvements can be made to achieve these goals while bringing economic savings.

We welcome hearing your comments about this book, and would be eager to hear of other organizations' experiences in this area.

John T. Willig

Editor's note: For simplicity, throughout this book, the acronym TQEM is used for Total Quality Environmental Management—the practice of applying Total Quality Management (TQM) practices to an organization's environmental efforts.

JTW

Section I

ACHIEVING WORLDWIDE COMPETITIVE ADVANTAGE

1

TQM AND STRATEGIC ENVIRONMENTAL MANAGEMENT

Gene Blake

Beyond the avoided costs for noncompliance lies an area of economic opportunity. Strategic approaches are necessary to tap these opportunities, but only recently have the principles of Total Quality Management been considered for environmental applications. This article identifies common principles in strategic environmental planning and thematic bridges to TQM philosophies. By applying TQM to strategic environmental planning, an environmental manager can thus address both avoided cost and environmental opportunity to improve overall corporate strategic advantage.

The application of "strategic environmental planning" to business principles is a relatively new venture. Although corporations have applied strategic principles for years, dramatically rising costs for environmental compliance have caused companies to consider whether strategic planning approaches also can be applied to more efficiently manage environmental responsibilities. The forces driving strategic planning are currently two: a heightened interest in the environment both within and external to corporations and increasing recognition of the impact environmental issues have on the quarterly and annual bottom line.

Gene Blake is a vice president with Stone & Webster Environmental Services in Boston and a cofounder of the Tufts University Center for Environmental Management and of Tufts' Master of Science degree program in Hazardous Materials Management. He also established the Tufts Environmental Management Institute, a summer studies program for environmental professionals.

Most companies have established environmental manager positions to address the adverse bottom line impacts. But an emerging trend in the job description of some environmental managers is the development of plans and actions to create competitive cost advantages, not just mitigate losses.

A third driving force in strategic environmental planning is emerging, especially for multinationals. International developments in political, economic, and environmental arenas offer complex challenges to environmental managers. The media and some economic analysts have identified the potential opportunities in the international marketplace for the enterprising businessperson, but receiving little attention is the fact that concurrent with the opportunities will be an unprecedented application of environmental principles and legislation. Our civilization has yet to witness the growth of a national or regional economy that is fundamentally tied to environmentally sound operating principles, but this challenge is being presented to countries throughout the world. Events such as the recent United Nations Environment Program in Brazil could offer a view through the looking glass toward a new eco-environmental planning concept. Although international conferences can offer a picture of where we wish to go and what obstacles we need to overcome, they are generally not a good forum for identifying exactly how we will accomplish our objectives in environmental management.

In fact, as our own economy emerges from its present lack of productivity, it too will be asked to evolve in the face of heightened regulatory scrutiny and imposing environmental protections. The provisions of the Clean Air Act amendments may cost business several billion dollars a year. RCRA corrective action cleanups and investigations will run into the hundreds of millions. The reauthorization of RCRA and the Clean Water Act will add to the freight that must be paid to operate in an environmentally conscious way. Whether or not one agrees with the direction of environmental legislation, the potential impacts to business appear stunning. We learned some time ago that there was no free lunch, but did we expect that the bill would be so high?

In the midst of the environmental legislative storm, some have suggested that an investigation of our definition of "quality" might offer a reasonable path toward more responsible environmental management. This perception has been underscored by a principle some now consider a trend: Environmental management should be viewed as an opportunity rather than as a problem to be solved. EPA's development of the Clean Air Act amendments with an emphasis on market incentives makes further use of business principles in environmental planning. It seems only reasonable, then, that other aspects of business practice be considered for their application to environmental management. Conversations have turned to Deming, Juran, Crosby, and other "Quality Coaches," who have dedicated substantial effort to defining the key elements of quality and the strategies for applying these principles.

The questions facing those who wish to apply these principles are: Do you believe that applying quality principles will help your business be profitable? And, do quality principles apply to the management of our environmental responsibilities? Though your view of TQM's ability to improve corporate profitability may not yet be resolved, I would like to point out some areas in which TQM and strategic environmental planning offer common ground for improved environmental management. If strategic environmental planning offers potential economic rewards, and if TQM is a means to implement that planning, you may have answered the first question.

Within the strategic environmental planning process there are at least five key principles for environmental managers and business executives:

1. Make environment a corporate commitment that each employee understands.
2. Put a total price on pollution, not just the cost of control.
3. Support the U.S. technological advantage for pollution control.
4. Fairly value sources of pollution beyond smokestacks and outfalls.
5. Be sure products are "green" before investing in them.

When one reviews the work of Deming and others, it is found that there is little distance between TQM and strategic environmental planning principles. In fact, good planning seems to be an application or outgrowth of TQM, rather than a separate activity. For instance, Deming is a strong advocate of worker participation in decision making. In his work *Out of the Crisis*,[1] he states that "constancy of purpose for improvement of product and service" is a guiding principle. Clearly, then, it is not enough to develop a corporate environmental policy within the upper stratosphere of your organization and translate that message via memo and meeting. You must have a plan to encourage the constant and continuous application of your environmental principles where the rubber meets the road—that is, with every company employee.

- *Make environment a corporate commitment*

The first step in implementing strategic environmental planning may not be the commonly taken approach of conducting plant audits, but might be training and encouragement of employees to recognize and control quality directly. This approach also speaks to Deming's third management principle, "cease dependence on inspection to achieve quality." Deming is implying that quality can be created not by inspecting the results, but by working it into every fiber of the product or service. Although I have heard many environmental managers logically espouse the credo that "there is no zero" when referring to a company's ability to control waste or pollution, Deming's work may imply that the acceptance of this philosophy runs counter to effective quality management.

Deming further empowers the worker by emphasizing the value of training. That is, environmental strategic planning is never "done for the day," but is a way of doing everything throughout the day, and training is necessary to assist the worker in the change in approach. A memo or slogan won't do. While this sounds like religion, most environmental managers will recognize that it *is* religion. Perhaps this is why Mr. Deming said, "It is time to adopt a new religion in America." Training is an investment in the corporate commitment to environmental management that will allow the corporate philosophy to be lived, not merely posted on a bulletin board.

- *Put a total price on pollution*

The second strategic environmental principle has driven both citizens and the business community to incorporate waste minimization or toxic use reduction into the workplace. By taking pollution issues from the end of the pipe back into the process and indeed back to the receiving dock, and by wholly evaluating their effect on your environmental compliance costs, you are beginning to do real strategic planning. The translation to Deming's work may be the following: asking employees to "do their best," Deming says, is not enough. People must know what to do. Also, when the incoming material is not of proper quality, or if the equipment used is ineffective, quality may not be controlled by asking workers to do their best. The waste minimization issue often involves capital investment; an interpretation of Deming's work can lead to the viewpoint that there is more to quality management than employee training. It reminds one of the old computer industry saw, "garbage in, garbage out." Changes in raw materials or production processes, based on a total pricing of your pollution, may lead to real quality management.

- *Support the U.S. technological advantage*

Supporting the U.S. technological advantage for pollution control appears to offer real potential to multinationals looking to compete overseas. Whereas companies may have hesitated to implement this advantage to date, or in some cases may have actually been prevented from doing so by host countries, a review of current trends in worldwide environmental enforcement underscores the potential advantage. Within the last year alone, Mexico's dramatic steps toward implementation of its environmental regulations have created a more level playing field for "clean companies" looking to compete in the marketplace.

- *Fairly value sources of pollution*

Fairly evaluating sources of pollution beyond the obvious, such as a smokestack or a pipe outfall, which is my fourth strategic principle, can be related to Deming's third point of quality management: cease dependence on inspection; require evidence that quality is built in. But his ninth management point, "break down barriers between staff areas," also applies. The transition areas within production or service companies offer wide gaps in quality; Deming encourages their elimination. The cost of pollution can be quite personal when all sources are not fairly evaluated and when the actions of the business sectors of a company are considered to be independent of one another. One company in New England managed its air and water discharges well, but avoided close scrutiny of groundwater pollution potential. By not fairly evaluating the company's discharge practices to include other than obvious sources, one company executive was one day placed in the awkward position of having to respond to his young daughter's inquiry about why the newspaper was saying that Daddy's company was a polluter. It's not easy to explain a lack of coordination in business sectors to children.

In Deming's twelfth point, he also encouraged removal of barriers that rob people of pride of workmanship. Worker pride is not easily maintained when the local headlines decry the environmental practices of the company. The economic implications reach far beyond fines and penalties.

- *Be sure products are "green"*

My fifth strategic point, evaluating the "greenness" of the products you employ in your processes, speaks to several of Deming's ideas. Clearly, the potential for a worker to implement quality is enhanced when the components making up that product share the same quality objectives. Related to this, Deming encourages a movement away from awarding business on the basis of price alone. An interpretation of this idea could be that by working with a supplier to encourage the development of the raw products or materials that will lead to improved environmental quality, and by supporting that supplier's investment in this development process by buying its products, full cycle environmental benefits are realized.

In the competitive equation, environmental strategic planning offers a means of setting apart from others your work, your product, your service. By evaluating environmental costs throughout your activities, a fair price may be obtained for the cost of doing business responsibly. But the implementation strategy for your plan may be its most important element. I encourage you to consider the application of quality principles. But beware, for Deming has warned that "a big ship, travelling at full speed, requires distance and time to turn." Quality principles are not for the quarterly-minded.

Note

1.   W. Edwards Deming, *Out of the Crisis,* Massachusetts Institute of Technology, Center for Advanced Engineering Study, 1986.

2

CORPORATE ENVIRONMENTAL MANAGEMENT SURVEY SHOWS SHIFT FROM COMPLIANCE TO STRATEGY

Tony Lent and Richard P. Wells

The Abt study of forty-one mostly Fortune 200 nonservice firms forms a new picture of environmental management. We present data indicating that environmental management is becoming central to corporate strategy and is being managed as an arena of competition rather than as a compliance-driven function. We look at environmental management's new role through four lenses: its relationship to strategic planning; its evolving management structures that show environment increasingly integrated into the main functions of the business; innovation in corporate environmental investments reflecting new drivers beyond compliance; and new management systems and measures of firm-wide performance that demonstrate that environment is being seen increasingly as an arena of competitive concern.

We argue that much of the change is driven by three realities. First, as customers integrate environmental values into their conceptions of product quality, they are buying more products with identifiably environmental attributes. This change translates environmental management, historically a cost center, into a potential source of sales

Tony Lent *is a consultant to Abt Associates.* **Richard P. Wells** *is a vice president and director of Abt Associates' corporate environmental consulting practice in Cambridge, Massachusetts.*

revenue, a change which cannot be underestimated. Second, recent life-threatening damage to the global ecosystem and atmosphere reframes environmental management. This moves firms toward a systemic and global approach matched to the globalization of competitive and market concerns, and it places environmental management in the strategic sphere. And third, pollution prevention in its cross-fertilization with total quality management is driving firms to focus on managing environment as an integral part of product management, and is helping them to reassess environmental performance as a contributor to productivity and innovation.

Environmental management is becoming fundamental to business and product strategy in a significant proportion of leading firms in nonservice industries. Of a sample of forty-one mostly Fortune 200 firms surveyed, fully three-fourths claim that environment is a central strategic issue.[1] (See "**Survey Findings**" box for more details of the study results.) The increasing influence of environment in business is due to rapidly emerging environmental markets; the public availability of environmental data; changed customer expectations of product and industry environmental performance; increasingly complex international environmental regulation; and the dawning realization that improving environmental performance provides many of the same productivity gains that focusing on eliminating defects does in manufacturing. Environment not only affects the tail end of firm operations but is also central in marketing, distribution, manufacturing, product development, supplier and customer relations, and profitability—core areas of corporate strategic concern.

This article presents a framework explaining the increasingly strategic role of the environment in corporate decisionmaking and it presents data that show environmental management is evolving into one of the core functions of business. It does so by examining five arenas:

- The broadening mission of environmental management and the new rules of the game;
- The ascendance of environment to the strategic level, looking at top management commitment and the expanding roles of senior environmental executives;
- The distribution of environmental management across the primary functions of the firm: product development, marketing, purchasing, manufacturing;

- Investment within environmental management, which shows the discipline focusing on business and product management issues and new external forces, moving away from a regulatory compliance focus; and
- The emergence of environment as a competitive arena, as exemplified by evolving management systems such as environmental total quality management (TQM), rewards and incentives for environmental performance, and the development of industry measures and benchmarks of environmental performance.

THE BROADENING MISSION OF ENVIRONMENTAL MANAGEMENT

Environmental management is one of the most rapidly changing areas of management today. The rules of the game, once simply interpreted as regulation, are now written by the joint committee of markets, competition, public opinion, the ecology, and government. These rules multiply as our knowledge of the nexus between industry and environment broadens. In response, environmental management programs change shape and multiply. As environmental challenges become more rigorous, the management resources applied to environmental areas become increasingly broad. This is causing environmental management to expand beyond its initial focus of effluents outside the firm, past plant floor boundaries, and across the main functions of the firm. It helps to start with a historical view of the evolution of environmental management.

Corporate environmental management was founded in the 1970s as Congress required technology-based standards first for water under the Clean Water Act and subsequently for air and hazardous wastes under the Clean Air Act and the Resource Conservation and Recovery Act, respectively. The response to these laws was a technically-based management approach that was tactical and defensive. The environment was introduced to corporate management as a cost-center.

During the decade that followed, environmental laws multiplied, dramatically increasing the expense and administrative burden of compliance. The high costs of compliance became a new driver leading firms by the mid-eighties to focus not just on pollution control but on investment in its reduction. Environmental management began its migration into other functions of the business when pollution engineers began to work on improving manufacturing processes, lowering pollution at its source, and lowering compliance costs.

Survey Findings

In corporate strategy we find environment taking on a central role. Seventy-seven percent of senior management define environment as critical or important to strategic decisions. Backing up this commitment, CEOs meet once a month or quarterly to address the issue. And the senior environmental executive often meets directly with the CEO.

In most of the companies contacted, environmental management has escaped its traditional borders. Environmental executives often have roles in other areas of the firm such as strategic planning, product development, R&D, marketing, and purchasing. Simultaneously, *nonenvironmental* functions are beginning to take on responsibility for environmental management: 63 percent of the sample indicated manufacturing management involvement; 57 percent, R&D and product development; 30 percent, purchasing; 28 percent, marketing; and 18 percent, finance and accounting. The involvement of outside disciplines in environmental management is a sure sign that the field is becoming more focused on designing environmental concerns into strategic and product planning.

Reflecting the discipline's new status is greater senior management involvement. More than 70 percent of firms in our sample have formed senior executive task forces to handle environmental concerns.

The role of the senior environmental executive is greatly expanded: 60 percent now have some input to strategy and many regularly attend corporate strategic planning meetings. In addition, their new responsibilities provide the first glimpse that the field is becoming pivotal in the main functions of the firm. Fifty-six percent of environmental executives reported having responsibility in R&D and product development; 30 percent have marketing responsibility; 18 percent, purchasing; and 20 percent, finance and accounting.

Looking within environmental management, we found changed investment priorities that reflected an expansion of environmental concerns beyond pollution control to the strategic sphere. The top four management challenges identified by senior environmental executives were pollution prevention, product development, compliance, and marketing. Regulation is no longer the motivating force for environmental management.

Fledgling and new programs planned for the next year underline this. The top four new efforts are marketing, product development, the measurement of environmental performance competitively, and monitoring global change issues. The areas of least new investment were compliance, auditing, and remediation.

Environmental performance is becoming a part of the product development process at a third of the firms in our sample. This indicates a shift toward integrating environment into product strategy and toward designing environmental risks out of the business instead of managing them at end of the pipe. In two cases we found environmental criteria institutionalized in corporate design standards. More than half of the firms questioned were experimenting with life-cycle analysis.

Pollution prevention is now the locus of most corporate activity. Environmental executives consistently rank this effort as making the greatest contribution to environmental performance. It is significant in providing firms with an initial framework and impetus for developing measurement systems and indices of successful performance beyond regulation. In pollution prevention, TQM and environmental management are cross-pollinating, making both more robust.

Investigating firms' environmental efforts, we find that they lack some fundamental tools and methodologies necessary for environmental management to make a significant contribution to corporate strategy and growth. Two are clear: Measurements that tie environmental performance to firm performance and the market, and financial indicators of success. Only a small fraction of firms measure corporate environmental activities' impact on the environment beyond compliance. Environmental activities' relationship to customer satisfaction, firm reputation, or sales revenues remains uncharted ground.

Although the data presented make it clear that environmental management is now a source of potential revenue, not just cost, firms have generally failed to weave a financial perspective into the function. Accounting systems are not yet able to model environmental costs in product standard costs. Not a firm in our sample was able to model how environmental activities affect both revenue and cost generation.

We conclude that measuring performance and applying financial tools within the discipline are two hurdles to its continuing maturation.

By the late eighties, the EPA still dominated firms' thinking on environmental management, when a new requirement, the Toxics Release Inventory (TRI), helped to catalyze a series of strategic shifts in environmental management. The TRI was a watershed for three reasons: first, the TRI gave firms a comprehensive reporting model to evaluate a broad array of outputs. The sheer volume of waste surprised many firms and helped reinforce the validity of pollution prevention. Second, the TRI began to harness market forces and voluntarism, moving away from the command and control model. It encouraged environmental management to act like any other market-driven part of the firm. Finally, the TRI focuses on a broad range of chemicals and environmental media instead of on specific ones, allowing firms to assess environmental impacts in the systemic way they actually affect business processes and operations. Previous laws diverted environmental management resources to a media-by-media approach.

The TRI set the stage for pollution prevention to become the dominant idea in environmental management, but it focused exclusively on *releases* of chemicals, not on their use or incorporation into products. Pollution prevention is now serving as an entry point for environmental management to move to increasingly strategic roles. Pollution prevention concentrates its effort on manufacturing process design and planning. From the learnings and benefits of pollution prevention, many firms have now begun to extend their efforts to product development—to design environmental problems out of products from their inception—as well as to supplier management. Supplier management of environmental performance is notable as the first example of environmental management moving entirely beyond the boundary of the firm.

Although these evolutionary changes are strategic in that environmental thinking now enters into product development, manufacturing, supplier management, and marketing, the management of corporate environmental activities remains largely tactical and nonintegrative—it does not have a firm-wide or general management perspective. Instead, it has maintained a risk mitigation mindset. That mindset has not collided with changed external realities until now.

Whereas environmental management evolved gradually from the seventies to the late eighties, the greener market, global change, and now competitive pressures have burst onto the scene in the past three years, rendering regulation just one of four drivers of environmental performance. Firms are responding to new markets for environmentally sound products; they are looking at their industry's contribution and response to global change; and they are beginning to see environmental performance as a key factor in competitive advantage. Corporate environmental management is searching for a way to fill its new strategic role.

The New Rules of the Game

In the last few years, in addition to increasingly complex regulations, three new factors have appeared on the scene that are raising environmental management to the strategic sphere of corporate management.

First is the market shift to environmental performance as a criterion for product quality and firm reputation. This shift translates corporate environmental performance into a revenue source—a benefit for corporations that have always thought of environmental management as a form of risk mitigation. Environmental performance now affects shareholders' and communities' goodwill toward the firm as well as employees' and customers' feelings about a company. This trend is pivotal in linking environmental management to strategy, because it places environmental issues at the center of a firm's mission in meeting changing customers requirements. It is also critical to understand the source of this demand on the part of markets and stakeholders.

Fifty-one percent of U.S. consumers made environmentally-based purchases last year across a wide range of product types.[2] The challenge now is to communicate and market environmental performance in a comprehensible way and for environmental management to measure its impact on sales. That BMW, a world leader in automotive technology, intends to recycle its cars by the decade's end is a sign that the demand for environmental performance is real. That the Big Three would team up to launch an R&D joint venture on recyclability is testimony that this trend is growing.

Spurring this demand is a public that now has access to data on firm performance made available through the TRI and through annual reports covering environmental performance. This information is scrutinized and rebroadcast by the investment community, the non-profit community, and by focused green-consumer advocacy groups.

The second fact is that environmental performance is beginning to be viewed as a contributor to competitive advantage much as manufacturing excellence has been in the eighties. That pollution prevention pays is an axiom of the discipline, but it misses the larger point by focusing on costs. The result of excellence in environmental management is higher productivity. Zero waste is a central theme of environmental management because of pollution prevention. And it is here that environmental management and total quality management merge. Firms that have already implemented TQM programs are seeing the parallel; when environmental "defects" are eliminated, from a product, not only is the defect eliminated but so is the process or technology that caused it, along with the overhead burden associated with managing the defect. The gain in wealth derives not only from a change to a benign product but from lowered management costs and resource-efficient operations. In the case of pollution prevention, firms spend fewer resources buying, storing, tracking, and managing pollutants; and more resources are expended on the product. These efforts result in more than cost savings; they come as well from a higher quality product and a market that rewards environmental leadership.

Do firms make this connection? Within environmental management there is a race to gauge environmental performance based on the assumption that it is a new competitive arena. Sixty percent of the firms in our sample were working on an environmental TQM effort, and 30 percent were trying to benchmark. Two even spoke of using environmental investment as a way to set an industry standard and gain leadership advantage.

Finally, the ozone hole and stakeholder reactions to it have played an important role. Before the Montreal Protocol, corporations maintained a medically based view of environmental affairs. This view relegated environmental management to the edge of business process, away from strategy. The corporate response to CFC elimination provided an opportunity for corporations and government to work together on an environmental issue with global impact. The risk-management/human-health framework that founded environmental management cannot contain the aggregate role that business now plays in the environment after this event. This shift reframes the mission of environmental management in a globalized and strategic management context.

Finally, environmental management is a strategic issue because it is the only discipline that begins to provide the tools through which sustainable economic performance can be discovered. Sustainable development is an idea that has been picking up speed in most developed countries outside the United States ever since the Brundtland Commission Report in 1987. The idea of sustainable development is basically that of doing business in a very resource-efficient manner so that future generations are guaranteed the natural resources necessary for survival. The business benefit is that managing for natural resource efficiency is one of the greatest engines of productivity improvement. Japan has always had a national economy about twice as resource-efficient as the United States, so it is not surprising that MITI, the Japanese industrial planning agency, has integrated sustainable development as one of its four priorities in the next century. Canada has also seized on sustainable development as a source of national advantage.

THE ASCENDANCE OF ENVIRONMENT TO STRATEGY

Seventy-seven percent of senior executive managements now see the environment as either "a vital part of most strategic decisions" (35 percent) or an "important part of many strategic decisions" (42 percent). Only 5 percent view environment as mainly a matter of regulatory compliance. (See **Figure 1.**)

But it is one thing to claim a policy or strategy on environmental management and another to integrate it across the entire business. If a firm embraces environment as central to its business, one would expect to see significant new responsibilities being shifted to senior environmental management and environmental initiatives driven from

Figure 1

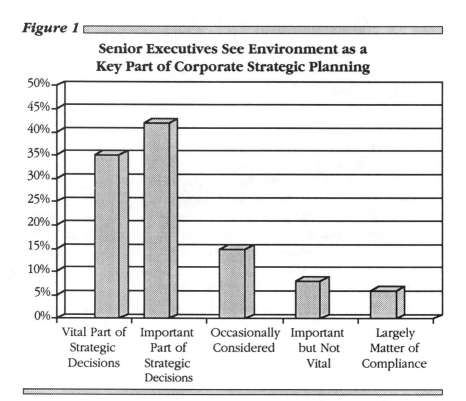

Senior Executives See Environment as a Key Part of Corporate Strategic Planning

outside of the traditional environmental management sphere. After all, the financial, marketing, and product expertise necessary to execute a change in strategy lie elsewhere in the firm. We find that both of these premises were supported by the information provided to us.

Top management is getting involved directly. CEOs are including environmental meetings on their agendas frequently. We find that 16 percent meet once a week or more, 25 percent address the subject at least once a month, and another 28 percent meet once a quarter. A concrete example of the new management commitment is the pervasive use of a senior executive task force to map environmental strategy and policy; more than 70 percent of firms in our sample had formed such work groups—possibly the most compelling evidence of a shift in thinking in the environmental area.

Environmental Executive Role Expanding

In addition to their traditional responsibilities managing compliance, public affairs, and oversight of plant performance, the senior environmental executive is newly involved in corporate strategy and has begun to gain responsibility across the main functions of the enterprise.

Seventy percent of senior environmental executives say they have some involvement in corporate strategy. This is borne out by their attendance in corporate strategic planning meetings: 5 percent are always included, 35 percent are regularly included, and 40 percent are sometimes included in these meetings. Only 15 percent are rarely or never included. They also are meeting directly with the CEO.

As firms begin to think more strategically about environmental issues, they are tending to integrate those considerations into the functional areas as a means of designing environmental risks out of the business and of capturing potential marketing rewards.

The environmental expert is gaining responsibilities in other functional areas as those parts of the corporation realize the potential impact of environmental issues to their operations. We looked outside the traditional environmental function and found that 55 percent of environmental executives now claim responsibility in the R&D and product development area; 33 percent say they have marketing responsibility; 18 percent are involved in purchasing; and 20 percent have responsibility in finance or accounting. This could indicate the beginnings of a shift in the locus from environmental management to other disciplines, or it could just indicate that environmental executives are serving as internal consultants to other functions. To follow up on the idea, we turned the question around after open-ended phone interviews disclosed that many new efforts were being headed up by nonenvironmental managers.

DISTRIBUTING ENVIRONMENTAL MANAGEMENT ACROSS THE FIRM

The boundaries between environmental management and other functions have begun to blur. This makes sense in a strategic model of environmental management, for if the environment is to be integrated into the core functions, they will need to work together to apply their expertise to the environmental front. Pollution prevention is one catalyst for increasing cross-functionalization because it focuses efforts on eliminating pollution at the root cause. This process leads to the involvement of manufacturing, planning, and purchasing after firms trying to solve problems within manufacturing find that alternative process technology and chemistry and product design are needed.

To assess the extent of boundary blurring in environmental management we asked firms to indicate in which functions *nonenvironmental* managers had environmental responsibility on a full- or part-time basis. If anything in our study indicated a structural change within environmental management, the number of nonenvironmental functions with growing environmental responsibility was it. (See **Figure 2**.) As pollution prevention is aimed at manufacturing, it makes sense that many environmental efforts are now spearheaded by manufacturing managers; 63 percent of firms had manufacturing management with environmental responsibility.

More than half of the firms in our sample had some environmental responsibility located in product development and R&D. Market, technology, and regulatory issues merge in product development. Criteria to increase potential environmental sales and minimize environmental risks can be handled simultaneously and integrated with other design-for-quality factors such as ergonomics, reliability, and ease-of-use.

Purchasing, quality assurance, and marketing follow in a second tier behind manufacturing and product development at between 30 percent and 25 percent involvement in environmental management. Purchasing management responsibility for environment is significant because it denotes a break from the company-centered approach to environmental management. This time the boundary of environmental management moves beyond the end-of-pipe/front-of-pipe model to the supplier—an entity outside the business.

Figure 2

Environment Increasingly Is Managed across Primary Functions of the Business

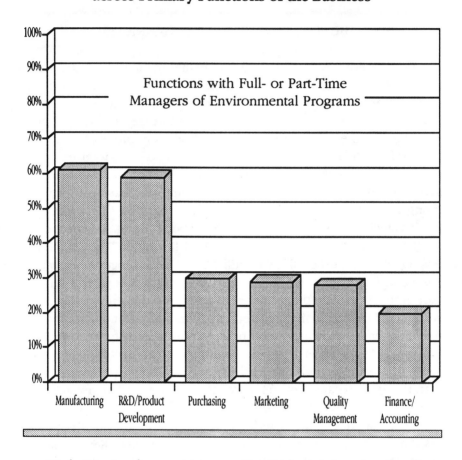

Functions with Full- or Part-Time Managers of Environmental Programs

Manufacturing   R&D/Product Development   Purchasing   Marketing   Quality Management   Finance/ Accounting

Marketing involvement is extensive. Perhaps it is a sign that firms are beginning to systematically assess environmental positioning as part of their marketing strategy. Fifty-eight percent of firms claimed to be marketing environmental product attributes, while 26 percent said they were actually marketing a niche green product.

Finally, the least involved in environmental management (with only 18 percent of respondents having environmental responsibilities) was finance and accounting. This is significant, especially if one recognizes that environment has both cost-and revenue-related outcomes. Until financial expertise is brought into environmental management, there can be no accurate measures of the impact of environmental performance on the bottom line.

Although the data are inconclusive, the pattern that emerges by looking at the involvement of nonenvironmental managers provides us with a rough map of the management "distance" between environment and the other functions. If managers in operations, manufacturing, and product development are gaining responsibility for environmental programs, then the transfer of specialized management knowledge will frequently occur between these arenas and environmental management. On the other hand, finance professionals who currently have the least overlap with environmental management may be least likely to lend expertise to the environmental function.

NEW PROGRAM INVESTMENTS
RESPOND TO CHANGING FORCES

As the external forces affecting environmental management change, so do its programmatic objectives. To capture this change we asked four sets of questions. The first was aimed at unearthing what senior environmental executives perceived to be their top three management challenges. We differentiated this from their top objectives, which we believed would focus too heavily on present efforts.

The second set was intended to draw a picture of where current environmental management dollars and resources were going, contrasted to perceived contribution to environmental performance. The third and fourth were aimed at differentiating between new and old investment in the field.

Because environmental management has been driven for the past decade by regulation and risk mitigation, three main functions— compliance, auditing, and remediation—not surprisingly consume the vast proportion of resources. However, the list of current management challenges provided a different view. Those mentioned almost equally out of 151 free-form responses were: pollution prevention, product development, and regulation, followed closely by marketing. Regulation is still a key force, but it is one among four.

Investing for Performance and Productivity

When we looked at new program investment, an interesting pattern emerged (see **Figure 3**). Although compliance, auditing, and remediation programs claim the lion's share of corporate environmental resources, over the last twelve months and during the coming year, environmental executives most frequently mention that they expect to make their new program investments in nontraditional areas such as environmental marketing, efforts to incorporate environmental concerns and attributes in the product development process (design for

Figure 3

New Environmental Program Investment Reflects Changing Focus

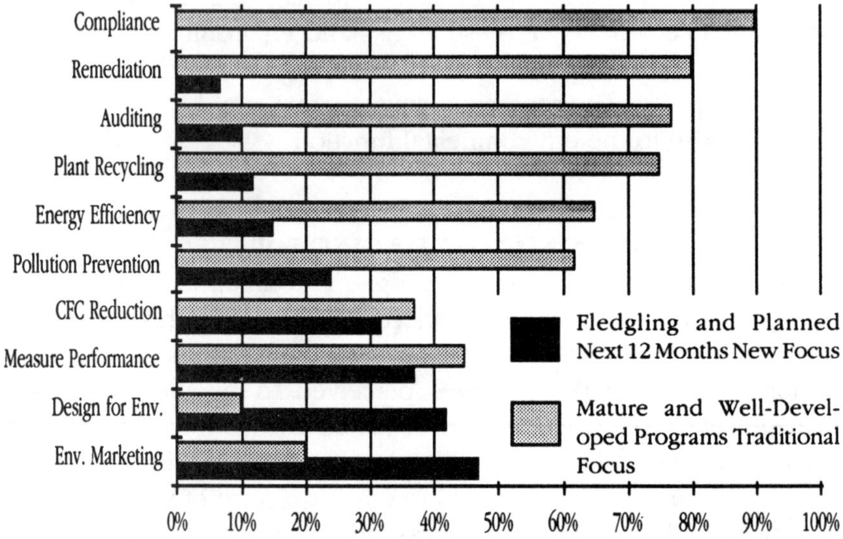
Compliance
Remediation
Auditing
Plant Recycling
Energy Efficiency
Pollution Prevention
CFC Reduction
Measure Performance
Design for Env.
Env. Marketing
Fledgling and Planned Next 12 Months New Focus
Mature and Well-Developed Programs Traditional Focus
0%
10%
20%
30%
40%
50%
60%
70%
80%
90%
100%

environment), and measuring and tracking the performance of the entire corporate environmental effort.

This new investment pattern has significance for two reasons. First, it mirrors the new drivers posited in the introduction: that environment is now a marketing/sales issue; that the prospect of global change is reframing environmental management for some industries; and that regulation, marketing issues, and global change taken together transform environmental management into a competitive issue. That it has become a competitive issue is demonstrated by the new efforts we see to measure and benchmark environmental performance.

Taken together, the changing pattern of investment suggests that environmental management is now an *arena* of firm *performance* that may be reinterpreted as a contributor to corporate wealth and productivity (cost, sales, and efficiency gains). In contrast, the risk management concept that has driven the structure and self-perception environmental management for the last two decades is antiquated, because it does not easily permit the transition to a new era in which environmental management can be a profit center.

To identify the most successful efforts, we asked, "Which programs do you believe make an outstanding contribution to environmental performance?" Here we would expect to see traditional programs providing the most benefit to performance, as they have been around for years and are well understood. The surprising finding is that pollution prevention ranked first. Compliance ranked fifth.

Even in traditional arenas of environmental management such as plant-level performance, we see that the focus has moved ahead of compliance. Only 6 percent focused their plant-level programs on compliance, having not added emissions reduction goals. Twenty-seven percent periodically reviewed operations, seeking opportunities for reduction, and around half have stated reduction goals and review operations to review progress against these goals. The most proactive segment (20 percent) additionally tied emissions reduction goals to performance evaluation and compensation for plant managers.

Design for Environment

Product development and R&D are the reservoir of sustained profitability for most leadership product companies and the intellectual source from which they renew themselves. During the eighties, with a raft of new competitive pressures across U.S. industry, firms began to refocus the product development function on manufacturing, bringing the customer closer to the product design process and, most recently, product cycle time reduction. Firms have gone through design paradigms so fast—from design for manufacturability, to design for assembly, to design for quality—that a number of different schools have merged under the heading DFX (design for X).

Design for environment (DFE)[3] looks well-positioned to be the next step in the renaissance of product development. This is extremely important to environmental management because product development is the one place in the firm where market currents, technology trends, and regulatory demands can blend into product features and attributes. It is the place where environment as a market issue and environment as an efficiency or regulatory issue can be integrated into product as well. Only when environment has roosted in the crow's nest of product development on an equal footing with the other design-for-X schools can full strategic planning for environment occur. Today this effort is in its infancy.

We looked at design for environment in three ways. Broadly speaking, we asked firms to evaluate the importance of environmental considerations in the design of product processes and packaging. We looked at product development itself to see when and how environmental criteria were included. And we tried to flesh out the extent to which certain measures of design for environment have been implemented.

Sixty percent of firms see environmental considerations as extremely important or very important in both product and packaging development and design. They have started to implement the use of environmental criteria in product design. Forty-six percent claim that environmental criteria are a part of the normal product development process. About 25 percent say that environmental criteria are used in the earliest phase of product development: product definition. Twenty percent even claim to have incorporated environmental criteria into their corporate design standards.

Although the concept of design for environment is readily grasped, it will probably be a multi-year task for any complex-product industry. Among computer manufacturers, for example, some leading manufacturers are starting with plastics used in the outer casing and solvents used in circuit board manufacture. These alone are taking more than two years to address. There are literally hundreds of parts in most durable products, and in nearly all cases the supplier knows nothing about the environmental performance of the component they are building. Is it possible to make it recyclable? How much energy is used in its creation? What are the transportation-related environmental burdens involved? How much of an energy sink is the part during its life? Will it leach in a landfill? These are questions being addressed material by material, part by part.

There is less of a consensus in defining methodology to translate environmental performance into product attributes. Whereas 65 percent of firms claim to use life-cycle analysis in product development and 43 percent say they consider virgin material use in product design, only 23 percent actually measure virgin material use and only 20 percent assess the environmental burdens associated with normal product use—both central aspects of life-cycle product analysis, so at present there is a disconnect between intent and implementation in this arena.

The conclusion that can be drawn from this disparate data is that environment is a growing part of product development. We find that the industries in our study and and the companies within them are at very different stages in implementing this idea, but the important point is that corporations seem to be moving. Greater than 60 percent of environmental executives now say that an environmental professional is called in to consult on product development issues. Based on the the greater than 30 percent who are planning a design for environmental effort in the future, it is clear that the field is gaining momentum.

ENVIRONMENTAL MANAGEMENT AS COMPETITIVE ARENA

Extensive top management commitment, the cross-functionalization of environmental management to include the primary parts of the firm, and new programmatic investment that moves towards the market, product development, and competition make the case that environment has become a critical management arena. Yet, to fully incorporate environmental performance into the wider definition of corporate performance, tools and methodology are sorely needed. They are necessary to ensure that environmental performance is communicated to and understood by the executive team and to ensure that environmental performance is identifiable as a goal firm-wide. To begin to achieve this, a means to measure and communicate success is needed.

What does environmental success look like? What are the units of measure? What is the impact of environmental design on sales? When environmental quality goes up, what happens at the bottom line? These are questions that most firms are just approaching. The integration of environment into the heart of corporate strategy will be hindered until environmental management can develop answers to these questions and a format for communicating them to executive management.

Our investigation in this arena covered TQM and pollution prevention, reward systems, emerging success measurements, benchmarking, and the integration of finance and accounting practices within environmental management to develop financial measures of success.

POLLUTION PREVENTION AND TQM—CROSS FERTILIZING

Pollution prevention is the main area of focus in many mainstream U.S. corporate environmental programs today, and it has probably done the most to catalyze firms beginning to manage environment as a competitive issue. Eighty percent of the firms in our sample were taking up the pollution prevention banner, including launching industrial recycling and instituting chemical and materials substitution programs.

Pollution prevention is helping move environment into the strategic sphere because it shares a number of characteristics with total quality management, the management methodology and tool set which has become gospel at most product firms in the last decade. TQM technique is being rapidly adopted by environmental management, which is providing environmental efforts with a path to wider legitimacy and top management acceptance. Because it follows in TQM's footsteps, pollution prevention is a natural. Like TQM, pollution prevention gets its start on the plant floor by looking at process improvement and design. Both efforts share a hatred for inefficiency and a focus on a continually improving ideal: in TQM's case, zero defects and in pollution prevention's, zero pollution. Ultimately, both fields aspire to the same ideal, zero waste in delivering value to the customer.

As TQM has done for manufacturing, pollution prevention pushes quality issues further up the organization. In TQM, the focus is on problems in manufacturing process, which leads to a reevaluation of supplier relationships in order to meet new quality criteria. We found this happening in environmental management as well, with 40 percent of firms instituting supplier screening programs based on environmental performance. Pollution prevention also helps to catalyze design for environment, the link between product development and environmental management, in much the same way as TQM moved manufacturing and product development closer together. The design-for-X movement in TQM came about when firms realized that their greatest leverage in improving process quality, and therefore product and organization quality, was to design it into products at the front end.

Another interesting phenomenon resulting from the synergy of TQM and pollution prevention: Environmental management seems to be moving deeper into the corporation via corporate TQM programs, and TQM programs are being increasingly used to manage corporate environmental efforts. The two fields are cross-pollinating and creating a shared language across the firm.

Sixty percent of the firms in our sample had either a corporate TQM program that was beginning to adopt environmental measures or an environmental program that was adopting TQM. This cross-pollination is helping environment cross the borders of strategy in two important ways. First, TQM is providing environmental management with a language of performance and quality that is widely understood by top management, whereas in the past the discipline has been trapped in the dialect of pollution engineering. Second, TQM is bringing to environmental management a customer focus that sets the stage to tie environmental management into firm performance on the revenue side of the equation. If this trend continues, environment can be managed as a profit center. But for this to occur, management systems and measurements of success have to get more sophisticated.

Reward Systems

For environment to become strategic, reward systems and incentives will need to reflect corporate commitment to the importance of environmental performance. Our findings in this area are mixed. About one-quarter of the firms in our sample have developed incentives for environmental performance that extend to managers outside of the environmental function. In about half of these cases performance is tied to salary. Of those tying financial reward to environmental performance, there is an even split between the use of quantitative versus qualitative goals. In the middle category are firms that have reward systems solely within environmental management (about 50 percent of the sample), most of which are tied to salary. Roughly 20 percent of all firms had no formal reward system for environmental performance whatsoever.

Benchmarking and Measuring Success

If any area indicates that firms are taking environment seriously as a competitive issue, it is the extent to which companies have begun to scramble to benchmark environmental success.[4] Measuring and benchmarking environmental performance was the one arena in which nearly all environmental executives stated they wanted to gain more expertise. During the period of our study, we found four separate industry efforts under way to develop best-in-class standards spanning the auto, electronics, and chemical industries. About 30 percent of firms are benchmarking exclusively inside their industry, and another 30 percent are looking outside their industry or at global leadership firms.

Seventy-six percent of environmental executives find developing a performance measurement effort either a *difficult challenge* or a moderately difficult one. What do firms measure? We found five kinds of measurement:

1. Compliance or regulation-related
2. Environmental performance-related or efficiency-related measures: those dealing with improved efficiencies, lowered costs, or reducing material and resource use
3. Risk measures
4. Measures connecting corporate environmental performance to the marketplace: revenues, customer satisfaction
5. Measures of upstream environmental impacts for virgin-resource use, habitat alteration, or global change-related emissions

The most ubiquitous measurements are those of compliance and the least common by an order of magnitude are efforts to gauge the environment-market link and measures of the upstream impact of operations. The most common measures reflect the historical importance of regulation. Nearly 97 percent of firms measure the success of their compliance effort. About 70 percent track performance of their environmental effort using either TRI chemical releases or Clean Air Act chemical releases.

Coming in behind compliance measurements are solid waste generation and energy use: both efficiency measures are utilized at 70 percent and 56 percent, respectively. A less frequent group of measurements in this vein were avoided costs of compliance, improved local community relations, and savings from pollution prevention, utilized by about 39 percent of the sample.

Risk-related measures had about 25-percent incidence and included measurements of avoided long-term liabilities, human-risk-weighted emissions during manufacture, disposal risks after useful product life, and normal use risks.

Virgin-resource use measures and global-change related measures are minimal. Roughly 23 percent claim to follow the impact of their operations on the environment upstream into virgin-resource use. An example would be the impact on forest of mining aluminum used in engine blocks. One firm in the forests products industry was actually tracking species diversity in the forests where it logged. However, tracking carbon dioxide emissions, a convenient yardstick of a firm's contribution to global warming, is practically nonexistent. This suggests that although global change issues are on the horizon and have already appeared in the form of the ozone hole, management practice does not yet reflect this driver.

Measures Missing To Link
Environmental Performance to the Market

Performance measurement is sorely lacking in efforts outside of regulatory compliance in programs that give firms a competitive edge. The TRI-related measures are just the start of this effort. Measures of success are also demanded by design for environment, vendor and supplier management, and especially by efforts that affect sales. Now the link is barely visible. Less than 18 percent of firms have initiated efforts to tie environmental performance to customer satisfaction, and only 12 percent claim to track sales as a result of environmental efforts. This is especially ironic when compared to the data that 56 percent of firms are promoting some type of environmental attribute, and 26 percent claim to have an environmental product line. Until firms link customer satisfaction and sales to environmental product attributes (the embodiment of companies' environmental performance and consumer demand for environmental quality), environmental management will remain closed off from marketing strategy. The challenge to environmental management is to prove that it can have a positive effect on the bottom line. This will necessitate further cross-boundary cooperation between marketing management and environmental management.

Environmental Finance and Accounting

Environmental finance and accounting is the ability to assign monetary values to revenues and costs resulting from environmental management efforts and the ability to implement traditional financial tools in environmental decisions with budgetary impact. Today most firms are tracking only compliance costs and have not begun in earnest to measure the financial performance of their other environmental programs.

For environment to move to the core of business strategy, top management needs financial indicators that show environmentally-driven costs and profits resulting from business and product-level decisions. If environmental costs are not tracked to the level of product-cost standards, product managers cannot make educated decisions weighing environmental features and benefits against other product attributes. If manufacturing managers are not provided with cost data associated with using, switching, or eliminating certain chemicals and processes, they cannot bring environmental issues into manufacturing decision making on par with considerations such as just-in-time inventory savings.

In the area of environmental finance and accounting, we find that efforts are at best in their infancy and more frequently embryonic. Most corporate environmental management programs lack access to the financial talent of the firm necessary to develop an adequate accounting system. This is an area where many environmental executives expressed frustration. Looking back to the data in Part III, we see that finance and accounting is the least involved of the main functions in adopting environmental responsibility, and, conversely, it is the part of the firm where environmental executives have the least input. Fewer than 40 percent of firms undertaking pollution prevention efforts measure their financial impact, which is incongruous considering that environmental executives perceive this effort to be their most outstanding.

Fewer than 10 percent of the companies in our survey had developed a way to apply environmental costs incurred to those departments or activities that incurred an environmental burden. And only one firm out of the forty-one surveyed has developed an ability to model environmental costs or savings into product standard costs.

The one bright spot was the adoption of either internal rate of return (IRR) or return on investment (ROI) criteria for environmental investments. Sixty-four percent of firms say they employ one or the other of these tools.

Clearly environmental management is a long way off from full-cost accounting. Because corporations have yet to develop financial tools in the environmental performance arena, there are no ways of communicating financial incentives or impacts of environmental activities. It is not that the environment does not affect the bottom line. The problem is that financial and accounting systems expertise, the wiring and grid necessary to communicate firm performance, does not yet extend to the new province of environmental management.

CONCLUSIONS

There is ample evidence that environment is an important strategic issue in business. Our survey shows that the key drivers of environmental management have evolved quickly over the last few years. In addition to regulation, emerging markets for environmental product quality, competitive pressure, and global change issues now play strong driving roles.

Reflecting these new external conditions, environmental management has started to change rapidly, becoming the object of strategic focus in a variety of large corporations, as our data has shown. Top-management task forces have formed to grapple with the task of developing environmental strategy. The role of the senior environmental executive is greatly expanded. And underlining the idea that environmental management is becoming an arena of firm *performance* running across the entire business, we find that responsibility for executing environmental initiatives is moving into the main functions of the business, manufacturing, R&D and product development, marketing, purchasing, and finance and accounting.

Within environmental management there is an increasing focus on managing environment at the product and business level. This focus is evidence that environmental management is moving far away from a predominantly risk-management and compliance-dominated world view that prevailed during most of the last two decades. As evidence of this shift, we have shown that new investment in environmental management is occurring in areas motivated by the new external drivers: environmental marketing, design for environment, the potential of global change, and environmental performance as competition.[5]

Investigating the emergence of environmental management as a core discipline, we find that both management systems and measurements of environmental performance remain underdeveloped. Although it is clear that environmental considerations are important to the market, there is almost no effort being made to demonstrate the impact that environmental activities have on sales. And though there are many ways in which environmental costs can be traced to products to provide financial indicators of environmental success, this has not been undertaken.

Environmental management is a strategic issue, no longer simply a cost center but an activity that can increase profitability. As such, the challenge is to manage environmental activities as a profit center. This is impossible until cost- and revenue-related outcomes of environmental performance are measured and linked. Financial expertise needs to brought to bear on this problem, and yet this is the discipline least involved in environmental management.

POST SCRIPT
Is the Emperor Wearing No Clothes?

This article was written in the fall of 1991 based on data gathered in the spring and summer of that year. Since that time a number of books and articles have appeared echoing the themes in this article. The President's Commission on Environmental Quality published two fairly slick volumes on corporate environmental initiatives.[6] INFORM published the results of more detailed and substantive case studies in *Environmental Dividends: Cutting More Chemical Wastes.*[7] Abt Associates wrote another article based on a more recent survey of corporate environmental management,[8] and Joel Makower recently published his excellent and highly-readable book, *The "e" Factor.*[9] All these works said basically the same thing—a combination of economic and social forces is shifting corporate environmental management from necessary burden to a competitive opportunity for business. Business has responded to this opportunity with a variety of creative initiatives that have transformed the role of environment in corporate thinking.

Yet, it seems appropriate now to step back and ask whether we have truly made progress, or whether the emperor is wearing no clothes, despite what many of us have said. Have we really made progress, or is what Abt Associates and others reported as a fundamental change in industry behavior really a superficial change at the margins of corporate reality? Unless we ask hard questions, we are not likely to make real progress.

The most disturbing answer is that we really do not know. We *can* say that releases to the environment of a handful of chemicals (300 out of a total of about 70,000 chemicals in commerce) listed in the Toxic Release Inventory have decreased, the production and use of chlorofluorocarbons (CFCs) have decreased, and the obvious opportunities for pollution prevention are being exploited. Beyond these areas we have anecdotes, but no systematic knowledge of whether true environmental improvement is taking place and of whether the "customers" for corporate environmental programs notice or care about the efforts that have been made. In a nutshell, we do not know whether we are witnessing only the harvesting of low-hanging fruit or something more fundamental.

The challenge now is to create conditions necessary to institutionalize environmental improvement as a fundamental shift in industry behavior. These necessary conditions include

- **Development of multi-dimensional customer-oriented measures of environmental success.** Experience with TRI has demonstrated, if it was not already obvious, that "what gets measured gets managed." The success of environmental programs must be documented in terms of results much more systematically than is currently the case. The survey reported in this article, as well as subsequent surveys, indicated that measurement of environmental results is haphazard at best— some companies track TRI releases, others track air toxics, yet others look at solid or hazardous wastes, regulatory compliance, or audit results to determine whether their environmental programs are yielding desired results. Very few companies look at their total environmental impact across environmental dimensions, and fewer still measure whether customers are satisfied with environmental performance.
- **Integrating environmental considerations in facility operations.** Our survey reported a strong tendency at many companies to integrate the corporate environmental function with other aspects of corporate operations. I suspect this

finding would surprise many facility environmental managers at those same companies. Whatever the rhetoric at the corporate level, facility level environmental managers remain isolated by their training, skills, and roles. They function as an internal regulatory agency charged with enforcing command-and-control requirements, not as members of cross-disciplinary teams that develop environmental solutions. Training for facility-level environmental mangers to help them adapt to their changing role is urgently needed.

• **Creating incentives for long-term investments that go beyond low-hanging fruit.** The INFORM study documents corporate pollution prevention actions, most of which involved little or no increase in capital investment and resulted in substantial cost savings and environmental improvement. Although INFORM performed an important service in making us aware that low-cost opportunities to improve environmental performance exist, they may have also created a false expectation that environmental improvement will always come easily. The fact is that sustained environmental improvements may require substantial R&D or other types of investments. To maintain momentum beyond the low-hanging fruit, we need to see environmental improvement in business terms, not just as a means of reducing short-term costs, but as a means of enhancing long-term profits. We need to see TQEM as a method to address customers' environmental needs, even if in the process we sometimes increase short-term costs. The method must include rigorous analysis of longer-term trends that link substantial environmental investments with reduced cost of liability and increased revenues.

Richard P. Wells

Notes

1.   Industries were selected in order to roughly match their contribution to GNP. Industries included were chemical, petroleum, automotive and suppliers, capital goods, consumer durables, consumer nondurables, defense, forest products, computers and communications. Two large retailers were included, but no other service industries were represented. Most firms have sales over $1.6 billion.

2.   Abt Associates. Results of survey of 800 U.S. adults between July and August 1990.

3.   *Design for environment* is defined here as all efforts to include environmental criteria into product design: design for dissassembly, design for recyclability, efforts

to include life-cycle analysis in product development, efforts to map customer demand for environmental performance onto new products, or efforts to reduce corporate risk by designing pollution out of products and processes.

4.   *Benchmark* in this paper includes the formal TQM methodology and also includes less rigorous though systematic efforts by firms to compare their environmental program within and between industries.

5.   When this research was undertaken, U.S. firms were often sharing the results of their environmental efforts. By the time this article went to press five months later, there was a decided tendency on the part of environmental executives to be quite concerned about discussing efforts like pollution prevention or design for environment. A shift had occurred whereby it was now seen as a source of competitive advantage.

6.   President's Commission on Environmental Quality, *Partnerships to Progress,* and *Total Quality Management: A Framework for Pollution Prevention,* January 1993.

7.   INFORM, Inc., *Environmental Dividends: Cutting More Chemical Wastes,* IN-FORM, New York, NY, 1992.

8.   Abt Associates Inc., "Total Quality Management: A Tool to Move from Compliance to Strategy," *Greener Management International,* January 1993.

9.   Joel Makower, *The "e" Factor,* Tilden Press, Inc., Washington, DC, 1993.

3

CERTIFICATION OF ENVIRONMENTAL MANAGEMENT SYSTEMS— ISO 9000 AND COMPETITIVE ADVANTAGE

Suzan L. Jackson

ISO 9000 has become the buzzword of many industries worldwide as they strive to gain competitive advantage by registering their quality systems. At the same time, environmental performance and improvement are becoming increasingly important in the global marketplace. Work has begun to integrate these two important concepts into a new one: certification of environmental management systems. This article explains the new standard and why companies need to recognize and react to their international environmental impact.

ISO 9000 is an international standard that describes elements of an effective quality system. It was written by Technical Committee (TC) 176 of the International Organization for Standardization (ISO). ISO 9000 can apply to any business, anywhere in the world, so its requirements are very generic. It specifies the elements of a system that needs to be in place in order to effectively manage quality, but it does not specify how those elements should be implemented. The "how" is left up to the user—ISO 9000 does not tell you how to run your

Suzan L. Jackson *is a consultant and instructor in DuPont's Quality Management and Technology Center in Newark, Delaware, specializing in the ISO 9000 Standards and Continuous Improvement. Her DuPont experience includes roles as a process engineer and manufacturing site quality coordinator. Her experience with ISO 9000 includes authoring site documentation, training all levels of personnel, conducting quality audits against ISO 9000, and consulting both within DuPont and externally on implementation of an ISO 9000 quality system.*

business. In this way, it is flexible enough to be useful to any type of business.

WHAT IS ISO 9000?

ISO 9000 is actually a series of five standards—ISO 9000 through ISO 9004. The first and the last of these standards (9000 and 9004) are advisory standards. Their purpose is to provide guidance to the user. The remaining three standards, ISO 9001, 9002, and 9003, are contractual standards to which a business may choose to register itself. Each describes a quality system model. A business chooses one of these three, depending on the type of business involved. (See **Exhibit 1**.)

Exhibit 1

What Is the ISO 9000 Series of Standards?

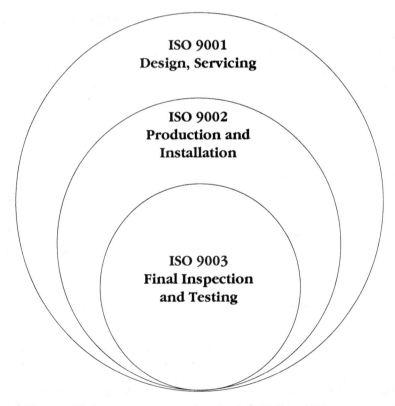

ISO 9001
Design, Servicing

ISO 9002
Production and Installation

ISO 9003
Final Inspection and Testing

Source: DuPont Quality Management and Technology Center, 1992.

ISO 9003 is the most limited of the contractual standards and is meant for businesses that only do final inspection and testing—no manufacturing, no design, no servicing. Due to its limited scope, ISO 9003 is used by only about 5 percent of the businesses that register their quality systems worldwide.

ISO 9002 contains all twelve of the elements of 9003 but adds to these, for a total of eighteen quality system elements. ISO 9002 is applicable for any business that either manufactures a product or supplies a service. About 75 percent of the worldwide registrations are to ISO 9002.

The most comprehensive of the three standards is ISO 9001. It adds two additional elements to ISO 9002—one on design and one on after-sales servicing. So if design/development or after-sales servicing is an integral part of your business, then ISO 9001 is the appropriate standard.

Quality System Registration

The ISO 9000 standards are being used worldwide to register quality systems. Registration occurs when an independent, accredited third party audits a company to certify that its quality system meets the basic requirements of the appropriate ISO 9000 standard. The use of an accredited auditing organization (a registrar) and an international standard means that this registration could be recognized by customers worldwide as proof that the company has a system in place to assure quality.

Quality system registration is quickly becoming a competitive advantage worldwide and even a market requirement in some industries. Companies all over the world are working to implement a comprehensive quality system and get it registered. Fifty-three nations have adopted ISO 9000 as their national quality standard. In the United Kingdom, where quality system registration has been in place for eight years, there are over 16,000 registrations to ISO 9000. Most other European countries have between 200 and 1,000 registrations to date, and the United States had 400 as of August 1992. (See **Exhibit 2.**) In the United States, the machinery, electronic, and chemical industries are all adopting ISO 9000 quite aggressively. (See **Exhibit 3.**) DuPont, leading the United States in ISO 9000 registrations, has 70 registrations in the United States and 160 worldwide.

Although many of these ISO 9000 efforts are market-driven, the companies using ISO 9000 are finding out that there are many internal benefits that greatly outweigh the effort required to implement such a

Exhibit 2

ISO 9000 Registrations Worldwide
Estimates—October 1992

United Kingdom	25,000	-	30,000
Germany	1,000	-	1,500
Australia	500	-	600
United States	400	-	450
Netherlands	200	-	400
Canada	200	-	250
Switzerland	200	-	250
France	100	-	200
Singapore	100	-	150
Spain	50	-	100
Japan	50	-	100
New Zealand	25	-	50

Source: DuPont Quality Management and Technology Center, October 1992

system. At DuPont, businesses have reported major cost reductions and improvements in product quality, productivity, and customer satisfaction due to implementation of ISO 9000 quality systems. One plant site increased its first-pass yield from 72 percent to 92 percent. A DuPont Electronics business reduced its site costs by $3 million, while improving on-time delivery from 70 percent to 90 percent and decreasing product defects from 500 ppm to 150 ppm. A chemicals plant reduced its product cycle time from 15 days to 1.5 days. Benefits like these have been achieved by businesses all over the world.

INTERNATIONAL ENVIRONMENTAL SCENE

Given the success of ISO 9000 worldwide, many businesses have begun to expand the scope of their quality management system to include other aspects of their business; environmental management has been one area of focus. Meanwhile, the European Community (EC) has realized that in order to facilitate free trade, environmental aspects must be managed. These two paths have converged in the formation of the Strategic Advisory Group for the Environment (SAGE).

Exhibit 3

United States ISO 9000 Registrations
by Industry—August 1992

Industrial & Commercial Machinery and Computer Equipment	86
Chemicals and Allied Products	80
Measuring, Analyzing, and Controlling Instruments	66
Electronic and Other Electrical Equipment and Components	53
Fabricated Metal Products, Except Machinery & Transportation	32
Stone, Clay, Glass, and Concrete Products	15
Paper and Allied Products	11
Business Services	8
Textile Mill Products	8
Primary Metal Industries	8
Other	33
TOTAL	**400**

Source: *Quality Systems Update*, August 1992.

STRATEGIC ADVISORY GROUP FOR THE ENVIRONMENT

SAGE was established by the ISO and the International Electrotechnical Committee (IEC) in 1991 to make recommendations regarding international standards for the environment. SAGE concluded that an environmental management system (EMS) was a critical element in achieving environmental excellence and in meeting future environmental needs worldwide. An EMS provides a way to achieve a company's environmental performance goals, using the company's environmental policies and principles as a base. For the chemical industry, an effective EMS is one element of Responsible Care. For any business, it is a part of sustainable development, defined by SAGE as "...operating activities [that] meet the needs of present stakeholders (shareholders, employees, customers, and communities) without impairing the ability of future generations to meet their needs."

SAGE's recommendations stated that a technical committee should be established in the ISO to develop an international environmental management system standard. Like all international system standards, it should be generic so that it could be used by any industry in the world. In addition, SAGE recommended that the new environmental standard should

- Fit with existing management system standards (i.e., ISO 9000)
- Describe best practices in environmental management
- Provide consistency worldwide
- Provide a model for elements of an effective environmental management system
- Not include performance criteria (these should be left to regulatory bodies)
- Include requirements for leadership commitment
- Be voluntary
- Add value to an organization when applied
- Be challenging, yet available to and within the capability of any business worldwide
- Include requirements for communication to stakeholders
- Link to ISO 9000 and other management systems standards through the use of common language to enable a single cohesive management system (see **Exhibit 4**)
- Be flexible

These characteristics encompass many of the characteristics of ISO 9000. Besides authoring the ISO 9000 series, TC 176 has also authored "Vision 2000: A Strategy for International Standards' Implementation in the Quality Arena During the 1990s," which describes the TC's vision of the future of quality system standards. One aspect of Vision 2000 is that a single international standard exists for consistent application worldwide. This single standard may then be supplemented by guidance documents to assist various industries in translating the standard's requirements for their own businesses. Vision 2000 advocates that these guidance documents be written by the same international committee that authored the standard to avoid proliferation of many different interpretative guides. TC 176 has in fact authored guidance documents for the process, software, and service industry segments.

SAGE's recommendations are in line with TC 176's Vision 2000 document. In addition to the above list, SAGE recommends that application guides be written when needed for specific industries to complement the generic international standard.

A SAGE subgroup has been formed on environmental auditing.

Exhibit 4

Strategic Vision for Integrated Quality Management System Standards

Standard Hierarchy

Generic Management Systems

Generic Management System

Mangement System Models for Specific Areas of Concern

Product Quality	Service Quality	Environmental Quality	Health and Safety Quality

Supporting Procedures Guidelines Criteria

Auditing
Customer Service
Life Cycle Analysis
Impact Assessment
Codes of Practice
Management Review
Performance Evaluation

Source: ISO/IEC/SAGE SG1 Document 46: Position Paper, September 1992.

SAGE notes that there needs to be close cooperation between this subgroup, other SAGE subgroups, and other groups working on international auditing standards. Specifically, the need for a strong link with ISO 10011, the set of international standards on quality auditing, is mentioned. This further integration of quality and environmental system standards would allow integration of management systems as well as integration of system audits, whether external or internal.

THE EC AND THE ENVIRONMENT:
COMMUNITY ECO-MANAGEMENT AND AUDIT SCHEME
The EC has proposed a regulation to encourage businesses to

continuously review and improve their environmental performance. This Community Eco-Management and Audit Scheme (previously named Eco-Audit) would be voluntary and would include two parts: an EMS and a verified public statement of performance.

As currently proposed, the environmental management system requirement could be met by internal auditors (if the company operates within an ISO 9000 system) or by external assessment. In either case, the auditors would have to meet the requirements of ISO 10011. The EMS would include, among other elements, written environmental policies and internal environmental auditing.

The public statement would report data to describe and quantify the company's environmental performance and would need some sort of validation. This validation, which would likely come from an accredited verifier, would verify that the data arise from a certified EMS and that it is compatible with the previous year's statement. Ideally, the same accredited organizations could verify the public statement, audit the EMS, and possibly also register the quality system against ISO 9000. In any case, the EC would like to avoid the need for a separate certification scheme, which could create greater costs and bureaucracy for companies.

The EC voted on the adoption of the Community Eco-Management and Audit Scheme in December 1992. Eleven of the twelve member nations voted for the proposed regulation; Germany voted against it. The proposal will be considered again in March 1993. Given this delay, registration within this scheme will be available in the fourth quarter of 1994, if it passes its March vote.

EMS STANDARDS: TWO APPROACHES

Currently, there are two different schools of thought on the integration of quality systems and the environment. One is to apply the ISO 9000 standards to environmental systems. The other is to create a separate standard for environmental management systems. Work is progressing on both sides of this issue and it is likely that the two approaches will coexist in some industries.

Applying ISO 9000 to the Environment

This approach is being developed primarily within the chemical industry. The United Kingdom's Chemical Industries Association (CIA) has published "Responsible Care Management Systems: Guidelines for Certification to ISO 9001—Health, Safety, and Environmental Management Systems in the Chemical Industry." The booklet is patterned after

ISO 9001 and is meant to guide organizations in applying their existing ISO 9000 registered quality system to the areas of safety, health, and the environment. This approach is consistent with Vision 2000 and allows for the same basic management system to be used for all areas of a business.

The guide was written with the chemical industry's Responsible Care program in mind. Although an EMS is only one part of Responsible Care, this interpretative guide could be helpful in integrating Responsible Care with existing and future quality and environmental initiatives.

The CIA's guide has a larger scope than just environmental management in that it also includes safety and occupational health. This was done deliberately in anticipation of safety and health management system requirements similar to the proposed environmental requirements (Community Eco-Management and Audit Scheme). The CIA's interpretative guidelines are currently being piloted by ten chemical industry companies in the United Kingdom. If these pilots go as planned, accredited certification of an EMS to these guidelines would be available by July 1994.

Environmental Management System Standard: BS 7750

The British Standards Institute (BSI) has developed and published an environmental management systems standard called BS 7750 (the British equivalent of ISO 9000 is BS 5750). This is a new and separate standard for EMS only, and includes requirements for environmental policies, review and assessment of environmental performance, continuous improvement, communication of performance to the public, and internal auditing.

BS 7750 parallels ISO 9000 in many ways, describing a similar generic model for a management system. The environmental standard has a larger scope than ISO 9000, but with ISO 9000 already in place, BS 7750 would be easier to implement. ISO 9000 provides a foundational quality system on which to build higher-level quality initiatives or broader management systems. Both ISO 9000 and BS 7750 have similar requirements in the areas of management commitment and involvement, internal auditing, the foundation of company policies, and the continual review of audit results versus those policies to encourage continuous improvement.

BS 7750 is currently being piloted in the United Kingdom by ten companies in the chemical industry over the next twelve months. Accredited certification to BS 7750 should be available by July 1994. BSI is also working on a management system standard for safety and health, which would be called BS 8750.

THE ISSUES AND THE FUTURE

Although these two different approaches seem at odds with each other, both are currently being piloted. With the SAGE recommendations for an international standard for EMS, it seems less a question of what will happen and more a question of when it will happen.

Either of the current approaches can work. Although both encompass the same basic principles, each has its advantages: A separate environmental standard means less interpretation is needed, whereas the application of ISO 9000 to EMS means greater potential for integration. Rather than become entangled in the argument of which approach is best, it would be more beneficial to simply acknowledge that EMS certification is coming and strive within each of our own organizations to apply these basic principles now.

Many of DuPont's European customers are already asking for or requiring an EMS. Besides this kind of market pressure, it is very likely that implementing an EMS will garner the same kind of internal benefits that ISO 9000 quality system implementation has. Ron Zelonka, DuPont of Canada's general manager-fluorochemicals and the chairman of DuPont of Canada's Business Environmental Stewardship Committee, has proposed that all of DuPont of Canada's fluorochemicals businesses certify their EMS; many of the businesses will start down that road in 1993. Regardless of the details of each business' EMS, Zelonka states, "the need for an environmental management system and the need to conform to the environmental management system (whatever the specific system is) will be common to all businesses."

With the increasing focus on quality system registration, the environment, and unrestricted trade worldwide, it is obvious that some sort of EMS certification will become necessary. Like ISO 9000, it is likely to be voluntary but highly market-driven. Given the implications of environmental matters on communities worldwide, it is also likely to be strongly driven by the consumer and the public. Environmental management system certification is on its way, in one form or another.

Section II

UNDERSTANDING TOTAL QUALITY MANAGEMENT

4

A POINT OF VIEW:
SEVEN PRINCIPLES OF
QUALITY LEADERS

Y.K. Shetty

Even though corporate executives believe quality and productivity are the most critical issues facing American business, many do not know how to achieve it. There are, however, several major corporations in the United States that are vigorously addressing this challenge. Companies known for quality have higher productivity and better profit margins and capture larger market shares. Quality gives them a sustainable competitive advantage.

Who are these quality leaders? Hewlett-Packard, IBM, Procter and Gamble, Johnson & Johnson, Maytag, Dana Corporation, Intel, Texas Instruments, 3M, Caterpillar, Delta, Marriott, McDonald's, Dow Chemical, Xerox, and General Electric are among the consistently productive firms that provide quality products and rank among the top in their respective industries.

What can other companies learn from them? Perhaps the most important lesson is that not all companies follow a single formula for success. Certain principles, however, are shared by all quality-conscious companies. Managers can apply these principles to their own firm.

Principle 1: Quality improvement requires the firm commitment of top management. Top management, including the chief executive, must make it clear that everyone must be personally committed to quality. Employees are initially skeptical when management says it is committed to quality; therefore, top management must

Y.K. Shetty is a professor of management at Utah State University's College of Business in Logan, Utah. He is co-editor of The Quest for Competitiveness *(Quorum Books, 1991).*

be consistent and reflect its commitment through the company's philosophy, goals, policies, priorities, and executive behavior.

Although top management's commitment to quality is critical, studies indicate that there is no common understanding of the term "commitment," and that managers' perceptions of their commitment often is not shared by their subordinates. In other words, top managers must clearly specify which actions will improve quality; they cannot delegate this responsibility. The steps that management can take to demonstrate commitment, involvement, and leadership include the following:

- Establish and communicate a clear vision of corporate philosophy, principles, and objectives relevant to product and service quality.
- Channel resources toward these objectives and define roles and responsibilities in this endeavor.
- Invest the time to learn about quality issues and monitor the progress of any initiatives.
- Encourage communication between management and employees, among departments, and among various units of the firm and customers.
- Be a good role model in communication and action.

Principle 2: Quality is a strategic issue. Quality must be part of a company's goals and strategies. Management's concern for quality must be consistent with and reinforce a company's other strategic objectives. This concern must be integrated into the way in which the organization conducts business, including its plans and budgets.

Quality must be a corporate mission with planned goals and strategies. The Ford Motor Company's mission statement says, "Quality comes first. To achieve customer satisfaction, the quality of our products and services is our number-one priority. Customers are the focus of everything we do." John F. Welch, Jr., chairman of General Electric, says that "Quality is our best assurance of customer allegiance, our strong defense against foreign competition, and the only path to sustained growth and earnings." Xerox, winner of the 1989 Malcolm Baldrige National Quality Award, says that "Quality is the basic business principle for Xerox...Leadership through quality is a strategy and a plan." AT&T chairman Robert Allen says quality is the foundation of his company's newly-found competitive prowess. "Satisfied customers vote with their dollars," he explains. "We're winning those votes by making our quality best in the world."

These and other companies, such as Hewlett-Packard, IBM, Westinghouse, and Motorola, systematically integrate concern for quality into every aspect of their business. Commitment to quality and commitment to profitability are inseparable. Quality is at the heart of every action and part of their strategies for gaining market share. Executives at these firms believe that proper attention to product and service quality will result in profitability.

Principle 3: Employees are the key to consistent quality. Effective leadership to improve quality entails a people-oriented philosophy and a concomitant commitment to quality. Poorly managed people convey their disdain for quality and service when they work and interact with their customers.

The human resource practices of America's quality leaders reflect an emphasis on good people policies. For example:

- They pay special attention to employee recruitment, selection, and socialization. They carefully select the employees best suited for company success and instill in them specific values concerning product quality and customer service. Employees also are intensely socialized on company culture—norms, systems, and procedures relevant to quality and customer service.
- They reinforce the socialization process with continuous training and education. Companies such as Westinghouse, Motorola, Xerox, and Ford believe that training involves more than teaching production workers statistical techniques. Training programs provide extensive awareness of quality, each employee's role in the process, and the importance of quality to the company. Statistical process control, problem-solving techniques, and the job skills to support quality improvement also are emphasized.
- They incorporate quality and customer service into performance appraisal and reward systems. These companies make sure that quality achievement—doing it right all the time—is an important element of the evaluation and reward system.
- They encourage employee participation and involvement. Employees are considered natural sources of ideas for ways to improve quality and customer service. Every person from the CEO to the hourly employee is involved, through informal interactions, suggestion systems, quality circles,

problem-solving teams, joint labor-management committees, and similar devices. Quality requires employees who have respect for each other and who take pride in their companies—and who have a real commitment to excellence. That commitment can be achieved only when employees are involved and empowered.

- They communicate effectively throughout the organization. Communication reinforces the deep commitment of management and creates an awareness and understanding of the role of quality and customer service. It attempts to instill a desire to consistently apply these concerns to on-the-job matters.

Principle 4: Quality standards and measurements must be customer-driven. Explicit quality standards for performance are essential. Quality is a complex concept and no single set of characteristics effectively defines product or service quality. Customers do have definitions of quality, however, and their definitions usually have several attributes that vary among industries and firms. A company's definition of product and service quality should include the criteria that customers use when they perceive value. Customers' perception of value involves the concept of relative value, which can be computed thus:

$$\text{Value} = \frac{\text{Quality}}{\text{Price}}$$

Therefore, a customer's product preference is determined by the perceived quality/price ratio of one product in relation to another competing product.

America's quality leaders systematically survey their customers (and their competitors' customers) and distributors to determine how they perceive the quality of their products and services. This and other information is used to profile the attributes of the company's current products and customers' expectations. Realistic quality standards are then developed and incorporated into every stage, from product design to service.

Xerox uses competitive benchmarking to improve its quality. This process involves measuring products, services, and practices against those of its toughest competitors. The goal that was formulated—to be superior in quality, product reliability, and costs—led to intensive customer surveys and the establishment of standards for product and service quality.

Measurement is essential to ensure that planned quality improvements actually are implemented. Customer satisfaction can be measured by formal customer surveys, focus groups, informal customer complaints, quality audits, testing panels, statistical quality controls, interaction with customers, and other methods. A combination of several methods often is used. Customer satisfaction should be continuously monitored to determine whether additional changes are required.

Principle 5: Many programs and techniques can be used to improve quality. Among the techniques and programs used to improve quality are statistical quality control, quality circles, suggestion systems, quality-of-work-life projects, automation, computer-based design and manufacturing, product design improvement, competitive benchmarking, and employee training. And some of the leading firms—such as Xerox, 3M, and Ford—admit to using a variety of techniques. The bottom line is that no single approach is best for all situations and companies.

Principle 6: All company activities have potential for improving product quality; therefore, teamwork is vital. Quality improvement requires close cooperation between managers and employees and among departments. Total quality management involves preventing errors at the point where the work is performed. Under this system, every employee and department is responsible for quality. Because product design, engineering, purchasing, manufacturing, sales, and service can affect product quality, each department should try to provide defect-free products or service. Concern for quality should not be limited to the quality-control department. Product quality is more than inspection—it must be built in. Successful companies remove barriers between specialists and create a climate for teamwork.

In 1980, Ford had a poor quality image. The company examined its sequential product-design process, which involved design, engineering, manufacturing, and marketing, with each group of specialists operating in isolation. Ford replaced this system with a simultaneous team approach to promote continuous interaction among departments, top management, and legal, purchasing, and service organizations. This approach led to improved quality and to the success of the Taurus and Sable models.

Hewlett-Packard, IBM, and 3M all employ a team approach to improving quality and speeding product development. Previously, suggestions often were received too late in the product development process to enable design changes before final assembly. Employee teams, representing all the departments concerned, now participate in the design process as part of an "early involvement program." Xerox, DuPont, and Procter and Gamble have similar programs.

Suppliers also must be part of the team. Quality components and materials are required to produce quality products. Successful firms carefully select suppliers and develop long-term relationships with them. Indeed, the quality renaissance has changed the relationship between companies and their suppliers. As genuine partners in the effort to improve quality, suppliers are now brought in during the early stages of new product design, are trained and given long-term contracts, and participate in quality and recognition award programs. For example:

- Motorola develops long-term relationships with its suppliers and regularly recognizes those who perform well.
- Ford's Team Taurus signed long-term contracts with suppliers and invited them to participate in product planning. Ford also gives awards to its best suppliers. Ford's "Q One" is an award for product quality and on-time delivery.
- Xerox reduced the number of vendors from 5,000 to 300 and gave them long-term contracts in return for better quality components. The firm trains suppliers in statistical process control, just-in-time manufacturing techniques, and cooperative costing, and includes them in product development.

Principle 7: Quality is a never-ending process. Efforts to improve quality must be planned, organized, monitored, and continuously revitalized. Many companies fail to make it a continuous process, often because they emphasize neatly packaged programs or hastily selected popular tools in the search for quick results.

Continuous improvements result only from an institutionalization of concern for quality—that is, when quality becomes part of day-to-day decision making. Therefore, quality goals, standards, measurements, training, and reward systems should be integrated into a company's regular plans, budgets, information system, human resource management practices, controls—its total management system.

PUTTING THE PRINCIPLES TO WORK

The experiences of America's quality leaders suggest that quality is not just a program; it is an all-inclusive, pervasive, ongoing way of doing business. It is achieved by making the improvement process a permanent part of a company's culture.

Companies should not blindly imitate or copy the practices of successful companies, but should tailor practices to meet their specific needs. The tactics are fairly simple and basic, but adapting and institutionalizing them—incorporating them in decisions, resource allocation, personnel policies, and operating systems—is a formidable challenge. To do so, a firm often must drastically change the way it operates. Progress demands patience, hard work, commitment, and discipline. But the payoffs are great, for enhanced quality can provide powerful leverage to achieve both competitive advantage and superior business performance. It is essential to maintain leadership in a rapidly changing and highly competitive global market.

5

THE TEAM APPROACH TO COMPANYWIDE CHANGE

Robert Janson and Richard L. Gunderson

One of the most serious challenges facing top management today is how to implement lasting change on a companywide scale. Deregulation, new technologies, foreign competition, and rapidly changing consumer expectations have converged to create a volatile economic climate that is forcing companies to shed old organizational structures—often rigid, top-heavy, and bureaucratic—in favor of new ones that are flexible, lean, and responsive to the marketplace. And more often than not, these structural changes are accompanied by significant modifications in corporate culture, management style, and marketing strategy.

Many forward-thinking managers are using a participative approach to bring about these changes. They realize that this is the best way to mobilize the kind of support they need to effect a major transformation, achieve positive results in the short term, and establish a solid foundation for their company's future. Yet despite their commitment to participation, many managers begin their change efforts haphazardly. And when they bring in experts to help them out, the questions they ask are almost always the same: Is there one best strategy for implementing change through participation? Is it really possible—or wise—to involve everyone in the change process? What form or forms should participation take?

At Aid Association for Lutherans (AAL), the largest fraternal benefit society in the United States, a five-step model for change through participation was used to help guide the company in its search for a

Robert Janson is president of Roy W. Walters & Associates Inc., management consultants based in Mahwah, New Jersey. *Richard L. Gunderson* is president and chief executive officer of Aid Association for Lutherans, an insurance company based in Appleton, Wisconsin.

new identity. The renewal effort, dubbed "Transformation," involved everyone from the board of directors to the shipping room clerk in order to achieve optimal results and maximum buy-in. Any organization can use the same innovative team approach to participation in order to design and implement reforms.

FIVE STEPS TO ORGANIZATIONAL RENEWAL

Though no two transformation efforts are exactly alike, all organizations undergoing change can increase their chances of success if they rely on a solid, conceptual framework. The following five-part model provides numerous opportunities for employee participation.

Step 1: Vision

Any company that wants to transform itself must begin by articulating where it wants to go and what it wants to become. A manufacturing firm, for example, may decide that it must improve product quality to become a leader in its field; a financial services company may strive for a more client-oriented approach. Whatever the objective, a company must state it—e.g., the company expects to be at the end of the change process, what values it will adhere to in its renewed state, and what principles will be used to guide the company during the transformation effort.

Envisioning a new future is not easy, but it is usually the most exciting phase of any renewal effort. And the more people involved in formulating the vision the better. At AAL, for example, more than 100 managers participated in drawing up the final vision statement, a process that helped foster a widespread commitment to change and a universal sense of ownership over the change process.

Step 2: Diagnosis

All companies undergoing change must also perform a "gap analysis," a formal diagnosis of where the organization currently is and what it needs to do to make its new vision a reality. This is the phase that provides focus for the change effort, because it helps identify the specific areas in the organization where the most work will be carried out.

Some organizational leaders try to perform this analysis on their own or with the aid of a few top advisors. Although sometimes productive, this method can be shortsighted. Unless a company is in a crisis situation—and a course of action must be decided upon at once—a go-it-alone approach can rob the change effort of the broad base of support needed to implement reforms effectively.

At AAL, several hundred people participated in the diagnostic phase, which involved a transformation team of twelve managers interviewing employees throughout the home office and the field. To identify areas of job discontent and organizational ineffectiveness, the team members asked three broad questions: What do you think are the company's basic strengths? What are its weaknesses? If you had the opportunity to change anything you would like, what would it be?

Though it took the team several months to complete its diagnosis, it generated a vast amount of information. And in the process, it helped stimulate "positive dissatisfaction" among the work force, which helped mobilize the kind of energy needed to see a major change effort through to the end. This was especially important at AAL, since the company was not in a state of crisis and there seemed to be no immediate need for fundamental change.

Step 3: Strategy

The next three phases of the change effort make up the action planning and implementation stage of the process. These phases operate concurrently in most companies, though changes in structure usually do not take place until there is a stated shift in strategic direction. In all three phases, however, the extensive knowledge gained in the diagnostic phase can be reported back to the entire work force, and suggestions for improvement can be solicited from all those interested in making a contribution.

The strategy phase at AAL involved setting up a new set of teams, each charged with examining one of the ten organizational variables identified in the diagnosis as key to the company's renewal: communications, control, culture, management style, marketing, mission, productivity, quality, structure, and technology. The purpose of these teams was to determine the practical possibilities for change and to suggest strategies for bringing those areas into close alignment with the future state envisioned for the company.

Step 4: Structure

Organizational restructuring is one of the most frequently recommended strategies to emerge during the planning and implementation stage of the change process. Many companies realize, for example, that they cannot achieve their newly stated objectives without becoming more decentralized, implementing a flatter organizational chart, or strengthening some business units at the expense of others. But structural change is also the most powerful and disruptive strategy that can be used in any change effort. That is why many companies make structural alterations early in the transformation process—when employees are most receptive to change—before working on modifying management style, marketing direction, or corporate culture.

There is another reason why this approach makes sense: Structural change often involves significant dislocation of personnel, especially supervisors and managers. At AAL, the redesign of the organization along product lines resulted in major shifts in job responsibilities for twenty-five of the company's top twenty-six managers. So AAL decided to tackle structural changes first—and brought a new team of managers on board—before finalizing any strategies for implementing changes in other areas of the organization. Most of these new managers were chosen from within through "job rotation" on a large scale, which gave the top qualified managers key jobs in the new organization. This restructuring gave everyone a chance to look at an operation from a new point of view.

Step 5: Tactics

The last phase of organizational change is logistical. It involves selecting the implementation tactics necessary to carry out the outlined course of action. Among others, these tactics may include work-flow analysis, job redesign, value analysis, or specific skills training. But the most effective ones are usually those that are consistent with the organization's existing culture or that seem to emerge as natural implementation strategies during the planning phases. The most powerful tool is agreement on a set of goals that motivate the behavior needed to carry out the vision and strategy. In AAL's case, a group of 100 managers was persuaded that the company had to downsize by 250 people in a five-year period while continuing to increase revenue, job satisfaction, and service.

Some tactics seem to work well in virtually all organizations. There are few companies, for example, that will not benefit from a work-flow analysis to determine whether jobs are being performed in the most satisfying and efficient manner. Nevertheless, the choice of tactics should not be made by those at the top of the organization—or by outside consultants. Instead, those charged with implementing the changes—and in most cases that means first-line managers and their subordinates—are usually in the best position to decide which tactics are the most appropriate.

ACHIEVING TOTAL PARTICIPATION

The five-step change model is intended for organizations that are seeking to involve as many employees as possible in both the planning and implementation stages of their change effort. But total involvement cannot be achieved all at once. In most cases, the participation process first takes root in the highest echelons of an organization before progressing down through the various layers of management to the rank and file. Does this mean that every transformation effort—no matter how participative in appearance—is essentially another "top-down" strategy imposed by senior management? No. Although it is true that the impetus for change almost always comes from the top, the reforms that make up the heart and substance of renewal can—and, in fact, must—emerge from other levels of the organization.

There is no way a company undergoing change can realize its participative aspirations unless workers, at all levels, are deeply involved in the process, and that means encouraging employees to take an active role in vision building, data collection, problem diagnosis, concept development, work analysis, and change implementation. In fact, the only way that involvement will become truly systemic is by having the workers themselves locate the "gaps" in the organization and select the proper methods that will be used to fill them.

At AAL, a new president who was brought in during a time of rapid change in the insurance industry instituted the change process. His initial strategy was to spend several months interviewing the company's 100 officers, a process that allowed him to confirm his first diagnosis of the organization and formulate a preliminary change agenda. Most important, it helped him become familiar with the management talent within the company and to build a strong political base in support of renewal. No decision was made to initiate change, however, until the president had confirmed his evaluation with the board of directors and with a group of outside consultants. By that time, a significant number of managers had already been involved in the process of analyzing the company's health and identifying major areas for improvement. That involvement accomplished two objectives: It verified the president's early suspicions that organizational changes were needed, and it developed a widespread sense of ownership over the issues that would later emerge as crucial to the renewal effort. This process was strongly supported by the outgoing chairman, who was the catalyst in helping decide that a major transformation was needed and that the new president was the person to lead it.

The participative process that AAL's new president inaugurated during the first few months of 1986 was duplicated over the next two years throughout every work unit within the organization. This participation involved not only the 1,500 underwriters, service representatives, and clerical workers located at the company's home office in Appleton, Wisconsin, but also the 1,900 district representatives—AAL's "dedicated" sales force—who staff more than eighty field agencies throughout the United States.

As will be pointed out later, some of the most significant and dramatic results achieved during AAL's Transformation were conceived and carried out by teams of workers at the lowest levels of the organization. But this was possible only because the program was allowed to become truly line-driven. Though staff managers had set the stage for the change effort, and consultants had provided the conceptual framework to set the program in motion, both were willing to relinquish control over the evolution of the process and allow it to unfold as a natural consequence of the participative approach. This is the main reason why participation was enthusiastically embraced at AAL, and why so many of the creative ideas unleashed during the process were able to be implemented with such success. In many cases, a participative approach to change—no matter how brilliantly conceived—fails to take hold because the process of renewal remains essentially staff-driven or, even worse, consultant-driven. In those companies, the need for control ends up diluting the process of its participative thrust, often prompting workers to balk at the expectation that they should assume responsibility for changes that will affect the long-term welfare of their organization.

Total participation, then, can be achieved, but it always involves a certain amount of risk. Why? Because when workers are empowered by their superiors to take action, the future of the organization cannot be accurately predicted. Managers still retain their leadership role and decision-making responsibilities, of course, but they must be courageous enough to yield when the participative process leads them into uncharted waters.

PARTICIPATION THROUGH TEAMWORK

Teamwork is one of the most natural and effective ways of bringing about participation. Not only are workers more productive when they collaborate on projects together in teams, but they inevitably find their tasks more rewarding and stimulating as well. When managers talk about participation through teamwork these days, many of them are referring to so-called self-managing work teams, an advanced stage of employee involvement in which groups of multiskilled workers produce an entire product or service with minimal supervision. This team concept has spread rapidly in manufacturing industries, and has even made some inroads into the service sector.

At AAL, for example, Transformation's effect on the company's Insurance Product Services (IPS) department was the creation of sixteen self-managing work teams. Each team, made up of twenty to thirty employees, now faces off against several field agencies in one of the company's four regional areas. It performs all the 167 tasks that were formerly split along functional lines among the department's 500 members, and it assumes the hiring, training, and vacation-scheduling responsibilities that were once carried out solely by managers.

Self-managing work teams like these are the final manifestation of the team-building approach, however. And in many cases, their viability depends on the fact that teams of all kinds were used as vehicles for participation throughout the change process. Much of the success of self-managing work teams at AAL, in fact, can be directly attributed to the experience gained by workers in the team-building process that took place in each phase of the organization's renewal effort. This does not mean that all organizations that rely on teams to bring about participation will inevitably end up with self-managing work units. But even organizations that do not embrace the self-managing concept will find teams useful at every stage of transformation. Why? Because no matter what form they take—quality circles, problem-solving groups, task forces, or self-managing units—teams make workers feel more involved, more accountable, more supported, and more committed to a common enterprise.

The team approach is the most effective way of making sure that everyone in the organization has a chance to be heard and understood. Not only does this allow workers to influence decisions that are made about the jobs they do, it also provides regular feedback to the transformation's leaders on what changes are working well, what changes are being resisted, and how changes can be revised to promote broader acceptance. Companies interested in using team building to enhance their participative approach should follow these guidelines:

- ***Encourage total involvement.*** The primary purpose of team building is to bring about participation. Therefore, make sure that all workers are given the opportunity to join teams, whether they ultimately decide to do so or not.

- *Establish parameters*. During the participative process, workers sometimes confuse their role in diagnosing problems, collecting data, and recommending solutions with management's responsibility for making final decisions. To avoid any misunderstandings, be sure to state up front what the purpose of participation is and what you expect teams to accomplish.
- *Organize around the customer.* All teams operate more effectively when their objectives are closely aligned with those of the organization. And for almost all companies today, the most important organizational objectives are to improve customer service and increase customer satisfaction.
- *Reevaluate your leadership talent.* When choosing leaders to manage the team-building process, concentrate more on style than on technical knowledge. The qualities to look for: creativity, approachability, and a demonstrated willingness to take calculated risks.

A CLOSER LOOK AT AAL'S "TRANSFORMATION"

AAL began Transformation, its renewal process, in 1986 during a period of unprecedented company prosperity. With assets of $4.6 billion and total revenue exceeding $1 billion a year, AAL ranked among the top 2 percent of all U.S. insurers. Bolstering its position was the aggressive introduction in 1982 of an administratively complex but highly successful universal life insurance product called Horizon, one of the first of its kind. Nevertheless, there were those in the company who saw unsettling shifts in the economy and the industry that could undermine AAL's future: increased competition from banks and other financial services organizations, a more sophisticated and demanding customer base, and shrinking profit margins. Another impetus for change came from the ominous appearance of an "expense gap"—the difference between the cost of doing business and the expense allowables generated in premiums—that was slowly beginning to emerge from the dynamics of servicing the company's new universal life product. Although it was initiated by senior management, AAL's broad corporate renewal effort was carried out with surprisingly few directives from the top. One stipulation, however, was that the company had to cut costs, presumably through downsizing. Another was that service quality to the field staff and, ultimately, the buying customer had to be improved to make the company more competitive. Finally, all changes were to be brought about through a high-involvement approach.

When the company began its renewal effort, few could have predicted the extensive changes that were to occur. Using team concepts throughout, Transformation was to move AAL from what was essentially a paternalistic and hierarchical organization to a company where decision making was pushed to the lowest levels. As part of this process, AAL's structure, work style, and culture changed radically, producing sometimes remarkable results. Overall productivity in a key service department increased 20 percent, case-processing time declined in one instance by as much as 75 percent (or fifteen days), and eighty-six positions in one department were eliminated through attrition and early retirement. Nowhere were these changes more significant than in the company's largest department, IPS, which provides all insurance-related services—from underwriting to claims handling—for the company's national sales force. Formerly organized along functional lines, where the skills and abilities of many employees were underutilized and many jobs tended to be boring because of their narrow scope, IPS also suffered from a severe lack of customer orientation. With as many as six layers of supervision, decisions were made at some distance from the problems they were intended to solve, which often negatively affected the timeliness and the quality of the response.

To address these issues, a new management team for IPS was brought on board in January 1987. Its premise: The department should reorganize along regional lines, provide one-stop processing to avoid the delays and lack of ownership associated with the "assembly line" model, and develop a strong team relationship with the field staff. A new mission statement was also adopted: "To enable the agent, the primary customer, to do an even better job of serving the policyholder, the ultimate customer."

From the start, IPS management intended to achieve these objectives using a high-involvement approach. Ten teams, totaling about 125 workers from all levels within the department, were chosen from lists of employees nominated by managers, supervisors, and co-workers. Three teams were charged with proposing, independently of one another, a new structure for IPS, while five other teams were to deal with specific change issues: physical resources, management style, management information, agent input, and impact on EDP systems.

With input from departmental management, the structure teams proposed a new organization for IPS in which each of the company's five sales regions would be serviced by three or four self-regulated work teams, each structured around three broad functions: underwriting and issue; loans, terminations, and dividends; and claims. To implement the plan, another set of teams was named, involving another 125 or so employees—again that represented a cross-section of the department—to prepare IPS for the transition to the new structure. This time, the primary purpose of the teams was to disperse the life, health, and disability functions of the "old" organization among the new "one-stop" teams, and to establish directives for the extensive cross-training that would be needed to bring the self-managing teams up to speed.

By December of 1987, the changes implemented in IPS had reduced the number of supervisory positions from sixty-two to twenty-two and eliminated almost fifty-eight full-time positions, resulting in savings of more than $1 million in salaries and benefits. At the same time, there were substantial productivity improvements. Despite a 12-percent cut in personnel, the volume of business processed rose about 10 percent from 1987 to 1988 and included the introduction of a new line of long-term health-care insurance requiring significantly different underwriting skills.

Most important of all, perhaps, is the impact the changes had on relations between AAL's home office and its field. Field agencies started to encourage service team members to attend their meetings, and in one region an experimental program was set up to partner specific IPS workers with field agents. Field attitude surveys showed that the number of salespeople agreeing with the statement "IPS understands the field" almost doubled between August 1985 and May 1989.

THE CHALLENGES OF PARTICIPATION

Despite the successes of Transformation, AAL's managers knew that companywide change could not be accomplished without problems. Primary among them was the stress created by the downsizing, the new demands of "fuller" jobs, and the aftereffects of rapid change. In response, the company made stress management sessions available to all employees, and continued employment, career counseling, and replacement were offered to those whose jobs had been eliminated due to organizational change.

Transformation at AAL also brought about increased awareness of another important issue: that despite the beneficial impact that participation usually has, not all employees embrace it wholeheartedly. A high-involvement approach always brings additional responsibilities, that some workers may feel unprepared to handle, and this can cause increased anxiety and feelings of inadequacy. At AAL, this realization led to the development of an advanced training program designed to provide employees with the skills they need to sustain a collaborative work style and to carry out management functions with decreased management support.

Any company interested in achieving the kind of results brought about by AAL's Transformation program must remember that the transition to a more interactive work environment often requires behavioral changes that employees cannot—and should not—be expected to bring about on their own.

Additional Resources

Baloff, Nicholas and Doherty, Elizabeth M., "Potential Pitfalls in Employee Participation," *Organized Dynamics*, Winter 1989.

Dalziel, Murray M. and Schoonover, Stephen C., *Changing Ways: A Practical Tool for Implementing Change within Organizations*, Amacom, 1988.

Janson, Robert, "Eight Steps toward Companywide Change," *Executive Excellence*, May 1988.

Kilmann, Robert, *Managing Beyond the Quick Fix: A Completely Integrated Program for Creating and Maintaining Organization's Success*, Jossey-Bass, 1989.

Potts, Mark and Behr, Peter, *The Leading Edge: CEOs Who Turned Their Companies Around—What They Did and How They Did It*, McGraw-Hill, 1987.

Weisbord, Marvin R., *Productive Workplaces: Organizing and Managing for Dignity, Meaning, and Community*, Jossey-Bass, 1987.

Wilkins, Alan L., *Developing Corporate Character: How To Successfully Change an Organization without Destroying It*, Jossey-Bass, 1989.

6

HITTING THE WALL: HOW TO SURVIVE YOUR QUALITY PROGRAM'S FIRST CRISIS

Barry Sheehy

The progress of a quality program is measured in years rather than months. And as with any great enterprise, there are moments of triumph and despair along the way. Baldrige Prize-winning Xerox describes its decade-long pursuit of quality as a series of steps—three steps forward and one step back. It is significant that Xerox was into the eighth year of its quality process before it won the coveted Baldrige. When charted on a graph, the three steps of progress appear impressive and the one step back seems inconsequential in comparison. Any business executive recognizes this as a normal development cycle—after all, nothing goes straight up forever without pausing to refuel or revector. Unfortunately, in the enthusiasm surrounding the launch of a quality program, the message regarding the inevitability of setbacks often gets drowned out. Consequently, when the first setback occurs—usually about a year to eighteen months into the program—the organization is unprepared.

The realization that things are not going as well as expected causes disappointment, anxiety, and, sometimes, panic. This first crisis occurs when the quality process is most vulnerable. The quality message is no longer new and has lost some of its excitement. The euphoria of the launch has given way to the realization that quality improvement requires a lot of hard work. The quality champions within the

Barry Sheehy is president of Achieve Performance Consulting, Inc., a division of the Achieve Group, Inc., in Mississauga, Ontario.

organization have been working with the needle above the red line for more than a year, and fatigue is beginning to show. To further complicate matters, much of the progress achieved in the first eighteen months is centered around quality awareness, infrastructure, measurement systems, and new skills. Some measurable gains have occurred, but the bulk of the effort in the first twelve to eighteen months centers on getting the organization ready to become a quality leader.

By month eighteen, newly established measurement systems are only just beginning to chart improvements. Cost-of-quality metrics are worsening rather than improving as the organization gets better at identifying and capturing poor quality. Incremental improvements resulting from suggestions and team activities, as well as standardization of processes, are occurring, but often go unrecognized and uncelebrated. Improvements—sometimes dramatic—in organizational cohesion, quality of working life, and employee skill levels are too often taken for granted. Organizations are like glaciers whose movement is hardly noticed by those standing on it. It usually takes someone from the outside, who previously knew the organization, to note, "My gosh! What's happened around here?"

North Americans are impatient—we are a hurry-up society. Our short attention span and compulsive need for immediate results is not conducive to a successful quality process. But rather than look for quick results, we must learn to focus on long-term improvement cycles. An improvement cycle for an organization undertaking a serious quality improvement effort usually runs from three to four years. If an organization sticks to its quality process and does not lose heart, most of its year-one objectives will have been attained by the third or fourth year of the process. It is then common for the organization to plateau while it seeks new, more ambitious objectives to drive the next improvement cycle. Each cycle will be shorter than the last as the organization masters the quality improvement process and builds upon past successes. (See **Exhibit 1**.)

What this graph does not show are the many crises that occur before and during each improvement cycle. By the time an organization is into the fourth or fifth year of its quality process, the executive team is well-seasoned and not easily panicked by these setbacks. But how does an organization react in the absence of experience? Sometimes not very well. This is why the first crisis is so dangerous. Think back to our Xerox example—three steps forward and one back. On a chart, that one step back seems like a modest technical correction, a quick downward blip on the chart. For those experiencing the event,

Exhibit 1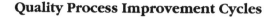

Quality Process Improvement Cycles

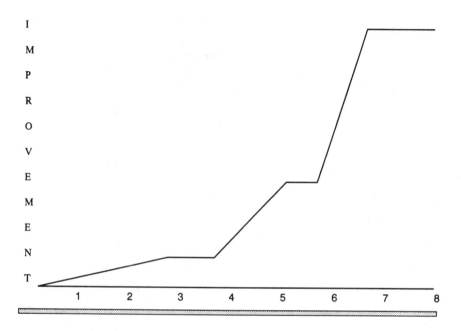

however, it can be terrifying. "Like a free fall from 90,000 feet" is how one vice president of quality described it. And warnings about the inevitability of setbacks provide little comfort when it actually happens. To quote John Keats, "Nothing is ever real until it is experienced"—and sometimes the experience is painful. "It's like being shot at," is how one executive puts it. "You can hear lectures on what it will be like until the cows come home, but when it actually happens you're still scared to death."

THE DUAL ORIGINS OF A QUALITY CRISIS

Why do quality crises happen? The two causes are change and rising expectations. Any successful quality process brings enormous change to an organization—changes in methods, processes, structures, attitudes, and, most important, behavior. During the launch phase of the process, emphasis is placed on the opportunities for improvement because they are easily articulated. The changes that will be brought on in the wake of these improvements are also discussed, but usually in vague terms because no one can describe exactly what these changes will be like. (The only exception is at the executive level; if your consultants are competent, they will have spelled out precisely the changes in executive behavior required to make the process work.) To the extent to which people understand the coming changes, it is subconsciously assumed that these changes will affect other people. "*They* will have to change"..."*They* will have to do things differently now, and about time, too"..."I've been telling *them* for years they need to change...." Managers assume employees will have to change, supervisors assume managers will have to change, employees assume everyone but them will have to change.

By month eighteen, however, it becomes clear that *everyone* in the organization will be forced to change. Sometimes this change is painful. Cherished assumptions and ways of doing business are being swept away, or at least threatened. Whole work units and functions are being reassessed. Supervisors who were content experts and order-givers are being forced into roles as facilitators and coaches. Middle managers who passed information up and down the organization are forced to become problem solvers for performance teams. Whole layers of middle managers and support groups are becoming redundant as activities are rationalized and the organization is flattened. Staff and headquarters groups that existed in splendid isolation from customers for years now find themselves dangerously exposed, as executives ask frightening questions: Who are our customers, and what are their requirements? In the eyes of our customers, are we meeting their requirements? Can these customers be better served by someone else? Should our function be decentralized? Popular managers, who are well-liked and have been around for years, suddenly decide they cannot adapt, and leave the organization. Incompetent managers are forced out and employees, instead of rejoicing, mourn the loss of "good old Charlie."

Employees whose powerlessness had bred a culture of complainers, suddenly find themselves *empowered* and *accountable*. They must now take responsibility for the output of their organization and for their own behavior. Every complaint is followed by the swift appointment of a task force to correct the problem. With this responsibility comes painful ambiguity as employees are forced to grapple with a business environment where there are few absolutely right and wrong answers. Black and white give way to gray, yes and no become maybe, and compromise is often the price of progress. Employees soon start to yearn for the simpler days when the organization's problems could be sorted out over coffee by blaming someone else.

Executives and senior managers also experience their share of trauma. In launching the quality process, executives usually welcome the idea of empowering employees to improve service, raise quality, and bring processes under control. What they are unprepared for is the resulting flood of challenges that come streaming in from empowered employee groups. As one executive put it, "Empowered employees are a pain the neck!" Venerable old systems find themselves under assault. Employee teams rampage through the organization, smashing idols and corporate icons. A few of these empowered teams may even march boldly across traditional boundaries, causing scattered turf wars to erupt. By month eighteen, corporate headquarters is beginning to look and sound like West Beirut.

In short, everyone has begun to recognize the fact that the quality process is real and sometimes painful. There is no longer any doubt that it will affect *all* of them. There is also an unconscious realization that if the process is not stopped, there will be no turning back.

The second cause of the typical quality crisis is rising expectations. At the start of the quality process expectations are usually low. Executives and employees map out their hopes and goals, but they are not really sure they are achievable. By month eighteen, some movement toward these goals is evident, but few breakthroughs have occurred; however, everyone in the organization is now aware of what a quality organization should look like and how it should behave. Everyone knows the difference between having quality and not having it. They can recognize good service and poor service. Unfortunately, this knowledge does not make people happy. Now they can see all the deficiencies in the organization that had been there all along but had been hidden or ignored. Now they can recognize when the boss delivers a mixed signal regarding quality or does not live up to the stated values of the organization. Everyone becomes keenly aware of poor internal service, and this puts considerable pressure on internal suppliers. Most painful of all, everyone can now see the gaps in their own behavior and the output of their performance team. All this dissonance creates anxiety and saps energy. People start to look back fondly on the good old days when things were predictable and ignorance was bliss.

IDENTIFYING AND DEALING WITH YOUR FIRST CRISIS

How will you know when the crisis has begun? The first hint is when one or two key individuals who are strong supporters of the quality process, start saying, "We are not perfect; look at how terrible we are." They are not the only ones feeling this way, and soon their chant becomes a universal chorus. All the uncertainties suddenly pour out as the organization tries to return to the security of the "old ways." Another warning sign of the impending crisis is excessive optimism by the quality champions within the organization. By month eighteen, all their hard work is beginning to pay off and they can sense that the organization is about to turn the corner. Do not, however, look to your quality champions to act as an early warning system for this crisis. They will be completely focused on the quality improvement process, and more than a little tired after eighteen months of hard work. They will probably be oblivious to the gathering storm and shattered by it when it occurs.

As the crisis builds, the theme of "We are not perfect; look at how terrible we are" soon evolves into "We are not perfect; therefore, we should stop our efforts to improve." Although this is not a rational response, it is a difficult one to combat. After all, you cannot prove that you are perfect because you are not, and never will be. As for keeping the process going, you have not amassed enough evidence by month eighteen to conclusively prove that the goal is worth the pain.

So how do you deal with this crisis? The first step is to recognize it for what it is—a last gasp by the old order to prevent a permanent shift in the culture. The second step is for the organization's leaders to tackle this as a legitimate crisis and not discount the event—it will not go away by itself.

The Chinese have an interesting way of depicting the word "crisis." They use two symbols; the first stands for *danger*, the second for *hidden opportunity*. The danger inherent in this first crisis is apparent. If nothing is done to arrest the chant of "We are not perfect...," the organization will march backward to its starting point, and then back beyond that. Bitterness, disappointment, and a sense of failure will pervade the organization, making it nearly impossible for it to respond to any strategic initiative for years to come. As with a beaten army, discipline and cohesion will erode, and the organization will be reduced to a rabble.

The key to successfully responding to the crisis is to acknowledge the danger by seizing the hidden opportunity inherent within it. And what is this opportunity? The chance to transfer ownership of the quality process from the champions to the organization at large—to have the process truly owned by every member of the organization.

Seizing the opportunity is a *leadership* function. To quote from Caesar's commentaries, "The leader is most required at the moment of crisis, when the issue is in doubt. Then the leader must be visible, inspire confidence, and impose calm and order." These few words summarize exactly what the leaders of an organization must do to respond to the first crisis—you cannot manage your way out of this situation; only leadership will do the trick.

How do you seize the opportunity hidden within the crisis? Every situation is a little different, but here are a few guidelines:

1. Acknowledge the crisis—do not ignore it.
2. Identify the hidden opportunity and set out to seize it.
3. Call together your executive team and make it clear that there is no going back. You are going forward, even if you have to go alone. Formulate a recovery strategy and make your executives part of it.
4. Meet with your managers, supervisors, and, if practical, your employees:

- Give voice to their fears and concerns.
- Do not try to argue with "We are not perfect, so we should stop." It is a sucker's game to try to refute this logic.
- Instead admit "We are not perfect," and then say that that is precisely why we are not going to stop. By giving voice to the "We are not perfect" theme and admitting it, you take away all its power—just like exorcising a demon by naming it.

5. Remind everyone of what has been accomplished. Do not let them discount these accomplishments; itemize each one and congratulate them on their achievements.
6. Remind everyone of the hopeful vision of the future that prompted you to launch your quality effort. Invite everyone to update the vision and review their commitment.
7. Ask for their advice on turning things around. Empower them to get things moving again.
8. Update your service/quality plan and then send it out to *everyone*.
9. Do not take counsel from your fears. Your courage and determination may be all that stands between a recovery and a rout.

Very early into the recovery process you will sense an eerie feeling, lasting from a few days to a few weeks, as panic subsides and the organization decides whether or not to follow you. You will not need to be told when it happens—you will know.

This first crisis cannot be avoided, but its impact can be rendered less lethal by taking some simple precautions at the start of your quality improvement process:

- Keep expectations under control by not making any promises that you cannot keep.
- Build an expectation of setbacks into your process. That is, tell people again and again that setbacks will occur and that this is normal.
- Provide adequate interpersonal skills training for managers, supervisors, and employees so that they can manage the tough human issues associated with change.
- Capture and document all improvements and benefits resulting from the program, no matter how small. Feed this information back to all employees.
- Plan a relaunch, including an executive retreat, at about month twelve. Use the opportunity to review why the process was started, and the goals and vision behind it and highlight the progress to date.
- Ensure that your service/quality plan has clear, attainable goals, time lines, and expectations.
- Do not put off all improvement activities until year two. If possible, plan and execute a few quick improvement projects in year one.

On the road to world-class quality there will be other crises, other moments of decision, but none will prove as difficult and as challenging as the first one. It is not so much a test of the organization as it is a test of its leadership. As Martin Luther King, Jr., said, "The ultimate measure of a leader is not where he stands in moments of comfort and convenience, but where he stands at times of challenge and controversy."

Section III

ORGANIZING AND INTEGRATING ENVIRONMENTAL QUALITY MANAGEMENT BEYOND COMPLIANCE

7

ENVIRONMENTAL LEADERSHIP *PLUS* TOTAL QUALITY MANAGEMENT *EQUALS* CONTINUOUS IMPROVEMENT

Abhay K. Bhushan and James C. MacKenzie

Xerox was one of the first U.S. companies to discover that environmentally sound practices not only result in good community relations, but also often more than pay for themselves. This case study describes the application of the quality process to environmental management at Xerox and shows how a focus on prevention, employee involvement, teamwork, and the use of quality principles and tools can improve profitability for any company.

I n 1980, Xerox formalized its commitment to the environment by establishing a corporate environmental health and safety department. This environmental commitment was greatly reinforced by the company's Leadership Through Quality program, launched in 1984, which led to Xerox Business Products and Systems winning the 1989 Malcolm Baldrige National Quality Award. The cross-fertilization of environmental and quality programs has resulted in environmental leadership at Xerox that represents the application of total quality environmental management principles.

In the 1990s, driven by customer requirements, competitive pressures, and resource conservation opportunities, environmental

Abhay K. Bhushan is manager of Environmental Leadership Programs for Xerox Corporation. James C. MacKenzie is director of Environmental Health and Safety for Xerox Corporation.

issues are becoming part of basic business strategy and are being integrated into the quality culture at Xerox. In this article, we will describe the application of the quality process to environmental management and show how the focus on prevention, employee involvement, teamwork, and the use of quality principles and tools can improve profitability for any company. We will also discuss the Xerox Environmental Leadership Program, how it is organized and managed, the projects that are part of the program, and the drive for continuous environmental quality improvement. Environmental leadership at Xerox is being reflected in all major business functions, including product and packaging design, manufacturing and operations, and marketing. Environmental communication is also a necessary part of the total quality environmental management approach.

FROM COMPLIANCE TO STRATEGIC PRIORITY

Traditionally, for most U.S. corporations, environmental programs have been driven by laws and regulations imposed by society, mostly influencing the periphery of the company's operations (see **Figure 1**).

Figure 1

Traditional View of Environmental Compliance

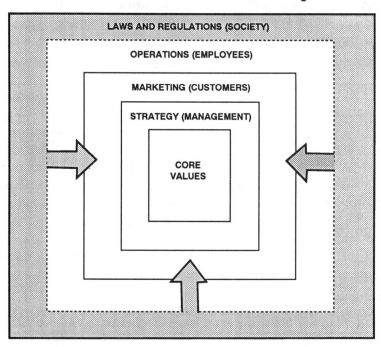

LAWS AND REGULATIONS (SOCIETY)

OPERATIONS (EMPLOYEES)

MARKETING (CUSTOMERS)

STRATEGY (MANAGEMENT)

CORE VALUES

A 1990 survey by Deloitte & Touche revealed that regulatory compliance issues dominate environmental concerns for most U.S. corporations.[1] However, as the vast majority of companies expect the regulations to become *more strict*, the reactive approach is yielding to proactive compliance as companies anticipate the changes in regulation.

During the last several years, there have been strong market and competitive forces affecting the basic business strategies as well as corporate core values. These forces include consumer boycotts, changing preferences, new customer requirements, and enormous resource conservation opportunities to make the business more cost competitive (see **Figure 2**). A more recent 1991 survey by Abt Associates revealed that 77 percent of senior management now defines environment as critical or important to strategic decisions.[2] Increasingly, nonenvironmental managers at Xerox and at other companies are being given environmental responsibilities, as environmental concerns are being built into products and processes.

Figure 2 ═══════════════════════════════════════

Emerging View of Environment as a Strategic Priority

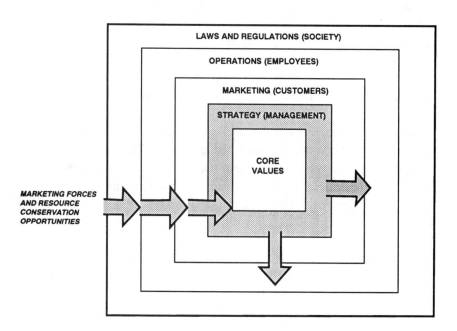

Xerox discovered before many other companies that environmentally sound practices not only result in good community relations, but also often more than pay for themselves. Preventing pollution, increasing efficiency, reducing waste, and conserving resources inevitably lead to increased competitiveness and greater profitability. In many cases, it is not just a free lunch, it is a lunch you are paid to eat! Looking back, it appears that the company went through two major phases in the continuing development of its environmental programs. The first phase of proactive environmental practices can be traced to several events in 1984 and 1985, and the second phase, which made environmental leadership a strategic priority, was formally established in 1990.

CORPORATE ENVIRONMENTAL POLICY
AND QUALITY CULTURE

Early in the 1980s, Xerox adopted its basic environmental policy: *Xerox Corporation is committed to the protection of the environment and the health and safety of its employees, customers and neighbors. This commitment is applied worldwide in developing new products and processes.* As part of the principles supporting the basic policy, environmental health and safety concerns take priority over economic considerations. Continual improvement is a commitment to quality in environmental protection and resource conservation. This is applied to both the company's operations and the design of its products, including design for optimal recyclability and reusability. Xerox is also committed to using every opportunity to recycle or reuse waste materials generated by the company's operations.

The worldwide implementation of this policy was accelerated when in December 1984, the world was horror-struck by the catastrophe (at another company's pesticide facility) in Bhopal, India, which caused several thousand deaths and over a hundred thousand injuries. This immense tragedy shocked most corporate leaders. David Kearns, then CEO of Xerox, concluded that management must act quickly and thoroughly to ensure the prevention of environmental mishaps at Xerox worldwide.

This emphasis on prevention was in line with the company's increasing focus on quality. In 1984, Kearns and senior Xerox management launched the Leadership Through Quality (LTQ) program. The LTQ process was cascaded from top to bottom *through the entire corporation*, and involved the training of all 100,000 employees worldwide. This process, a major culture change for Xerox, embraced quality principles, management practices, and the use of quality tools (see **Figure 3**).

At Xerox, management encourages teamwork to facilitate the quality process. Each person is responsible for quality, which means understanding and fully meeting customer requirements. The term "customer" is defined very broadly to include not only the end customers for Xerox products and services, but also anyone for whose benefit work is performed. This includes internal Xerox customers as well as surrounding communities and society. Management behavior visibly reinforces the quality process with openness, trust, respect, patience, and discipline.

To make Xerox a total quality company, intensive training is provided in the use of quality tools to all employees. This includes interactive skills, teamwork, benchmarking, quality goal setting, measurement and monitoring, and systematic defect- and error-prevention processes, as well as the use of statistical and analytical tools. Communication and recognition programs were established to encourage employees to use the quality process. A method for measuring the Cost of Quality—actually the cost of lost quality—was developed to reinforce the preventive approach. It was, therefore, natural to apply the quality process with its emphasis on prevention to environmental issues, as part of total quality management.

Figure 3

Xerox Corporate Culture of Leadership Through Quality

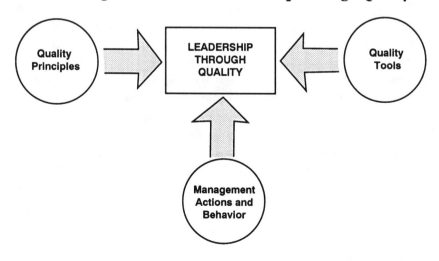

FOCUS ON PREVENTION

In January 1985, the environmental health and safety group was directed to identify and eliminate all potential environmental hazards in the company. An environmental assessment was performed at all Xerox locations worldwide. The worst potential outcome of any hazard was assumed. Unacceptable risks were eliminated, chemical storage was minimized, and hazardous chemicals were avoided in processes wherever possible. Safe building evacuation standards that are routinely applied in the United States were required at all locations worldwide. A program was begun to eliminate, or in a few cases secondarily contain, underground storage tanks. The following examples illustrate the preventive approach to pollution and environmental hazards:

- At one location, Xerox discovered a large storage of arsenic and selenium near warehouses that contained food and pharmaceuticals. Though the probability of disaster was low, the risk was also unnecessary. The storage site was moved to another area and the amount of chemicals deemed acceptable at any one location was greatly reduced.
- At a Xerox facility situated near a nursing home, the stored tanks of chlorine were first reduced, then removed, and finally chlorine was eliminated altogether from the manufacturing process.

Concurrently, Xerox surveyed worldwide locations at which industrial solvents had been used at any time in the past. This survey focused on possible groundwater or soil deposits of such solvents either adjacent to or underneath each facility. Where such deposits were found, action was taken immediately to prevent the material from migrating. Appropriate government agencies were notified, and remedial plans were developed and implemented with the consent of the agencies. At locations not covered by environmental laws, Xerox took voluntary remedial action, applying the same policy worldwide. In emphasizing management's commitment to environmental protection, David Kearns said, "If we cannot afford to protect the environment, we should get out of the business."[3] In keeping with this commitment, Xerox spent over fifty million dollars in proactive environmental remediation.

As a cornerstone to quality, a prevention program was implemented to protect the environment and is ongoing at all operations.

This includes institutionalizing procedures for reviewing all processes and process changes from an environmental standpoint. Systematic environmental audits are conducted at least annually at all manufacturing facilities, and less often at office locations. Instead of just looking for potential hazards, all practices must meet the higher standards established for the corporation. These standards greatly exceed the local requirements in many of the countries where Xerox has operations.

Work of this nature is admittedly costly. However, failure to prevent or remediate an environmental problem early can be orders of magnitude more expensive. Ultimately, it can result in potentially huge fines and generate public ill will that can seriously hurt business. The costs of lost quality can be very substantial. Even with strong corporate direction, the task at Xerox was difficult in the mid-eighties as environment was not a top priority for most managers. Xerox was facing stiff competition from IBM and Kodak at the high end, and the Japanese at the low end of the copier and printer market. Initially, many managers viewed the additional expenses mandated by higher corporate standards as unnecessary. This initial resistance was overcome by strong leadership from Xerox senior management, who mandated the environmental initiatives and also provided much of the needed funding. In retrospect, with the increased focus worldwide on the environment and the ensuing stricter regulations, Xerox managers are glad to have made these investments. Not only did the environmental initiatives reduce future liabilities, but in many cases operating costs were also reduced as a result of environmental improvements.

The preventive approach often yields unexpected benefits. In 1967, because of potential health hazards associated with disposal of photoreceptor drums made from aluminum with a selenium and arsenic alloy coating, Xerox decided to reclaim these parts. What started out as a way to avoid a potential hazard became a profitable business decision. Xerox discovered that the photoreceptor drums could be remanufactured to the same quality as new ones at a fraction of the cost. This remanufacturing philosophy has gradually expanded to include many other machine parts. Today Xerox is reclaiming about one million finished piece parts worldwide each year, representing a total value of $200 million. As 3M and others have demonstrated, *Pollution Prevention Pays.*[4]

QUALITY PRINCIPLES AND TOOLS

The institution of the preventive environmental programs coincided with the rollout of the Leadership Through Quality (LTQ) process at Xerox.[5] The programs benefited from the quality culture that was developing—especially management's recognition of the need for quality environmental management. LTQ established quality as a basic business principle for Xerox and trained employees on the use of fundamental quality principles:

- Understand customers' existing and latent requirements.
- Provide all external and internal customers with products and services that fully satisfy their requirements.
- Employee involvement and teamwork, through participative problem solving, is essential to improve quality.
- Error-free work is the most cost-effective way to improve quality.

Customer Focus

Customer satisfaction was established as the number-one objective of Xerox Corporation. This objective applied equally to environmental matters. Internally, it is essential for the various operating groups and Environmental Engineering to work as a team in understanding and complying with regulatory requirements, selecting environmentally friendly materials, minimizing waste, recycling, and conserving resources. Long-range goals and product specifications reflect good environmental principles in terms of materials, design, waste minimization, resource recovery and recyclability, and, therefore, Xerox's customer acceptability.

In addition to traditional customers for the company's products, a quality environmental program must also meet the requirements of other important customers. Government agencies at municipal, county, state, and federal levels have regulations that must be complied with. Xerox has established a proactive practice of frequent and open communication with all agencies—in terms of disclosing ongoing and future activities of broad environmental interest as well as reporting compliance with legal requirements.

Employee Involvement

The cultural change, mastering the LTQ process, and the evolution of a common language among all Xerox employees took place over several years. These changes were in direct support of the expanding environmental programs, as well as product design, manufacturing, and marketing activities. Through employee involvement, Xerox was successful in identifying many opportunities for environmental quality improvement. Empowered with the quality process, employees started a number of initiatives, from local grass-roots recycling efforts to worldwide, all-plant programs. These opportunities are yielding millions of dollars in added profits each year.

Environmental initiatives are prime outcomes of employees using the LTQ tools of problem solving, the Quality Improvement Process (QIP), and teamwork. Xerox management encourages the formation of cross-functional teams to focus on quality improvement projects. Often, these Quality Improvement Teams (QITs) focus on environmental issues, discovering that they can help business results and the environment at the same time. Employee enthusiasm for projects that include environmental benefits is generally higher than that for other types of projects.

Quality Improvement and Problem Solving

The Xerox Quality Improvement Process encompasses planning, organizing, and monitoring for quality (see **Figure 4**). In the planning phase, the focus is on identifying what is to be done and for whom, and in arriving at realistic expectations and specifications. In the organizing phase, the focus is on defining how the output can be produced, selecting measurements for success, and determining if the work process is capable of producing the desired results. If the work process fails this test, then the problem-solving process (PSP) is applied.

The problem-solving process includes the steps of analysis, generating potential solutions, selecting, planning, and implementing solutions, and then evaluating to see how effectively the problem has been solved. A number of analytical tools such as control charts, process flow, cause and effect (Ishikawa or fishbone diagrams), statistics, pie charts, and force-field analysis are used to help in analyzing and generating solutions.

To see how this process is used at Xerox, consider the example of how our European Manufacturing Operation's Packaging team addressed the problem of developing environmentally acceptable packaging that would meet imminent global legislation. The root cause problem analysis (see **Figure 5**) shows the environmental and legislative concerns associated with functional packaging, including corrugated board, cushioning materials, plastics, and timber (pallets). Focusing on cushioning materials, the team identified many potential solutions and selected Corrupad and Molded Pulp, based on identified customer requirements (see **Figure 6**). These materials are made from post-consumer recycled waste and are easily recyclable.

Figure 4

Xerox Quality Improvement and Problem-Solving Processes

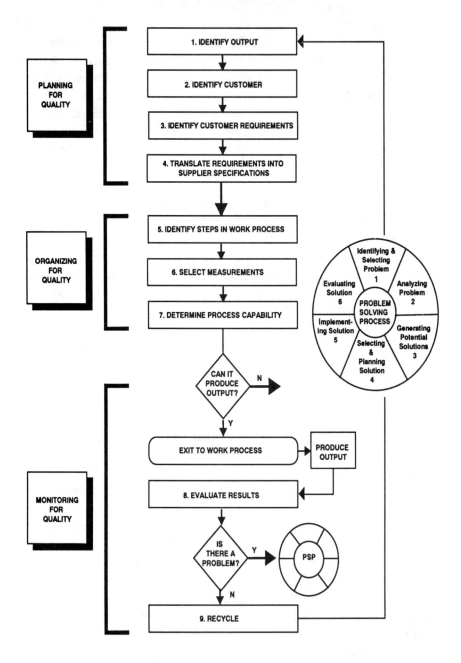

Figure 5

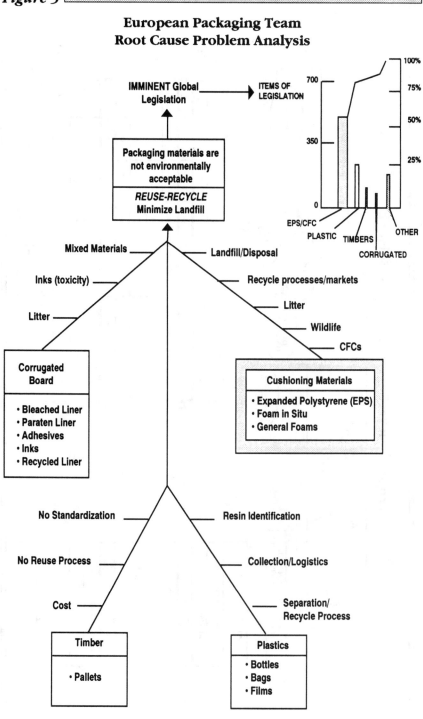

European Packaging Team
Root Cause Problem Analysis

Figure 6

European Packaging Team Selecting Solutions

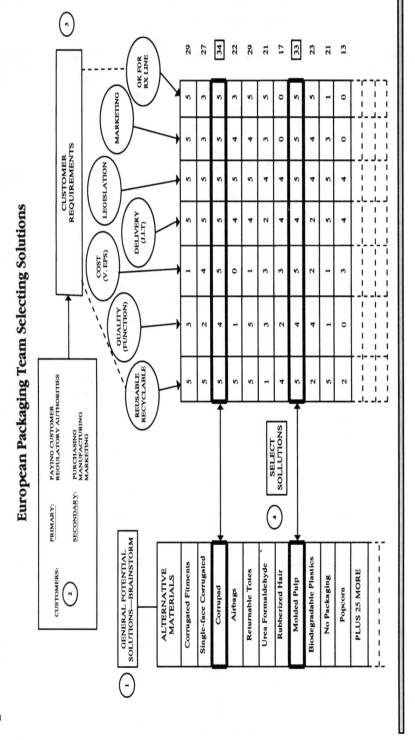

The solution has been implemented successfully and is resulting in improved customer satisfaction, easier regulatory compliance, and cost savings of about $2 million a year for Xerox. The packaging team won both internal (Xerox Team Excellence) and external (Silver Star, Starpack 91) awards for its innovative solution.

In the final monitoring-for-quality phase of QIP, the results are evaluated to see if the output fully satisfies customer requirements. The focus is on identifying any required changes and additional opportunities for quality improvements. Quality improvement is a continuous process that is significantly enhanced by benchmarking and a program for systematic measurement and monitoring.

Benchmarking and Measurement

Benchmarking is an important element in the quality process. It involves identifying the industry leaders and best practices in each area of environmental improvement, then studying their methods, metrics, and results and identifying their goals. Best practice is any method used in any work process whose output best meets customer requirements. Xerox goals and practices are then based in part on what is learned from the benchmarking activity.

The benchmarking process provides increased insight and motivation to the teams working on quality improvement projects; it ensures setting of higher, realistic and measurable goals; and it leads to superior performance. Benchmarking is immensely valuable in developing good measures of performance and combating the NIH (Not Invented Here) syndrome. The Japanese term *dantotsu*, which means "best of the best," incorporates the essence of this process.[6]

Reward and Recognition

Another aspect of the quality process is reward and recognition for team excellence and individual excellence. Five environmentally-oriented QITs won the 1990 Team Excellence awards. The projects undertaken by these teams included improved environmentally sound packaging, reuse of pallets and packaging, marketing recycled paper for Xerox copiers and printers, and waste reduction and recycling at the sites. Added public recognition and environmental awards were provided to the teams to encourage increased focus on environmental excellence.

Individual top-level awards were given for energy conservation, initiating the National Office Paper Recycling Project, and a patented two-phase vacuum extraction cleanup process. Environmental values are being internalized within Xerox as part of normal management processes.

ENVIRONMENTAL LEADERSHIP AND
SUSTAINABLE DEVELOPMENT

The second phase of environmental intensification at Xerox was aided by the increased awareness and enthusiasm from employees and customers stimulated by Earth Day 1990. In October 1990, the Xerox Environmental Leadership program was formally approved by senior corporate management and communicated to all managers and employees by Paul Allaire, the CEO of Xerox. This action brought increased focus on waste reduction and the growing recognition among management that proactively protecting the environment and "doing the right thing" is the safest and surest way to long-term profitability. Management commitment is vital to the success of any Total Quality Environmental Management (TQEM) program.[7]

Environmental Leadership Organization

A senior management Environmental Leadership Steering Committee was formed in late 1990 to guide the environmental programs (see **Figure 7**). This steering committee has representation from the heads of major functional groups as well as the worldwide Operating Companies (field marketing sales and service). The Steering Committee has been meeting on a quarterly basis to provide added focus and resolve program content and funding issues. Quarterly reporting on the program elements to the Steering Committee and to the CEO and his staff provides a measurement of progress toward the established goals. The manager of the Environmental Leadership programs has the responsibility to coordinate and help improve the environmental initiatives companywide, to facilitate communication to employees, customers, and the public about such initiatives, and to benchmark the progress of other companies in order to provide a yardstick for Xerox's efforts.

Teamwork, communication, recognition, and information sharing via the extensive Xerox corporate electronic network are being used to build new environmental initiatives. Several companywide electronic mail distribution lists and information databases have been set up to facilitate coordination and communication among teams and individuals on new environmental initiatives. These include the "Xerox Green" distribution list and database with more than 300 committed individuals working on various aspects of the environmental leadership programs worldwide.

Asset Recycling and Design for Environment

As a prime example of these new initiatives, Xerox has adopted a

***Figure* 7**

Environmental Leadership Organization

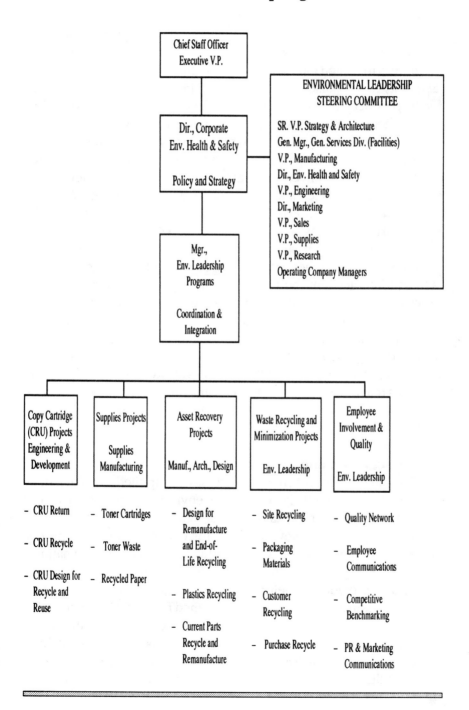

"cradle-to-grave" requirement for design architectures that addresses environmental concerns throughout product life cycles. Environmental requirements addressing every aspect of a product's life cycle have been adopted to minimize environmental impact and provide savings through parts recovery, remanufacturing, and recycling (including plastics recycling). The key objective in our "Asset Management" program is to design into our products all the elements of environmental quality at the outset. Thus design will include the total life strategy for the product—not only form, fit, and functions, but also disassembly, remanufacture, reuse, recycle, and final disposition. Environmental requirements are being incorporated into product specifications, architecture standards, and long-range plans. Enforcement is achieved via the Product Delivery Process, with mandatory reviews. The environmental policies and standards documented in the *Corporate Functional Guide* and *EH&S Standards* are implemented via regular management practices.

Decision making based on life-cycle costs is not easy, as many of the tools and techniques are not fully developed. Even more difficult is taking into account the full environmental costs of a product or a process. This is not established or accepted practice, and our focus on the near term seriously impedes the full consideration of life-cycle environmental costs. Nevertheless, Xerox has made a good beginning in considering these costs and making decisions that enable economical remanufacturing and result in significant savings. Procedures and practices resulting in improved asset management are likely to provide annual savings of hundreds of millions of dollars a year in addition to protecting the environment.

Packaging Reuse and Recycle

The quality improvement process was applied by packaging engineers to substantially reduce the environmental impact of our supplier and product packaging. In addition to the development of Corrupad cushioning as a substitute for expanded polystyrene discussed earlier, another team developed a comprehensive multinational supplier packaging program (88P311) to standardize packaging and pallets and provide for their reuse.

Suppliers are being educated and trained for the 88P311 packaging recycle/reuse program and the Xerox purchase recycle initiatives. The training package includes detailed instructions accompanied by a video. This program will avoid about 10,000 tons of waste and save up to $15 million annually. Other environmental packaging innovations include the use of corrugated shipping containers with an outer surface layer made exclusively from repulped, non-deinked office wastepaper for supplies packaging, and mixed wastepaper brown (MWP Brown) recycled packaging containers.

Recycled Paper

Xerox, Rank Xerox, and Fuji Xerox all offer xerographic paper with post-consumer recycled content. In 1990, a Xerox team developed and introduced a recycled copy paper in the United States and Canada composed of 50 percent recycled fiber and 10 percent post-consumer waste. Rank Xerox introduced an "environmental paper" in Europe that is manufactured without using chlorine bleach and optical brighteners, and meets Greenpeace's Group A criteria.

Another Rank Xerox recycled paper is doubly qualified for Greenpeace Group A criteria because it uses 100 percent recycled wastepaper *and* is made without using chlorine bleach or optical brightening agents. This paper has also been awarded Germany's coveted "Blue Angel"—the country's emblem of environmental acceptability—which requires that at least 50 percent of the content come from "low-grade" wastes such as newspapers, phone books, and magazines.

Waste Reduction and Recycling

A major project involving almost every employee is waste reduction and recycling at every facility. This program is being institutionalized through the formation of conservation and recycling teams at the different facilities. The Xerox Site Waste Reduction and Recycling Team, a core group, provides guidance and service to the individual teams at each location. The program emphasizes the Reduce, Reuse and Recycle waste reduction hierarchy as well as the purchase of recycled material to close the loop in recycling (see program logo, **Figure 8**).

Xerox is investigating new uses for waste toner from the company's manufacturing operations. Several promising solutions, including masterbatch pigmentation for plastics, asphalt additives, gaskets, and plastics lumber are in various stages of implementation. Tons of waste toner will be diverted from landfills to constructive uses, resulting in expected savings of over a million dollars a year.

Recognizing customer concerns about disposable products, Xerox has developed cost-effective procedures for retrieving and recycling customer-replaceable copy cartridges. Furthermore, the company has

Figure 8

Xerox Facilities Waste Reduction and Recycling Program Logo

now established design standards for its future products, including copy cartridges and toner containers, that provide an integrated approach to extended life, reduced cost, recycling, and remanufacturing compatibility. Customers participate in partnership with Xerox in copy cartridge return, parts reuse, and paper recycling programs.

Partnerships

Working in cooperation with others is an important aspect of the Total Quality Environmental Management approach. This includes consultants, competitors, suppliers, government agencies, and environmental organizations. Xerox worked early on with several environmental consulting companies to develop innovative procedures and techniques for environmental remediation. In 1990, the company became a founding sponsor of the National Office Paper Recycling Project, one of eight companies to join the U.S. Conference of Mayors in developing a comprehensive national strategy to maximize recycling of office waste paper and reduce the volume of paper being sent to landfills.

The U.S. Environmental Protection Agency (EPA) has initiated several major partnership programs for U.S. businesses that Xerox has joined. These include EPA's Green Lights partnership program for energy conservation as well as EPA's "33/50" program for emission reductions of seventeen industrial toxics: 33 percent by the end of 1992 and 50 percent by the end of 1995.

In 1991, Xerox and Rank Xerox joined other companies worldwide in supporting the International Chamber of Commerce Charter for Sustainable Development. This charter embodies sixteen principles for environmental management that we are using as a guide in improving our environmental performance. At Xerox, sustainable development means satisfying present needs without compromising the ability of future generations to meet their needs.

Setting Goals and Monitoring for Improvement

Total Quality Environmental Management must contain the essential element of continuous improvement, or *Kaizen.*[8] Continuous quality improvement builds on benchmarking, measurement, and monitoring of progress toward goals. These goals are regularly reviewed and changed as required to meet benchmarks, as improvements are made internally or by the industry. The goals should be as high as possible but realistic and measurable.

As an example, when the goals for site recycling at Xerox were first set in early 1990, it was a 50 percent waste reduction and recycling goal by the end of 1992. At the time, this seemed to be an uphill task. By early 1991, many of the larger manufacturing sites were already exceeding the 50 percent goal. The goal was then revised to be continuous improvement quarter over quarter, and year over year. By the end of 1991, quite a few sites had reached 60 percent; the manufacturing site in Oklahoma City reached 78 percent in third quarter; and the site in Venray, Netherlands, exceeded 82 percent. The initial Xerox goal of 50 percent by 1992 was based on industry benchmarking. While overall, it may still be a reasonable goal, internal and further industry benchmarking showed that this was not a high enough goal for individual sites that can aspire to 90 percent by the end of 1992.

To ensure total quality environmental management, important environmental concerns such as ozone depletion were identified, and the quality process was applied to make improvements. Xerox has been eliminating the use of ozone-depleting chlorofluorocarbons (CFCs) in packaging, service materials, and manufacturing operations. A goal was set to eliminate CFC usage in all operations (except refrigeration and air conditioning) by the end of 1991. Whenever possible, Xerox now uses natural, biodegradable cleaners and water in place of chemical solvents in machine-refurbishing operations. From

1982 to 1990, solvent air emissions at the Webster Refurbishing Center dropped by over 90 percent by substituting d-limonene (citrus-based cleaner) for solvents. Similar results were obtained in a photoreceptor postlathing cleaning process by substituting citric acid cleaner for trichloroethane. These practices avoid 1.5 million pounds of chlorinated hydrocarbon waste annually with an associated half million pounds reduction in air emissions. In the spirit of continuous improvement, Xerox has been developing a CO_2-based cleaning process (blasting by solid CO_2 pellets) that appears even more effective and environmentally sound than soap and water and citrus-based cleaners.

The company has also taken a number of measures to reduce or eliminate hazardous waste and emissions. For example, by substituting soap and water solution, methylene chloride was completely eliminated from photoreceptor cleaning operations. Methylene chloride is one of the TRI (Toxic Release Inventory) chemicals monitored by EPA. It is a suspected human carcinogen that easily vaporizes. Substituting non-toxic cleaning alternatives for methylene chloride has saved Xerox $400,000 a year in hazardous waste disposal costs. Methylene chloride is also used in a coating operation related to polyester-based photoreceptors. In 1989, Xerox began installing a state-of-the-art recovery system, at a cost of several million dollars, to remove methylene chloride emissions. This system, when completed this year, will eliminate about 90 percent of the methylene chloride emissions.

COMMUNICATION AND OUTREACH

The development of the Environmental Leadership Program as a companywide initiative has brought increased focus on communication and outreach for environmental issues. Environmental communication and marketing at Xerox are part of our total quality approach (see **Figure 9**). The communication is focused on customer and employee education and very selective advertising and promotion for product and company positioning.

For customers, Xerox created brochures that describe the company's environmental philosophy and policy, as well as its notable accomplishments. A booklet, "Facts About the Safety of Xerox Products," has been developed to educate employees and customers on product safety. The Summer 1991 issue of *Benchmark*, a quarterly magazine for Xerox customers, focused on environmental concerns and initiatives with the theme "Preserving Planet Earth." A number of new initiatives, such as copy cartridge return and recycle, use of recycled paper, and office paper recycling, directly involve the

Figure 9

Environmental Communication and Marketing
as Part of a Total Quality
Environmental Management Approach

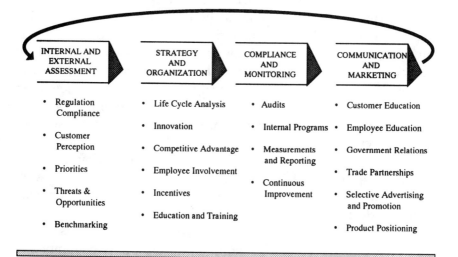

INTERNAL AND EXTERNAL ASSESSMENT	STRATEGY AND ORGANIZATION	COMPLIANCE AND MONITORING	COMMUNICATION AND MARKETING
• Regulation Compliance	• Life Cycle Analysis	• Audits	• Customer Education
• Customer Perception	• Innovation	• Internal Programs	• Employee Education
• Priorities	• Competitive Advantage	• Measurements and Reporting	• Government Relations
• Threats & Opportunities	• Employee Involvement	• Continuous Improvement	• Trade Partnerships
• Benchmarking	• Incentives		• Selective Advertising and Promotion
	• Education and Training		• Product Positioning

customers, and these are described in a new brochure, "Paper Recycling: A Perspective."

Employee communication has immense benefits for any company. As employees become better informed and educated on environmental issues, they are a most important agent for change. Motivated employees avoid waste and save money for the company. Well-informed employees also provide effective communication to customers and the general public. Employee communication initiatives at Xerox include management communiques from the CEO, an Environmental Health and Safety newsletter, and articles focusing on the environment in employee publications. To reinforce the company's environmental commitment, these publications are printed on recycled paper. Additional communication channels include the company's extensive electronic mail network, employee forums, and videos. Regular Earth Day celebrations at different locations also reinforce employee communication and involvement.

With the growth of environmentally and socially responsible investment funds, there has been increased focus on environmental communication for shareholders. The Xerox Corporation 1990 Annual

Report carried a four-page special Environmental Leadership section. In 1991, the quarterly reports to shareholders continued the focus on environmental issues, and environment will be a regular feature in future annual reports. An added benefit of communication via the reports to shareholders is that all employees, as shareholders in the Employee Stock Ownership Plan, receive this communication.

The surrounding communities and the general public are being kept informed of Xerox's initiatives through regular press releases, press briefings, participation at industry conferences and seminars, and other direct communications. Open, honest, and factual communication with the news media is essential to enable them to meet their responsibilities and provide fair representation of the corporation's environmental posture. Motives, hazards, risks, and responsibilities can be accepted only if they are understood by all. Our environmental program includes communication with our neighbors by means of newsletters, open public meetings, town meetings, and a well-publicized phone number of the Director of Corporate Environmental Health and Safety.

So far, there has been little advertising on environmental issues, as the focus remains in making the necessary environmental improvements. In the future, the environmental message will be carried via our regular product advertising, and possibly some selective advertising that is informative and educational. By benchmarking and learning from others, Xerox is avoiding the pitfalls of green marketing, such as in the case of the biodegradable plastic bag that undermines consumer confidence.[9]

FINAL THOUGHTS

At Xerox, our TQEM goal is continuous improvement, until we can virtually eliminate pollution and waste. Zero Defects, Zero Disposal, and Zero Pollution are goals that we can strive for in our quest for sustainable development. We will continue to benchmark the world's leading companies for each of our environmental initiatives, and learn from these companies to equal or exceed their environmental performance, and to be the "best of the best."

To be sure, new initiatives will be added as we intensify our focus on the preventive approach, and new quality tools will be developed to address life-cycle cost analysis. As in the drive for quality throughout the company, environmental management is seen as a race without a finish line, demanding continuously renewed effort and commitment.

Notes

1. Deloitte & Touche, "The Environmental Transformation of U.S. Industry: A Survey of U.S. Industrial Corporations—Environmental Strategies, Management Policies & Perceptions," September 1990. (Study with Stanford University Graduate School of Business Public Management Program). For further information, contact Deloitte & Touche, 275 Battery Street, San Francisco, CA 94111.

2. Abt Associates Inc., Wells, R.P., and Lent, T., "From Compliance to Strategy," 11th Annual International Strategic Management Society, Toronto, October 25, 1991. For further information, contact Richard Wells at 617-492-7100.

3. David Kearns, Xerox CEO, quoted in June 1990 issue of *XeroxWorld*, a monthly publication for Xerox employees.

4. 3M Corporation's 3P (Pollution Prevention Pays) and 3P Plus programs are widely acclaimed and discussed in a number of publications, including Joel Hirschhorn's book, *Prosperity Without Pollution*, Van Nostrand Reinhold, 1991.

5. Xerox Leadership Through Quality program is described in a number of publications, including *Leadership Through Quality Kit*, available for purchase from Xerox (Contact: Customer Service Lead, 1-800-828-5881).

6. Camp, Robert C., *Benchmarking: The Search for Industry Best Practices That Lead to Superior Performance*, ASQC Quality Press, 1989. This is an excellent book on benchmarking based on the author's experience at Xerox.

7. Smith, A.C., "Ten Steps Toward Integrated Environmental Excellence," 1 *Total Quality Environmental Management* 3 (Autumn 1991). "Environmental quality leadership must begin with top management" was listed as the first step.

8. Imai, M., *Kaizen—The Key to Japan's Competitive Success*, Random House, NY, 1986. Xerox is also using the Kaizen process for continuous improvement of its product line.

9. *Green Business: Hope or Hoax*, edited by Christopher Plant and Judith Plant, New Society Publishers, 1991. This book discusses some of the green marketing pitfalls.

8

ENVIRONMENTAL MARKETING'S NEW RELATIONSHIP WITH CORPORATE ENVIRONMENTAL MANAGEMENT

Walter Coddington

Issues of environmental marketing track back to issues of environmental management—i.e., to issues of overall corporate environmental commitment and responsibility. It is absolutely essential that a commitment to corporate environmental improvement be in place before an environmental marketing program is launched. Additionally, marketers can and should play a central role in the greening of the corporation. The marketer brings at least two important skills or strengths to the environmental improvement process—strengths of perspective and strengths of skill set.

Growth of the consumer packaged goods industry in the United States has been managed largely by marketers who depend on market research, scientific and technical breakthroughs,

Walter Coddington *is the founder and president of the New York-based environmental marketing consultancy Coddington Environmental Management, the first full-service marketing management and communications consultancy, whose clients include House of Seagrams, Miller Brewing, Pepsi USA, Ragu Foods, United Media, Glidden Paint, General Electric, Bristol-Myers, and Del Laboratories. This article is excerpted in part from* Environmental Marketing: Positive Strategies for Reaching the Green Consumer *by Walter Coddington (1993, McGraw-Hill).*

quality and financial controls, trade relations, and promotion to accomplish their mission.

Today, however, another major influence acts on the marketing planning and implementation process—the environment. More specifically, I am referring to the environmental impacts of the manufacturing, management, and marketing processes as measured by scientists, regulators, grassroots environmentalists, investors, and the consuming public. Marketing activities that recognize the environment as a business development responsibility and business growth opportunity are what I mean by "environmental marketing."

Eldon Enger and Brad Smith, in their book, *Environmental Science: A Study of Interrelationships*, inform us that "environmental science is an interdisciplinary area of study...[one] that must also deal with areas of politics, social organization, economics, ethics, and philosophy." And so it is with environmental management. The environment has an impact on every business cost decision area from raw material, pollution prevention, and waste management costs to research and development, administrative, and marketing costs. A company's environmental marketing initiatives are, therefore, usually accompanied by—if not driven by—a gradual change in corporate culture and the way in which the company does business: a shift from compliance-oriented environmental management to proactive environmental management and marketing planning.

In response to regulatory and activist pressure for corporate environmental stewardship, many U.S. businesses are doing the bare minimum required by the law. According to Martin Charter, editorial director of *Greenleaf*, a number of U.K. companies are using, for example, the CATNIP principle (Cheapest Available Technology Not Involving Prosecution) versus the BATNEEC principle (Best Available Technology Not Entailing Excessive Cost). This is legally adequate but strategically regressive. Whereas, for example, the outgoing U.S. government administration's Council on Competitiveness focused on ways to help industry get off the environmental hook by halting new environmental regulations and weakening others, Japan prepares to supply the global market with alternative energy sources and green products and processes. More forward-thinking managers are identifying and seizing new environmentally-related business opportunities, ranging from pollution prevention and more efficient technologies to environmental education and "green" product promotion. Similarly, conservative executives among the ranks of "follow the crowd" corporations focus on the $130 billion to $140 billion estimated cost of complying with environmental regulations, whereas "leadership" company marketing executives at Procter & Gamble, Canon, and others hasten to gain a competitive edge in the market by leveraging their environmental improvement initiatives.

The environmental marketer adds the environment to the standard mix of decision-making variables. But the environment is a unique variable, for it is omnipresent, serving as a backdrop against which all strategic decisions are made. No matter what the specific subject is—product and packaging design and development, labeling and advertising, or promotional strategies—the environmental marketer takes environmental considerations into account.

Thus environmental marketing is also about a change in marketing perspective. But it is even more than that. It demands a new set of procedures for implementing the strategies that arise out of environmental impact consideration, resulting in a fundamental change in how we do business.

For most consumers, altruistic concern about the contamination and degradation of their natural physical environment is accompanied by personal and practical worries about the impact of this environmental damage on their health and safety and on that of their loved ones. The highly charged nature of consumers' environmental anxieties makes it doubly important for marketers to exercise extreme care when they incorporate the environment into their business decisions.

ENVIRONMENTAL MARKETING AND ENVIRONMENTAL MANAGEMENT

Paradoxical as this may sound, environmental marketing is about more than environmental marketing. It's not enough, for example, to make environmental claims about a product or a package, even if these claims are truthful, if the manufacturer has a negative or suspect environmental record. Environmental messages will inevitably be viewed as attempts to deliver a message about the manufacturer's overall environmental commitment. If the two communications are perceived by consumers as being inconsistent, even apparently innocuous environmental product or packaging claims run the risk of backfiring.

Issues of environmental *marketing* thus track back to issues of environmental *management*—i.e., to issues of overall corporate environmental commitment and responsibility. It is absolutely essential that a commitment to environmental improvement be in place before an environmental marketing program is launched. Otherwise, the marketing program will be neither credible nor sustainable.

This does not mean that a company's environmental performance must be perfect before beginning environmental marketing. Performance needs time to catch up with policy. Not every process and product design will reflect the highest standard of environmental sensitivity. Still, before an environmental marketing program is launched, a corporation has to have begun the process of incorporating environmental considerations into the length and breadth of its management operations.

Environmental marketing's umbilical connection to environmental management broadens the role of the marketing executive. The messages used to target the [external] customer or consumer will be based on the environmental activity engaged in by the [internal] company. Marketing executives who want to practice environmental marketing should actively participate in internal environmental management decision making through such activities as involvement with the corporate environmental management task force. Typically this involves functioning in the dual role of (1) scout who reports to the corporation on relevant external factors and (2) advocate who promotes higher levels of environmental understanding and stewardship within the organization.

THE ROLE OF THE MARKETER ON THE CORPORATE ENVIRONMENTAL MANAGEMENT TASK FORCE

The marketer's participation on the corporate environmental task force or the environmental improvement team benefits both the environmental management process and the marketer's own environmental marketing activities.

The environmental task force is the hub of most environmental management programs or processes. The marketer can and should play a central or leading role on that committee. Marketing executives bring two strengths to that activity: (1) perspective and (2) skill set.

Strengths of Perspective

Because they usually focus on marketplace issues, marketers contribute a special sensitivity to the external implications of environmental management decisions. This allows them to contribute to the environmental management process in three important ways:

- They can identify the marketing implications of corporate

environmental exposures and initiatives. Marketers provide a much-needed "voice from the marketing front" (i.e., they can help management to understand the all-important marketing implications of a company's environmental strengths and weaknesses).

- Marketers can help to identify new business product and service opportunities that arise out of those same environmental exposures and initiatives. (More than one company has used its own hazardous waste cleanup obligations as a springboard for entry into the hazardous waste remediation business.)

- Marketers can work to ensure that when corporate environmental policies are developed, the marketing implications are given due consideration. It is much better to have input before the fact than to be left to gnash one's teeth after the damage has been done.

Strengths of Skill Set

More often than not, the job of environmental management director has fallen to engineering or technical professionals. "Vice president of environment, health, and safety" is a typical title.

Considering the nature of their training, it is not surprising that these people have tended to take a straightforward, linear approach to their work. What is the simplest way to get from Point A to Point B? That is often the technician's approach to problem solving, and it has been the way environmental management has traditionally been handled.

But linear thinking is not what environmental management is about. For one thing, environmental management places a premium on communication (including encouraging people to modify their behavior)—and communication is not an ability that technical specialists are renowned for possessing. (Let me say, however, that I firmly believe it will be the conscientious and capable scientists and engineers who will mitigate the consequences of our excessive consumption.)

Environmental management also requires enormous finesse at traversing the corporate bureaucracy. It is the environmental managers' unenviable task to coordinate activities across multiple divisions and departments—again, not a linear activity.

Finally, environmental management requires managers to work with information coming at them from a host of different disciplines—legal affairs, manufacturing, purchasing, marketing, and so on.

Few of these skills fit the profile of the typically trained or oriented engineer. The marketing executive, however, *is* often superbly qualified:

- As a matter of course, marketers must coordinate their activities across multiple departments (e.g., R&D, manufacturing, packaging, sales, public relations).
- In mapping their strategic directions, marketers take into consideration variables that come at them from a multitude of directions. What is the competition up to? What is coming out of research and development? What are the demographics and psychographics of the marketplace, and how are they changing? What are the best advertising media? Both marketing and environmental management decisions are made in similar conceptual "vortices." In other words, marketers bring to environmental management the holistic approach to strategic planning that the consideration of environmental impact and initiatives demands.
- Finally, marketers are professional communicators. This skill is enormously useful in virtually every aspect of environmental management—on the task force itself, and in such areas as environmental management training, emergency response training, community relations, and other domains that put a premium on communications.

The bottom line is that marketers contribute a unique and invaluable combination of experience, perspective, and communication and organizational skills to the environmental management function.

Benefits to the Marketer

In addition to benefiting the corporate environmental management process, marketers' participation in environmental management enhances their ability to do their jobs as marketers.

- *Forewarned is forearmed*—By being involved in environmental management activities, environmental marketers have a greater sense of the seriousness and depth of their company's environmental commitment, thus enabling them to gauge their environmental product and marketing positioning accordingly.

- *No limits to knowledge*—A popular phrase from the 1980s was, "You can never be too rich or too thin." Well, marketers can never be environmentally attuned enough, either.

By participating in environmental management, marketers become steeped in a wide range of environmental issues. Their expertise becomes, so to speak, "organic." This can only benefit them as they devise their own environmental marketing plans.

THE SYNERGY BETWEEN ENVIRONMENTAL MANAGEMENT AND ENVIRONMENTAL MARKETING

There are close structural similarities between environmental marketing and environmental management.

At least six forces drive the implementation of a corporation-wide environmental management strategy: (1) regulatory pressure; (2) social responsibility; (3) concerns about actual or potential liability; (4) community relations; (5) shareholder pressure; and (6) "leadership"— i.e., the desire to set an example as an environmentally responsible company.

There is a close correlation between these six considerations and the drivers for environmental marketing:

- "Pre-empting regulation"—i.e., behaving in such ways as to avoid regulatory action, is also a response to regulatory pressure (actual or potential).
- "Competitive image advantage" is the direct consequence of behaving in a "socially and environmentally responsible" manner.
- "Activist group pressure" can create negative publicity. So does its parallel, "liability."
- "Retail relations" and "community relations" are similar in that both involve stakeholder-relations issues.
- "Shareholder pressure" translates into demand to develop its corollary, "business opportunities."
- Finally, "vision" and "leadership" are near cousins. If there is no vision, there is no leadership.

Because environmental management involves many of the same issues as environmental marketing, the two activities are deeply synergistic.

As I make the case for increasing the involvement of marketers in the company's overall environmental improvement management process, I must also point out that marketing and sales professionals in most U.S. companies have been the least interested in anything environmental. This is unfortunate, given the contribution they could make and the inevitability of their involvement in environmental marketing practices. Consider this real-life scenario:

> Each day, another business is approached by a customer who says, "What are you going to do about the waste your product generates in our facility?" Concerned that the competition will gain a competitive advantage by responding quickly and with commitment to the environmental challenge, management turns to marketing and says, "Do something!" But what does the marketer do? An environmental claim with no backup (i.e., overall corporate environmental policy or commitment) invites customer and regulatory backlash. Inaction nets you a dissatisfied customer. The wrong action could have a negative impact on the bottom line.

Marketers need to immerse themselves in the study and practice of environmental science, stewardship, and economics *now*. If they do not, they will join the ranks of Mobil Chemical (Hefty garbage bags), General Electric (Energy Choice light bulbs) and other companies that have engaged in "green product" promotion without doing their environmental issues and management homework.

9

SYLVANIA'S GTE PRODUCTS PROBLEM STOPPERS: #1 EMPLOYEE INVOLVEMENT TEAM

Darlene W. Caplan

Anyone doubting the dedication of North American workers to total quality and continuous improvement on the job should have witnessed the 1992 National Team Excellence Competition.

Competition was stiff and included such world-renowned companies as AT&T, Florida Power and Light, Thiokol Corporation, British Columbia Telecom, Atlantic Electric, Harris Corp., Weirton Steel, Rockwell Houstin Operations, Diamond Star Motors, United Technologies, Principal Financial Services, and Weyerhauser Co.

The winner of the 1992 Association for Quality and Participation's National Team Excellence Competition was a nine-person work team called the Problem Stoppers from Sylvania Lighting in York, Pennsylvania. The Problem Stoppers won for eliminating glass waste at York by recycling it in the plant, which not only saved the company about $142,000, but also proved to be an outstanding example of total quality environmental management and responsibility. This article details their award-winning efforts.

The Sylvania Lighting plant makes over one billion light bulb bases annually. The excess glass from the manufacturing process, more than 800,000 pounds a year, had to be shipped to a hazardous landfill. The Problem Stoppers changed the process to

Darlene W. Caplan *is quality services manager of Sylvania Lighting in York, Pennsylvania.*

eliminate the forming of unusable glass waste. Now, the molten glass is cooled into pellets and recycled in the plant.

The TQM climate that spawns such responsible and enthusiastic teamwork at York is created through "patient persistence—complete dedication to the team approach and the willingness to take risks with your people," says Jim Tyson, general manager for the Lighting/Industrial Strategic Business Unit, which includes the York plant.

The Total Quality Business Strategy of the York Sylvania Lighting plant—the way the business is managed, measured, and evaluated—is known as the Building Blocks to World Class, patterned after the Malcolm Baldrige National Quality Award (MBNQA). Each block represents an element of the MBNQA criteria. As the benchmark for national quality, the Baldrige was selected as the vehicle for York's self-assessment, self-improvement strategy.

Fifteen elements were Pareto-analyzed to be the areas of greatest improvement opportunity and impact, with the philosophy that in improving these elements, the other elements would naturally improve. Action plans to address these target elements were created by cross-functional, multilevel task forces from the six plants that comprise the Lighting/Industrial Strategic Business unit, which includes the York Metal Base plant and six other manufacturing facilities. Each plant in the unit chose two to three target elements to improve.

Progress is measured continually and the journey culminates with a general manager's Quality Improvement Award presented to the most improved (against their own baseline scores) plant's employees at year end.

The fundamental elements of the Building Blocks to World Class are the cornerstones of Employee Involvement, Education and Training, Employee Well-Being and Morale, and Documentation, driven by Senior Executive Leadership, with the ultimate goal of Customer Satisfaction.

TEAM OVERVIEW

The Problem Stoppers is a multilevel, multifunction team that uses both an employee participation group and Total Quality Task Force approach to problem solving. The team uses project leadership through individual member project leaders to focus on several projects simultaneously.

The Problem Stoppers meet for one hour every week but much of their project work (e.g., data gathering and resourcing) is performed during the workday. One additional hour per team member is allotted for this type of investigation and analysis. This information is then reported back to all members during their regularly scheduled weekly meeting and acted on by the entire team.

The team is facilitated by rotation of the leadership role (every two months or for the life of the primary project). The team leader serves as a member, and sometimes as one of the project leaders at the same time. The role of recorder is static, as he or she has computer access, but in his or her absence, there are two backup recorders. Minutes are issued on a regular basis, immediately following each meeting, and are distributed to all team members, area supervisors from all shifts, internal resource people involved in the current projects, product line managers, and the quality manager who coordinates employee involvement.

Because the team is cross-functional, many varied interests prevail. To keep the attention and involvement of all members, the team attacks several problems at once, each with a project leader from the area in which the problem exists. The project leaders have prime responsibility for driving their project through implementation and evaluation stages.

When approaching a new problem, the team employs traditional problem identification techniques as a full team, and creates their problem and goal statements. They analyze root causes as a full team but the data collection responsibilities rest on the project leaders, enabling efficient collection due to the proximity to their work areas. The data is verified typically by more than one member to ensure reliability.

Because all stakeholders are continually informed and involved in the problem-solving process, formal presentations are not usually required. Typically, the operations manager is invited into the meeting to discuss the team's findings and listen to the implementation plan, the justification and/or cost-benefit analysis, and in the case of large capital expenditures, for sign-off and approval.

The team has the authority and responsibility to invite outside resources, customers, or vendors into their team meetings to obtain information. Team members may approach any internal resource people for data collection or information purposes.

PURPOSE, VALUE, AND SELECTION PROCESSS

The team brainstormed a main problem list of thirty-four problems and used the triple-choice method to reduce the list. Triple choice is a group prioritizing process by which every team member may select a predetermined number of problem ideas from the main problem list, eliminating temporarily those with no votes. The team proceeds to prioritize the remaining problem ideas through two more rounds of selection, until the problem ideas of the highest group interest are determined. In this case, the team narrowed the list down to three problems: dirty bathrooms; glass furnace waste (cullet); and baffles.

The Problem Stoppers evaluated the three problems by using a criteria chart to select a problem that the entire team could invest in and one that would be beneficial to company, employees, and to the community. The remaining problems were evaluated using the criteria of

- Potential solvability
- Cost of implementation
- Importance to team
- Implementation time factor

The Problem Stoppers team selected furnace cullet waste as their problem for two reasons—environmental impact and cost. Disposal of the excess waste furnace cullet was costly as it was considered hazardous waste, necessitating disposal into a hazardous waste landfill and negatively affecting the environment.

Glass cullet is the by-product of the glassing process. When light bulb bases are manufactured, molten purple glass is poured into the base as the insulator before the brass eyelet is inserted. What glass remains following the process hardens into large unusable glass lumps, which must be placed into a hazardous waste bin to be disposed of in a hazardous waste landfill.

A problem statement was created by answering the question, "What is wrong?" The problem statement was: Excess usable furnace cullet is being dumped into the hazardous material hopper. Consequently, a goal statement was written to demonstrate the team's intention and objective: Reduce the amount of furnace cullet and/or make better use of the glass cullet. The statement techniques are used to focus the group on each selected problem.

Stakeholders were identified to be those directly involved in the process: glassing machine and batch house operators; mechanics; area supervisors; and set-up utility workers. All were involved in the data collection process, prototype evaluation and monitoring, and prototype modification recommendations, and they acted as resource people.

With its focus on the Building Blocks to World Class, the team developed an action plan to enable continuous improvement. The

Problem Stoppers problem selection affected eight of the blocks, but most dramatically Public Responsibility, Continuous Improvement of Process, and Employee Involvement.

PROBLEM AND CAUSE ANALYSIS

To analyze the problem and determine its cause, the team used the following methods:

- Possible causes brainstormed list
- Cause and effect fishbone diagram
- Analysis chart
- Process observation video analysis
- Stakeholder survey
- Outside "experts" interviews
- Log/report studies
- Pareto analysis

The primary cause for the disposal of furnace cullet into the hazardous waste hopper was determined to be its size and consistency.

The most effective methods of uncovering the cause of this particular problem was through glassing machine operator interviews and team member observation.

The glassing operators explained that when they are busy working on more than one glassing machine or when a mechanical problem is experienced, the molten glass continues to flow from the glassing furnace. This glass is diverted to a water bath used to cool the glass. Because of the time involved, the glass runoff builds up over the water level and hardens into a large, unbreakable lump of glass that is nonrecyclable in the glassing process and necessitates disposal in a hazardous landfill.

DATA COLLECTION

The Problem Stoppers used several techniques in gathering necessary data: video observation/analysis; charting; interview; review of glass disposal reports; monitoring/analysis of daily batch house reports; and resource consulting.

The team photographed the hazardous waste hopper to verify its contents, then videotaped the glass shoveling process that is used to dispose of the glass cullet to observe the handling methods.

Operators and the safety manager were questioned regarding safety/ergonomic issues involved in the shoveling disposal process.

The team interviewed the industrial engineering environmental manager to discover the number of pulls (hopper removal to hazardous waste landfill) and to generate potential manufacturing process use for the excess glass cullet. In addition, the accounting department was polled to determine the costs associated with disposal and labor costs and the manufacturing process engineer was consulted as a resource to assist the team in investigating different types of conveyors as a potential solution. Outside vendors were contacted and interviewed, and quotations were requested by the team.

SOLUTION SELECTION

Possible solutions were generated through the brainstorming method following the data gathering and analysis processes.

Solution potentials were to install water lines, water curtains, water jets, a drag chain conveyor, or a lead screw conveyor. To analyze these ideas, each was tested and rated on a scale of 1 to 5 (5 representing the most effective) with the following results:

a. Water line - helped, didn't solve
   * rating = 2
b. Water curtain - improved, didn't solve
   * rating = 3
c. Water jets - improved, didn't solve
   * rating = 3
d. Drag chain - (analyzed/researched) - would solve
   * rating = 4
e. Lead screw - (analyzed/researched) - would solve
   * rating = 5

The two preferred potential solutions were found to be the drag chain conveyor and the lead screw conveyor. The team investigated installation of each and found, due to space limitations in the glassing room, that the lead screw conveyor was the preferred potential solution. The lead screw conveyor was prototyped, installed, monitored, and evaluated by the team with feedback from all stakeholders. The evaluation led to many modifications.

The lead screw conveyor solved the root cause of the problem by removing the furnace cullet from behind the furnace, keeping it free of contamination. Assisting in the design and installation of the prototype, the team concurrently evaluated the cullet and the performance of the conveyor.

A cost/benefit analysis performed by team members showed:

- $80,800 a year savings (labor, scrap, scrap disposal);
- 800,000 pounds of recyclable glass put back into manufacturing process (avoidance of hazardous waste disposal); and
- $76,407 implementation cost of eight conveyors.

Thus, the payback period is less than one year for this solution.

The solution benefits were found to be: cost savings, reduced hazardous waste, ergonomic safety, less downtime/more production, 100 percent reusable cullet, increased automation, improved housekeeping, and increased employee satisfaction and involvement.

SOLUTION CAUSES PROBLEM TO SOLVE

The Problem Stoppers' solution to the unusable glass furnace cullet problem spawned an additional problem. The increased amount of usable glass cullet could not be effectively and quickly dried, resulting in wet cullet unacceptable for the manufacturing process.

The resident engineering department proposed the purchase of a new dryer system at the cost of $65,000, which was then budgeted. The York Metal Base plant's product line manager approached the Problem Stoppers to request that they address the problem for two reasons:

- The team solution to the initial problem, though positive, caused the new problem.
- Team solutions are usually more cost-effective and efficient than one functional decision in the case of equipment purchase/modification.

The Problem Stoppers are an Employee Participation team (EP) that functions by traditional guidelines. EP teams self-select problems on which to work through the arduous process described above. Management does not suggest problems for the team to attack.

Total Quality (TQ) is the Sylvania team structure in which a task-oriented team is established to address a particular goal, problem, or challenge and dissolves following the resolution and implementation.

Though not a TQ team, the Problem Stoppers decided to accept the challenge because they determined the problem was not solved satisfactorily unless solved from "cradle to grave." The team viewed the wet cullet problem as Phase II of the furnace cullet disposal problem.

The team accepted the challenge and through group problem-solving methods proposed and implemented a solution of updating and modifying the present dryer system at a total cost of $3,228. This modification eliminated wet furnace cullet by reducing the moisture content, increasing dryer capacity, and improving material handling, which enabled virtually all of the cullet to be recycled. This second tier solution netted a cost avoidance of $61,772.

The Problem Stoppers' solutions thus resulted in a savings of approximately $142,000.

TECHNIQUE SHARING

Information and technique sharing is part of the Sylvania Lighting TQM culture. The Problem Stoppers have shared their problem-solving techniques and success with their largest customer through an in-house presentation and a customer visit. The team, after having visited this customer, hosted employees in-house to explain their employee involvement process.

The Problem Stoppers were selected to present before GTE Electrical Products Corporation President Dean Langford, and several other corporate staff members, as an element of the TQM process.

As part of Sylvania Lighting's public responsibility philosophy, the team has shared group problem-solving methodologies with the membership of the Mid-Atlantic People Involvement Network, several Association for Quality and Participation chapters, BMY Military Systems, York International Corporation, Mack Truck Corporation, and Alloy Rods Corporation.

Ace Parmelee, vice president of Electrical Components and Materials Division, GTE Products, summarizes, "The results achieved by the Problem Stoppers prove that the people who do the work on a day-to-day basis best know how to improve the process, and when they work together as a team the results are impressive. When cross-functional people work together, it's always tough to beat their results."

10

ENVIRONMENTAL COMMUNITY RELATIONS: A VITAL COMPONENT IN TQEM

Cynthia Leslie-Bole and Stephen J. Nelson

In the current regulatory climate, environmental professionals are becoming increasingly involved with a side of the business that has often been given low priority in the past: communicating with the public about environmental and health risk issues. This article describes effective approaches to such communication, and demonstrates their implementation success.

The challenges of publicly communicating environmental and health risks have only recently become a significant part of a manager's or environmental professional's responsibilities, because historically, companies were not required to publicly release information concerning hazardous materials. Trust and confidence in the ability of corporate officials and governmental agencies to protect the public made detailed disclosures unnecessary.

Today, however, the climate has changed considerably with community-right-to-know (CRTK) regulations mandating public disclosure of environmental issues and the risks they pose. Consequently, reports of waste discharge monitoring, chemical spills and releases, emissions, and hazardous chemicals inventories are now public

Cynthia Leslie-Bole is the environmental communication director for ERM-West, a full-service environmental consulting firm in Walnut Creek, California. She is also a founding member of NAPEC California. Stephen J. Nelson is a principal engineer at ERM-West.

documents. Because many major environmental statutes also grant private citizens the right to sue for enforcement of regulatory requirements, public special interest groups, community organizations, and local governments are gaining status as additional parties that are involved in environmental aspects of plant operations.

Accompanying the more activist regulatory environment is the increased public expectation of openness that goes hand-in-hand with the "information age." Anyone who doubts that the environment is the issue of the 1990s should pause to consider that 100 million people participated in the April 22, 1990, Earth Day, and "green" consumer trends are beginning to influence the products people buy and the businesses they support. As a result of this increased awareness, environmental communication with the public has become, of necessity, an integral part of total quality environmental management.

Because members of the community now have a right to know about chemical hazards, and environmental communication is an integral part of total quality environmental programs, an increasing number of businesses are now assuming a proactive community relations stance on environmental issues. These companies are finding that proactively managing the increased attention from community groups can enhance corporate credibility while building public trust and support, thus laying a foundation for more effective industry/community partnerships on environmental issues.

Proactive environmental communication can also actually reduce overall compliance costs by generating public support for less costly alternatives, less onerous permit conditions, and faster project approval processes. Because governmental agencies respond to elected officials, improved community perception can directly lead to reduced political pressures to take enforcement actions. Similarly, improved public perception can decrease the possibility of private party actions to force compliance.

Finally, community relations can be particularly significant for companies (such as food processors and health products manufacturers) whose sales are tied to consumers' perceptions of the company as providing safe and environmentally benign products. In these cases, an improved environmental image can lead directly to increased sales and profitability.

BUILDING A COMMUNITY RELATIONS PROGRAM

When initially planning a community relations program, it is important to consider that communicating with the public is inevitable;

people form images and impressions of plants and facilities as a result of their contacts with employees and neighbors, observations they make as they drive past, information presented in news articles, and images formed by corporate advertising campaigns. The primary variables are the degree and amount of planning and coordination provided for these messages; a managed community relations program is simply an effort to organize and integrate these impressions in a logical and consistent manner.

Community Relations Principles

The goal of an effective community relations program is to establish an educational dialogue with community members so that an informed, collaborative public results. Because public perceptions are often based on incomplete or incorrect information, the primary objective in community relations should be to provide accurate and timely information and create a dialogue between interested parties. The credibility of any community relations program will be quickly tarnished if it becomes a one-way public relations program or an effort to "sell" an idea, concept, or solution to the public; instead, community relations programs should be based on a two-way information exchange, in which the company listens and responds to public concerns, needs, and priorities while also providing information about plant operations and environmental issues.

Credibility is clearly a company's most valuable resource in the context of community relations, and there are several essential steps for building credibility. Credibility starts first with listening to be sure that the messages and concerns of the other parties are fully heard and understood. Effective dialogue and information sharing can begin only after this basis is established. Information must also be presented accurately and reliably, even if it is not always favorable to the company involved. In general, it is best to err on the side of overdisclosure because the concerned parties, rather than the company, are best able to judge what information is relevant to them. Companies engaging in dialogue with the public must also be committed to acting on the input received because lack of commitment will be easily detected by others. It is therefore important to be honest about what *cannot* be done to satisfy community needs as well as what can be done, as unkept promises can destroy credibility.

Finally, bear in mind that no matter how effective a company's community relations program is, consensus may not be possible because of differing attitudes and values. In these cases, credibility is enhanced when the company works to understand where the differences lie and respects the community's right to disagree with the company's perspective on the issue.

The R.A.C.E. Process for Community Relations

The R.A.C.E. process is a useful, four-step, iterative approach that can be followed in developing and implementing a proactive environmental community relations program. The R.A.C.E. steps are as follows:

- **Research:** The purpose of the research step is to determine the current perceptions of the facility and to identify community concerns. This is the information-gathering stage, and common data collection tools include questionnaires, news clippings, interviews, and meetings with local agencies.
- **Analysis:** In the analysis stage, community relations objectives are defined and a management plan is formulated. In this effort, the data collected in the research stage are evaluated, critical audiences are identified, key message points are determined, and short-term and long-term strategies are developed. The product of this analysis stage should be a community relations plan that reflects a clear understanding of community needs, concerns, and current perceptions of the company.
- **Communication:** With the analysis completed, the communication stage, in which dialogue is initiated with the public, can begin. This can be accomplished by a variety of methods, including community meetings, fact sheets, plant tours, interactions with schools, and citizen advisory panels. Before initiating the communication stage, however, spokespeople must be trained in presentation and media relations skills to avoid having an ineffective communication attempt undermine the credibility of both the community relations program and the company.
- **Evaluation:** After communication efforts have been implemented according to the community relations plan, the effectiveness of the program should be evaluated. This step can include follow-up surveys, media monitoring, more questionnaires, and feedback from employees and neighbors. If the evaluation indicates that the program was not effective or that additional follow-up is appropriate, the program should iterate back to the analysis step, incorporating the data resulting from the evaluation process.

A COMMUNITY RELATIONS CASE STUDY

The Acme case study can be used to illustrate the benefits that can accrue from a proactive approach to community relations using the R.A.C.E. process. The Acme site is a former electronics manufacturing site characterized by PCBs in site soils and solvents in the groundwater beneath the site. By the time an active community relations program was implemented for the site in 1988, the community had become closely involved in several soil and groundwater contamination investigations in nearby industrial properties. The community was generally well-educated and decidedly environmentally "active."

The most vocal neighborhood organization near the Acme site was a local homeowners association. The association's members included environmental professionals and activists who were highly sophisticated in their dealings with regulatory agencies, responsible parties, elected officials, and the media. When the community relations process began in 1988, the association was antagonistic toward Acme and the regulatory agency overseeing site remediation. They were concerned about property values, health risks, and the length of time required for cleanup. In fact, the association had filed letters of complaint regarding the lack of progress toward actual remediation at the site and had even threatened to have the regulatory agency removed as the responsible agency for the site.

Although many legitimate factors contributed to the delays in the remediation process, Acme had never made an effort to explain these factors to the association or to enlist the group's assistance. Because of the adversarial relationship that had developed, it was assumed that the association would obstruct Acme's proposals and oppose any remedial action that did not call for costly excavation and removal of all contaminants on site. In response to these challenges at the Acme site, Acme followed the R.A.C.E. formula to create a proactive community relations program. The phases of the R.A.C.E. program for the Acme site are described below.

Research. The first step in the community relations program was to conduct information-gathering with technical staff, the client, and regulatory agency project managers to identify project history, goals, and strategies. After becoming familiar with environmental issues and community attitudes in general, Acme identified the key players in the community—that is, the people who could make or break acceptance of Acme's proposed study approach and remedial plans. A meeting was arranged at the home of the association's president; the group's resident Ph.D. toxicologist and the head of the group's emergency planning committee also were invited. Acme spent many hours listening to the association's perspectives and concerns and discovered that their biggest single complaint was that they had been left out of the process. Other key players in the community were also interviewed, including elected and appointed officials and representatives of environmental and other neighborhood groups. The information gathered from the interviews was then combined with that gleaned from reviewing historical media coverage and regulatory agency files to develop a profile of the community and its key concerns and priorities.

Analysis. The community profile developed in the research phase provided the basis for analyzing who the primary publics/audiences were, developing the key messages that needed to be conveyed to those audiences, and formulating a plan for how the messages could most effectively be communicated to those audiences. The result of the analysis phase was a community relations plan that met regulatory requirements while outlining an ambitious, proactive strategy for involving the association in all phases of the remediation project.

Communication. During the communication phase of the project, Acme issued fact sheets, offered an information hotline, maintained a mailing list and information repository, hosted public meetings, and had numerous informal contacts with community members, in particular with those representing the association. To accommodate the association's desire for inclusion, they were asked to contribute to the preparation of fact sheets, assist with the scheduling of public meetings, review technical documents, and participate in developing remedial alternatives screening criteria. The association's toxicologist was even invited to perform peer review of the risk assessment work plan and preliminary results prior to submission of the document to regulatory agencies. In some cases this accommodation strained short-term deadlines, but in the long run, it prevented the major delays that would have occurred if the association had not bought into the process.

Evaluation. Program evaluation began the moment community relations activities began. Every communication piece or event was reviewed to determine how it could be improved to better serve Acme's and the community's needs. Acme solicited feedback from the association continually, and as a result, built rapport and established a collaborative working relationship with the association where formerly only antagonism existed. At one point, the association even sent an unsolicited letter to the regulatory agency citing the Acme project as a model for managing site remediations. In the end, because of Acme's proactive community relations activities, the association, Acme, and the regulatory agency were able to work cooperatively toward the shared goal of remediating the site in a way that protected public health, improved the environment, and was economically feasible for Acme. By building this problem-solving partnership, delays and increased remediation costs due to public opposition were ultimately avoided, and remediation strategies acceptable to all parties were pursued.

CONCLUSION

As the Acme case study illustrates, a proactive approach to environmental communication with the public, when guided by the R.A.C.E. process, can result in collaborative problem solving and information sharing between community members and company representatives. As trust and credibility build on both sides, win-win solutions to controversies become increasingly possible. In this process of environmental community relations, however, it is crucial to remember the following:

- The emotional aspects of environmental issues can be as influential as technical issues and must be acknowledged.
- Facts and statistics will not necessarily win arguments or alter perceptions.
- Meaningful involvement of community members is critical.
- Creating trust, not minimizing risk, is essential for gaining public acceptance.

When these concepts are used as the foundation for a proactive environmental community relations program, a corporation's total quality environmental management program is enhanced. In addition, a positive public image is cultivated based on openness, environmental responsibility, and full compliance with the spirit as well as the letter of the public disclosures mandated in the current regulatory environment.

11

MEASURING FOR SUCCESS IN COMMUNICATIONS FOR PERMITS

Thomas R. Blank

Today, U.S. corporations are discovering the merit of combining the principles of total quality environmental management (TQEM) into their measurement and communications programs. This approach has been particularly productive in the permitting process that is necessary for starting, expanding, or sustaining plant operations—a procedure that can easily be thwarted in the absence of a prominent and aggressive communications component. The need to benchmark and measure such a communication program's progress is critical both for internal management and for environmental regulators concerned that an applicant demonstrate a high degree of public involvement.

America sees itself as an egalitarian society, and nowhere has this view become more apparent than in the field of the environment. Although no party to an environmental controversy recognizes an opponent as having equal standing, today's paradigm accords relative equality to each perceived stakeholder. This means that when the issue is environmental impact, the corporate chieftain who has invested millions of dollars of stockholders' funds in a plant expansion has the same standing as a lone citizen next to the plant. Valid scientific evidence presented to a regulatory body carries no more weight than the anecdotal evidence pieced together by neighbors. In short, the relative equality of stakeholders has produced a kind of "decision gridlock" because few winners or losers are determined— the game just goes on and on.

Thomas R. Blank *is senior vice president of Hager Sharp, Inc., in Washington, DC.*

Today's environmental paradigm demands consensus for any legitimate stakeholder to realize progress. Permit applicants, whether they are public or private entities, become the losers when consumers fail to achieve consensus. In the absence of permit decisions, projects that will provide necessary services such as waste disposal go nowhere, and infrastructure projects such as new highway construction also remain at a standstill. The winners, then, are not only the local opponents to a particular project, but also the national groups whose political agenda suffers if such projects are brought on line. The best example is Greenpeace's national opposition to hazardous waste incineration. The organization is clearly working on a national environmental policy agenda, not on a specific community's quality of life. When Greenpeace works at the local level, it is because the group's agenda has been considered and rejected by legislators and regulatory agencies at a higher one.

To successfully move from the losers' column into the winners' column, the central challenges confronting the permit applicant include building credibility for the permit process, for the applicant, and for the project technology or approach. The applicant must also sap credibility from opponents to facilitate consensus building for its position or project. *Given that permitting processes can take years to unfold, and that communications programs have become an integral and vital component of their success, it is necessary to devise a way of benchmarking and measuring progress toward the desired consensus such programs should help produce.* Only by devising such a program can the communications function become truly integrated into a company's overall TQEM program and produce added value.

BUILDING A CONSENSUS TO PROCEED

The reality is that despite recurrent opposition from national environmental advocacy groups and local citizens, some businesses and local citizens are forging a community-by-community consensus on acceptable ways to manage the risks of industrial operations.

This consensus-building process, painstakingly wrought over months and years, is the foundation on which we will realize the environmental benefits of the tens of thousands of environmental regulations now on the books at the federal, state, and local levels.

This consensus has yielded progress when it has been based on the realization that laws and regulations alone do not equal a cleaner environment. Rather, it is permit holders implementing laws and regulations day after day that leads to such benefits as cleaner water, cleaner air, and increased waste disposal capacity.

There will not be a cleaner environment in the absence of the proper implementation of sound environmental policy. In fact, the only winners, when implementation of environmental laws and regulations is "held up," are those people who opposed them in the first place—the extremists who talk a good game about their commitment to the environment but who would rather see no solution to environmental problems than a solution that is not their own. Their political agenda is usually clear-cut: to stop all industry and economic development dead in its tracks.

In Logan Township, New Jersey, for example, where a hazardous waste incinerator has operated for more than twenty years, a set of New Jersey regulations requiring mitigation payments to the local jurisdiction, coupled with a mutual desire to settle an existing lawsuit, laid the groundwork for consensus on how to manage risk in a local community.

Orchestrated in the early 1980s, this was one of the earliest attempts at mitigation. The law necessitated interaction between the community and company. The result has been a lessening of tensions, a better understanding of the level of risk involved, and an array of economic benefits to the local community. This case, settled in 1983, also established the principle of profit sharing as a key strategy in forming a consensus between industry and citizens.

Critics dismiss such agreements as little more than bribery. In doing so, they display their true feelings about the groups whose interests they claim to represent. Firsthand experience with such citizens' groups in Louisiana, New Jersey, Pennsylvania, Virginia, and elsewhere has shown that these groups generally are quite capable of articulating their own best interests convincingly and efficiently.

THE RESPONSIBILITY TO LEAD BELONGS TO BUSINESS

Environmental extremists are not the sole challenge facing business in its attempt to implement sound environmental policy. The public sector itself is often divided on the quality of its own laws and regulations. Instead of valuing and supporting the role of the private sector as implementors of environmental policy, regulators often view regulations as a means of controlling innate bad behavior rather than as a set of defining rules that reflect a consensus for both environmentalism and economic growth.

Environmental policy activists nurture the fallacy that zero pollution and zero risk in industrial operations is possible to achieve, thereby putting the perfect ahead of the good and holding up most regulated approaches to pollution control.

In this climate of misperception and misinformation, the burden falls on business to meet some very real challenges. TQEM, with a strong communication component, can achieve the desired result. Before stakeholders as diverse as the national news media, plant communities, and state and local government officials, businesses must be prepared to implement communication programs during permit processes that forcefully argue the following:

- That the legislative and regulatory permitting processes reflect an acceptable social consensus on risk—and that they yield a fair answer, meaning a proper balance between environmental and economic concerns;
- That the permitting and regulatory processes with which corporations must comply will work to effectively guarantee health and safety—and that the technical specifications of a permit application will provide the guarantee;
- That, in the absence of corporate efforts to implement laws and regulations, the policy process has no meaning and environmental progress is not achieved; and
- That *local* citizens (not national activist groups) have a right to influence and change industrial operations that may present a risk to them.

CHARACTERISTICS AND MEASUREMENT

Businesses are succeeding best at achieving consensus when they involve the public in their plans in a substantive way. Community-by-community progress on environmental issues, however, takes time.

What follows are the characteristics and measurements that must be achieved in a total environmental quality permitting communications program. The communications component of the TQEM program has three parts: issue identification, credibility building, and consensus building.

Issue Identification

Issue identification begins with benchmarking and continues throughout the permit application process. It is here that credibility building begins, as you must be able to prove you are addressing the issues that are critical to the stakeholders. It is important here to remember that the permit applicant is a stakeholder and, therefore, has standing to help identify issues to be addressed in the communications program.

Benchmarking occurs before the time that the permit application is submitted and the intent to seek a permit is publicly announced. To best define your benchmark, begin with the research that will form the foundation for your communications program. The issues that emerge in the research phase will need to be addressed and the applicant will need a solid base to support its reasoning for initially selecting them as targets. Focus groups, polls, and a careful review of news media reporting about industrial, environmental, and economic development issues are the measurements.

It is a good idea to conduct several focus groups. These groups of eight to ten people should include individuals whose physical environment will be affected when a project comes to fruition. In such a group (generally participants do not know each other), a discussion of both personal and community values can be conducted. The group sponsor can also learn about participants' attitudes toward economic development, trust in government, and social issues such as the environment. Focus groups are especially useful research tools in situations in which emotions play a major role in determining the outcome. Suffice it to say that, in permitting processes, emotion plays a major role.

Polling data is another component of benchmarking that is advisable depending on the scale and scope of a project. When permits for a "greenfield" facility (meaning one that is new and when the applicant has no track record) are being sought, polling is highly desirable. These data should be compiled several times during the permitting process, beginning before any public announcements and then at set intervals afterward.

Regulators are also a factor in issue identification. First, the technical data requirements for the permit application can be construed by regulators as the raw materials needed to determine whether a particular project will adequately protect public health and safety. Therefore, what the raw data are, how they are gathered, and what they show are all issues. Put them on your identified issues list. Secondly, regulators are the people who deal most intensely with the public and other stakeholders; therefore, their input on issues, especially on the prioritization of issues, must be sought early in permit development.

The issue identification process broadens once a permit process becomes publicly known, either in the form of a public announcement of intent or by the actual submission of an application. Public meetings and hearings will be factors, as will various small group meetings and community presentations. Keep records of the issues brought to your attention in these ways. In today's environmental climate, any major project will see the formation of some sort of citizens' advisory committee, and such groups' proceedings are sources of issue identification raw data.

To be successful over the time when a permit application is being developed, submitted, reviewed, and acted upon, it is necessary to maintain credibility for the issues you say are central to your stakeholders. Employing these issue identification processes in a well-designed strategy that begins with benchmarking and traces the progression of issues over time will assure that you address the issues that matter most to your project's stakeholders. Keep careful records of your measurements and you can successfully prevent accusations that you have failed to address the issues stakeholders care about most.

Building Communication: The Key to Credibility

Environmental managers know that the public consistently judges a company and its interests by using a blend of image and substance on various issues. Your communications efforts must prove two things: (1) the laws and regulations will ensure health, safety, and environmental protection; and (2) you, as the applicant, have both the desire and the capability to achieve near-perfect compliance.

Your credibility will result from the public understanding the engineering and the regulatory issues of the permitting process, and from persuading key stakeholders that you are capable of proper and responsible implementation. Let me emphasize that credibility comes from public understanding and not from good compliance alone. Proper implementation, of course, is proven by applying and communicating the tenets of TQEM. Your communications program will be critical to your proposal being judged favorably by government authorities who are themselves subject to public pressure and scrutiny.

It is imperative that the communications professionals who are designing and implementing your program have previously worked under fire. Remember, when the public understands the laws, regulations, technology, overall project concept, and ethical approach of the company as well as you do, they will become supporters. It follows, then, that a program that will achieve this must be crafted by communications professionals with a solid understanding of the regulatory and technical issues involved. With the opposition, the politicians, and the news media continually scrutinizing your venture, you cannot afford communications mistakes that whip up public opposition or unsettle permitting officials. Your communicators must have the instincts and flexibility to revise strategy as events dictate while maintaining sight of the overall technical objective—permit issuance. In short, they themselves must have the training and experience to be credible with stakeholder audiences.

Credibility Building:
Regulatory and Community Relations Processes

Corporations most often fail to secure permits because a loss of credibility occurs along two lines. First, the permitting process itself is perceived as inadequately designed to properly protect the public health and environment. A damaging component of this perception is that local citizens believe they play only a minimal role in the permitting process and that their efforts have little impact.

The second line of credibility loss comes with regard to the applicant itself. Usually, this is tied to operating history and compliance issues.

To use the communications program to deal with the first of these credibility issues, a commitment must be made to adopt the regulatory process itself as the communication program's centerpiece. By doing so, the applicant can engage the public in a dialogue about the public policy and technical logic underlying the regulatory parameters. Doing so then becomes a measurement of the program itself—i.e., whether or not the applicant has successfully kept the stakeholder focus on this set of issues. Finally, such an approach is the best way to integrate communications under a TQEM program.

A second set of measurements relates to timing. When did the applicant choose to involve the public? Early involvement usually accords more credibility to the applicant, especially with regulators. For instance, when the public was engaged, had a plant expansion been definitely determined, or was this site one of several being considered?

A corollary measurement to timing is the issue of what decisions are not made at the time the applicant chooses to involve various stakeholders, especially the public. For instance, if the permit is for wastewater discharge there may be various technologies that can meet compliance standards. Choosing to involve stakeholders in the ulti- mate choice will bring that decision and, therefore, that permit application a higher degree of credibility. Of course, the applicant accords the stakeholders only an advisory role and retains the right to make the final technology selection.

As was mentioned previously, in instances in which major permits are being sought, there is usually some sort of citizens' advisory committee involved. The makeup of that committee is a key measurement in credibility building. Insuring that it is truly representative of the community stakeholders and even including opponents where they will buy in is important. The applicant must then carefully relate the work and advice of the committee to the actual permit application. Even if such committees turn renegade, regulators give points for trying, and formation is a measurement plus.

Finally, an overall measurement of the communications program is the thoroughness of the channels or media used. In other words, a press release from time to time is probably not sufficient to demonstrate a substantial commitment to stakeholder involvement and would not derive the maximum credibility for the overall TQEM permitting process. A range of techniques that will likely include direct mail, advertising, news media relations, presentations, and speeches is necessary. Use of each of these techniques or tools is a measurement because you can show that your approach includes a wide range of communications media and tools.

Credibility Building for the Applicant

In permitting, the communication component must be designed to enhance and accord credibility not only to the regulatory and community relations processes but also to the permit applicant as an entity—separate and distinct from the permitting process at hand.

A threshold issue is environmental regulatory compliance, with a key measurement being how an applicant chooses to communicate compliance history to stakeholders. Has it been done willingly and openly, in a way that is accessible to lay audiences? A presentation on compliance history will very likely be part of almost any permit application, and it directly overlaps with both facets of credibility building.

Another major measurement of the communications program is whether it builds credibility for the company's personnel and for the company's financial soundness. Is there a projection of existing goodwill determined by charitable contributions, for example, and ongoing community presence as shown by economic benefits such as jobs? The most intangible, but one of the most important, measurements is the demeanor exuded by the applicant in its dealings with stakeholders, especially the local community. Remember, there are both an emotional aspect to success in permitting and an aura of integrity and ethical behavior that must be maintained to insure credibility.

Moving toward Consensus

Regulators, financial analysts, and senior corporate executives will want to know if you are making progress toward getting permits issued that will allow you to expand operations and to maintain existing ones. The key measurement that will indicate this is movement toward a consensus. The research done at and before application will be a benchmark here. However, it should be expected that after a permit application is announced, polarization will occur. The news media and various emotional public meetings will show this negative progress. In other words, the distance from consensus will grow greater apart between the time of your initial communication research and the immediate aftermath of a public announcement. Over time, however, there are a number of measurements that can be used to determine how progress can continue.

A measurable movement toward a consensus can be seen by keeping and analyzing the records of interactions with stakeholder groups. Begin with the news media. If the gross amount of coverage has dwindled over time and the story has moved from the front pages, the controversial aspects of the project have lessened. Reports and assessments of employees or other project personnel who regularly interact with the public or local opinion leaders can also be useful. Quantity of interaction can usually be seen as positive progress toward consensus. If polling for issue identification is ongoing, the results will almost assuredly show some marked change from the original benchmarking. Absence of litigation is another measurement that is sometimes useful. This is by no means an exhaustive list, but it suggests the kinds of things that might be included as a unique set of measurements is devised for each permit process an applicant might undertake.

WHAT PERMIT PROCESSES ARE AMENABLE TO THIS INTEGRATED APPROACH?

Not every permitting process is suited to this integrated TQEM approach. Those that are, however, include

RCRA Part B. These are perhaps the most controversial of environmental permits because of the many misperceptions about hazardous waste, the industries that generate it, and the companies that manage it. In addition, Part B permits have so many "minor permits" that include such a wide array of issues that it is necessary to involve each stakeholder in an organized way before external forces do it on their own.

RCRA Corrective Action. There are already regulations that require the permit applicant to publicly notify potential stakeholders. Though these regulations can be seen as routine, they really constitute an as yet unexploited opportunity for applicants to further public understanding about their operations.

SARA TITLE III. Too few companies have used their compliance requirements under Right-To-Know as a credibility-building opportunity. Rather than communicating the information in proper perspective, opponent groups have been able to use the raw data to create unnecessary fears.

NDPES. Water pollution is always a potentially volatile issue. It is one area, however, in which industry has done a particularly good job of improving performance. For purposes of building corporate credibility, this is fertile territory. Given that "excursions" are routine events in this case, it is also ripe for exploitation when presented by opponent groups.

Environmental Impact Statements. Here again, a myriad of issues are covered and should be communicated in an organized fashion. Also, most EIS processes include at least one public hearing, at which the applicant should attempt to keep focused on the technical issues and off the more emotional ones. An upcoming public hearing can be a useful linchpin on which to engage the news media, citizens' groups, and others in a discussion about the technical issues of your proposal.

Wetlands Permits. These are emerging as a serious controversy of the 1990s and a favorite target for opponent groups. Creating some understanding of wetlands characteristics and technical determinants can be a key factor in lowering public concerns.

Clean Air Act. Now that the dust has settled on the legislation, the fighting about the regulations is beginning. The result is some lowering of the credibility of the law itself; and those regulated by it must show that its amendments are incorporated in their particular situation.

Overall Compliance. If a program of TQEM is being used, overall compliance is the vehicle for a communications program that will yield credibility for an operator or an applicant. Compliance can be an excellent motivator for incorporating a communications function into ongoing plant operations.

There are other kinds of projects that encompass massive permitting processes—such as real estate development, transportation infrastructure, and solid waste facilities—in which communications is a key component. However, a program of total quality environmental management may not be evident given the nature of these particular projects.

CONCLUSION

Permit processes, by their very nature, seek to implement uniformity, and from this attribute comes their value and strength. In seeking environmental permits, however, these processes are ill-equipped to deal with the reality that each stakeholder has defined a certain uniqueness for that stakeholder's own situation. Failure to address that perception of uniqueness, which is seen as an effort to impose uniformity, are the seeds of disaster for those entities seeking to make environmental permitting processes yield the desired result.

A blending of stakeholder values with technical and regulatory requirements is vital to progress. The communications component of a TQEM approach to permitting can be and should be the linchpin for winning permits and expanding plant operations. In deference to the uniqueness of each permitting situation, specific actions are not included in this article. Rather, we have attempted to suggest the component parts of a communications program and how to measure progress toward successful implementation of each. The overall value is that each stakeholder can evaluate the progress and the efforts made by the applicant toward consensus. In permitting, consensus is the objective. Many stakeholders, however, will also place a value on demonstrated effort. When consensus is elusive, measurable efforts are a persuasive and valuable tool, especially with regulators.

■■■ Section IV ■■■

BENCHMARKING AND
MEASURING FOR SUCCESS

12

WHY—AND HOW TO— BENCHMARK FOR ENVIRONMENTAL EXCELLENCE

Marcia E. Williams

Benchmarking your company's environmental program against that of another company or organization is one of the more effective means of assuring it is on track toward environmental excellence. If used properly and objectively, it provides a means of gauging the progress of your environmental program while allowing both companies to benefit from new and innovative ideas for improvement. Benchmarking is capable of measuring program efficiency, program design, and program outputs. Benchmarking also provides environmental managers with the unique opportunity of sharing successes and failures with respect to program integration into operations. This article describes the steps involved in designing and implementing benchmarking to assess the design of an overall environmental management program.

There are many forces driving environmental excellence and the need for improved benchmarking. First, there has been a dramatic increase in the amount of environmental legislation and regulation. The U.S. Congress authorizes environmental laws on

Marcia E. Williams *is president of Williams & Vanino, Inc., a Los Angeles consulting firm that specializes in helping companies establish and strengthen proactive environmental management programs and respond proactively to upcoming regulations and legislation. Previously, she served as divisional vice president of environmental policy and planning at Browning-Ferris Industries, and had a distinguished eighteen-year career with the U.S. Environmental Protection Agency.*

a five- to eight-year basis and each reauthorization brings new requirements along with record new expenditures. With over nine major environmental laws, this works out to one major reauthorization each year. As a result, the U.S. Code of Federal Regulations is now over two feet tall and contains over ten thousand pages of regulations developed to implement the environmental legislation. Each year over one hundred new major regulations are developed. Moreover, states are now producing legislation and regulations at a much faster pace than the federal government. State regulations often go beyond the federal regulations and are not always consistent from one state to another.

The additional legislative and regulatory focus is combined with broader and stronger enforcement. Recent modifications to the EPA Civil Penalty Policy have resulted in much higher penalty assessments. In addition, there has been a significant increase in the amount of federal and state criminal enforcement, including targeting of corporate executives. The enforcement database network has become increasingly sophisticated as EPA links its information databases to those of other federal agencies, including OSHA, U.S. Customs, and the SEC.

As enforcement activity is increasing, individual enforcement actions have become far more creative. For example, some states link tax credits to compliance status. It is also likely that government enforcement agencies will use compliance history as a positive incentive by linking it to other outcomes that are of significant interest to corporations. One example would be to link permit modification priority to compliance status. Other examples would be to link the ability to trade marketable permits to compliance history and link government procurement of products to the environmental compliance history of the company. Although these specific examples are not yet in place, these and similar ideas are under discussion.

The federal government and states are also increasing their use of disincentives. One of these disincentives goes under the name of fitness laws. Fitness laws use corporate compliance history to preclude companies from doing certain types of business with the government agency or in the political jurisdiction. Thus, fitness laws greatly increase the real penalty for noncompliance.

Liability concerns take many companies beyond regulatory requirements and force more proactive environmental actions. Federal and state Superfund laws have shown that compliance with today's regulations is not enough if environmental damage results. Lender tightening, nonavailability of insurance, and third-party legal suits are part of the liability issue. This pressure on corporations is aided by new information disclosure regulations that focus only on mandating the proper sharing of information with the public. The mere act of having to disclose information has pressured industry to modify behavior.

These direct government pressures have continued to feed other entities, which become new pressure points on companies. For example, investors are worried about the long-term quality of their investments and want to be socially responsible with their money. Lending institutions are also applying pressure. Knowledgeable lending institutions increasingly worry about the credit risk associated with investment based on the environmental soundness of the venture and the likelihood that it will be significantly affected by future environmental requirements. Customers and suppliers are also exerting pressure. Companies that have strong environmental programs (often Total Quality Management companies) want to do business only with other environmentally sound suppliers. The customer-supplier relationship is becoming much more closely linked under the umbrella of TQM and sustainable development.

Many companies today are also finding that there are positive incentives driving environmental excellence. Competitive business position is one, including knowing where new business opportunities are likely to be created and knowing which existing business areas or product lines are likely to become obsolete. Positive public reputation is a second motivator. Most companies now realize that effective public affairs and advertising strategies can be built only if baseline performance is admirable. A company's environmental rating is becoming like a company's credit rating or bond rating. Companies have quickly assessed the fact that good corporate environmental behavior can lead to other benefits as diverse as helping the company recruit the best employees and helping the company achieve faster approval of needed regulatory actions.

SETTING STANDARDS OF EXCELLENCE

Although the best environmental management programs are designed and tailored to fit a company's own corporate culture, there are six key components of any strong environmental management program. It is useful to articulate these areas before discussing benchmarking in detail, so as to lay a foundation for potential environmental benchmarking topics. The six areas are management and organization, continuous assessment and measurement of performance, information flow and communication, technical expertise, strategic planning, and adequate resources. Key features for each of these areas include the following:

Management and Organization

- Senior management (including the CEO and board of directors) whose commitment to achieving environmental health and safety (EHS) goals equals its commitment to achieving financial performance goals.
- Assurance that the messages sent from the CEO are received and believed by everyone throughout the company.
- An environmental leader who is part of the senior management team.
- An EHS program that encompasses all business segments, domestic and international.
- A corporate culture that includes compliance and environmental excellence. Also, it is important to create a culture in which it is more important to find problems than to hide problems. Once problems are known, they can be fixed.
- Establishment of clear environmental policies and implementing procedures along with high employee awareness and commitment. This includes the development of an environmental health and safety policy that is signed by the CEO and commits the company to EHS excellence and full compliance.
- Line manager accountability for EHS performance. This insures that environmental health and safety is fully integrated into a company's ongoing business operations.
- Effective companywide teamwork on solving EHS issues.
- The operation of proper reward systems. EHS compliance should rank equally with productivity and profitability in terms of emphasis in performance evaluations.

CONTINUOUS ASSESSMENT AND MEASUREMENT OF PERFORMANCE

- Continuous and thorough self-policing regarding EHS compliance and risk management at the facility level. Risk management includes those items that, although not covered by specific regulations, may still create environmental liability for the company.
- Regular computerized tracking of facility-level findings and action plans, as well as tracking the important permit requirements. The concept of sophisticated audit follow-up is crucial.

The only thing worse than not finding problems is finding problems and failing to fix them in a timely and adequate manner. Many companies convince themselves that there is a difference between "paperwork violations" and more significant violations. However, most regulatory officials view paperwork violations as significant because they show inherently sloppy housekeeping.

- Regular reporting to division and corporate line managers and EHS staff on significant issues. This is tricky because it is critical to transmit the right amount of information on environmental performance. It is just as problematic to transmit too much information as it is to transmit too little information.

- A corporate audit program of all divisions/facilities directed at ensuring the integrity of the self-policing, tracking, and reporting system.

- A set of measures, including but not limited to, audit results. These measures can be used to measure overall environmental health and safety progress.

- Regular corporate program evaluations that assess the effectiveness of the full EHS management program.

Information Flow and Communication

- A formalized information system, computerized if possible, to track needed actions. The system should be comprehensive and include all action items facing the company. The system should also include an automatic tickler function.

- Availability of all needed EHS information. This includes availability of outside databases and regulatory status information.

- Frequent reporting of information to various levels of management.

- Appropriate records retention controls in place.

- Formalized programs in place for sharing environmental performance with external customers.

Technical Expertise

- Training is performed regularly, comprehensively, and effectively in order to develop expertise in EHS compliance and risk management matters. Virtually all employees must be sensitive to the environmental components of their jobs. This includes senior management. Many companies institute training programs that teach a subject but don't really relate the subject to

an individual employee's job. Effective training recognizes the critical nature of job-based training.
- Necessary EHS experts are available to all operating, purchasing, planning, and marketing functions.

Strategic Planning
- A proactive government and regulatory affairs program at the federal and state levels to track emerging EHS laws and regulations and to communicate important developments throughout the company. Without such a function the company is always in the position of playing catch-up.
- Formal EHS risk assessment and management so the company is constantly assessing its own internal operations to identify areas of vulnerability, whether these are driven by existing regulations or not.
- Strategic environmental planning for EHS compliance, risk management, pollution prevention, and toxics use reduction. There are many ways to go about this. Some companies develop strategies for each facility; other companies develop cross-cutting strategies for each major environmental law.
- A formal link between facility/division environmental action plans and the budget.
- Procedures to evaluate new projects prospectively for the adequacy of environmental resources and capital.
- Environmental considerations integrated into the formal business strategic planning process. This also allows a company to develop a critical link between its business operations and a proactive legislative/regulatory program.

Resources
- Adequate human resources and operating budgets to support EHS needs. Many aspects of environmental health and safety performance are determined by line operating personnel and marketing staff. Resources must be adequate in these areas or environmental performance can suffer.
- Best available pollution control, safety equipment, and preventive maintenance programs.

BENCHMARKING
Benchmarking is the practice of comparing programs or processes with the intent of establishing reference points for continuous im-

provement. Many companies that are considered environmental leaders today achieved that status through the use of a benchmarking process. In addition to its application on environmental management systems, benchmarking can be used on very specific aspects of company operations. Although each company has its own specific mix of products and services, many operating functions are performed at multiple places within the company, within an industry, or even cross-industry.

Some simple examples based on the waste industry can clarify the concept. An example of issues that could be tracked at different locations within the same company is the generation of vehicle waste and vehicle fuel economy per truck mile of operation. Within the waste industry, different companies could benchmark the quantity and quality of leachate generated on a monthly basis adjusted for climate condition. A cross-industry example would be energy usage or solid-waste generation within office buildings by size of building.

In each area in which there are similar functions being accomplished, benchmarking allows a company to do several critical things.

- It helps the company develop good performance measurements.
- It allows a company to determine how one operation within the company, or the company itself, stacks up against itself, competitors, and noncompetitors. Such an analysis sets the stage for performance improvement.
- It provides an opportunity to gather innovative ideas for how to improve a given function. The key to success in this area is understanding which innovative ideas have the capability to work within a company's basic operating culture.
- It can help identify and set priorities for performance improvement.

Although there are some general steps that a company must go through when benchmarking, there is no one set way to benchmark. Benchmarking can be as formal and elaborate or as informal as a company wants. Most of us have participated in benchmarking all our lives. One obvious example is the height and weight chart that appears on the wall of a doctor's office. Another example would be standardized test scores. In each case, we can compare ourselves to averages or to "best in class."

Benchmarking allows a company to step outside its own culture to see new solutions that might be available. For example, a company may have been wedded to a rigid set of product specifications. When it sees how other companies handle similar situations, however, it may discover that changing the product specifications could reduce the amount of product waste without hurting the product.

Benchmarking, by its very nature, encourages its participants to be inquisitive and to ask questions. Initially these questions will often focus on the company being benchmarked. As the process continues, however, most companies begin to ask hard questions of themselves. Though most of the focus of benchmarking is to benchmark against industry leaders, companies can also learn by benchmarking other good (but not best-in-class) companies, especially outside of their immediate industry. No one company is a leader in everything. Many times ideas picked up during a benchmarking process can be embellished when they are carefully applied to a new company.

STAGES OF A BENCHMARKING PROGRAM

The benchmarking process has five key stages: planning, collecting information, analysis, implementation, and assessment. It is critical to remember that benchmarking is an ongoing process and is not static. It is a process, not a project.

Planning

The first stage of the planning effort usually starts when the "customer" identifies the needs. The customer could be a CEO, someone within the environmental health and safety department, or someone within another part of the organization. At this stage several things need to occur. A cross-functional team is usually established to work on the project. The team is selected to cover an appropriate mix of functional areas and is given training on team dynamics and the fundamental approach to benchmarking. Once established, the team works with the customer to determine the fundamental reasons for benchmarking. For example, a program to set priorities for which divisions are most in need of EHS attention is very different from a program to develop a more cost-effective way of implementing the EHS program. The customer and the team must begin with firm objectives. Two good questions to answer as a starting point are

- What are the important areas in which improvement is needed?
- What are the areas of the company that are key to its success?

The scope of the benchmarking effort requires a clear definition of topic areas, as well as a clear decision as to what will be measured within each topic area. It is possible, however, to do either quantitative or qualitative measurement.

Once the scope of the review is determined, the next step requires the development of a list of questions that will help collect the specific measurement data. As this list will be key to the project's success, it will be useful to test this instrument internally before going to outside companies. In that way, one can make sure that the instrument will result in the exact data that are needed. It will also ensure that the desired data are in fact collectable. A test of the instrument also provides the company with the ability to eliminate bias in the way the questions are phrased. Such bias is not unique to benchmarking programs and must be carefully evaluated for any questionnaire or survey effort.

An example would be useful. It may be desirable to determine whether the CEO of a company is active as an environmental health and safety leader. One way to phrase the question would be to ask directly, "Does your CEO support environmental issues?" However, that is a leading question. A better way to frame the question might be to ask what the CEO's priorities are, or how environmental messages are communicated at the company in question. This allows the responder more latitude in the development of a response.

Another important element in the planning process is to determine how many organizations—and specifically which organizations—a company wants to benchmark. It is also important to consider how to reach out to obtain the cooperation of the companies and organizations of most interest. In many cases you may already know who you want to benchmark. Certainly this is the case if a company wants to run an internal benchmarking program. However, in an external benchmarking program it may be possible to obtain the help of others in identifying proper benchmarking targets. For example, suppliers or other customers (both traditional and nontraditional customers) can help determine industry leaders. Also, regulators might be helpful in identifying companies with excellent environmental records. Shareholder groups such as the Investor Responsibility Research Center might identify companies that have strong external EHS communications.

Collecting Information

The first step in collecting information is to determine how the information is to be collected. One could use visits, phone calls, literature research, and so on. There are a number of published sources of information. The U.S. Environmental Protection Agency, individual states, and many other groups have set up various types of clearinghouses. These clearinghouses can often be useful, for example, in the area of pollution prevention. Another published source includes surveys that have been performed on items of interest. Many consulting firms have recently published studies showing how different companies approach their internal environmental management programs. Company annual reports and environmental reports can also be useful sources of published information. Another published source includes business and environmental trade press articles.

In addition to published information, there are numerous workshops, conferences, and roundtables at which various companies share experiences on different environmental topics. Global Environmental Management Initiative (GEMI) has held two annual meetings to discuss a broad range of topics. Many trade associations set up specialized workshops. Some companies have obtained benchmarking information by developing survey instruments that they mail to other companies. (These companies will almost always share overall results with participating companies.)

Often the best way to get benchmarking information is to engage in one-on-one exchanges. In these cases it is important to begin by deciding who should go on the visits, how much time will be needed, and how the information will be collected and recorded. It is critical to make careful notes on the information in real time so that important information will not be forgotten after the session. One-on-one sessions can involve formal presentations or informal question-and-answer formats. The sessions can emphasize one-way communication or two-way communication. Whatever method is used to collect benchmarking information, it is important to develop a way to store the information so that it will be easily retrievable for analysis.

Analysis

The starting point is to develop a format for capturing the information that can compare your company against the benchmarking targets. After data are systematically entered into this format, the comparison can proceed. Analysis usually involves the development of goals, recommendations, and implementation strategy. A cross-functional team can be crucial in developing the implementation strategy.

Implementation

Implementation requires the project team to prioritize recommendations and implementation steps. The success of the project depends on an effective communication effort throughout the company. Finally, it is important to develop a tracking system that can measure implementation progress.

Assessment

Because benchmarking is an ongoing process, it is useful to continue it on a regular basis. New benchmarking efforts can use the same comparison companies and/or the same benchmarking topics. To the degree the same benchmarking topics are used again, it is helpful to keep baseline performance measures in addition to any new measures to help evaluate progress. An ongoing benchmarking program assures that "best" remains an ever-moving target.

TOPICS FOR BENCHMARKING

There is no limit to the number and types of benchmarking topics that have been undertaken by companies. At the broadest end of the scale, many companies have looked at the overall components and functioning of their environmental health and safety management program and assessed their program against other leaders in the field. This type of an assessment is often a qualitative, not quantitative, benchmarking program. Another ongoing broad program is a project being undertaken by GEMI in looking at how different companies are implementing each of the sixteen principles in the International Chamber of Commerce Business Charter.

At the other end of the scale, many companies have chosen to perform benchmarking on very specific initiatives. These include topics like refuse reduction, injury and illness tracking, energy usage, CFC reduction, and pollution prevention.

The following example shows how the benchmarking process provides companies with a disciplined method for improving specific areas of EHS performance and illustrates the benefits of implementing a benchmarking program.

The Browning-Ferris Experience

In late 1990, Browning-Ferris Industries (BFI) initiated a benchmarking process for its environmental program to better assure that its environmental policies and programs were consistent with those of leading companies. The process involved planned visits to companies recognized as innovators in their own search for environmental excellence. Each company was visited by a team of four or more environmental professionals representing key environmental departments within BFI's corporate and regional structure.

The scope of these visits was not so structured as to limit the topics of discussion, but several key themes were emphasized as fundamental to bring back to the company:

1. Audit process design, protection, and issue closure;
2. Process for reviewing and implementing policies;
3. Environmental program staffing and professional development;
4. Measuring environmental progress; and
5. Information flow between operating units, regions, and the corporation.

Four companies were selected and visited between December 1990 and April 1991 by teams of BFI's environmental professionals. Each visit required approximately six to eight hours of time and typically involved the top environmental manager and one or more support staff of the company being visited.

Discussions generally began with how the company's environmental program was structured and staffed in comparison to numbers of facilities, personnel, and revenue. It was also important to understand how the organization evolved and how this structure was effective in achieving integration of environmental compliance and stewardship into the various operating units. Most of these companies, which, like BFI, were highly decentralized, revealed that their program structure and policies changed dramatically when the company changed from a centralized to a decentralized organization. Nevertheless, the degree of decentralization with respect to operations was much greater than the extent of decentralization of the environmental program. In other words, some centralized control over the environmental program was maintained not only to assure compliance with applicable laws and company policy, but also to establish and measure progress toward environmental goals (e.g., pollution prevention) that go beyond compliance.

The extent and breadth of these benchmarking discussions with the four selected companies were extensive and extremely beneficial to BFI. Key insights that BFI obtained through this benchmarking process included

1. The structure and staffing of BFI's environmental program appeared consistent with that of the other companies.

2. Environmental policies at BFI needed to be streamlined and focused on broad environmental objectives applicable across all business segments rather than being procedural in nature.

3. BFI developed ideas for strengthened self-reporting and tracking mechanisms that allow facilities to report and track their environmental actions yet provide some regional compliance oversight with applicable laws, rules, and permits.

4. BFI's audit program appeared to be consistent with other company audit programs in terms of formalized reporting of findings, but appeared to be advanced in terms of a formalized action closure plan. With respect to attorney-client privileges, BFI's program, which contains such a privilege, was in the minority.

5. Strategic planning was found to be highly formalized in the four companies reviewed; this vastly strengthened their environmental programs. BFI's program gained several insights for improvement.

6. All companies had a senior officer responsible for environmental affairs with broad coverage over all business segments.

CONCLUSION

As BFI and other companies pursuing environmental excellence are discovering, it is important to know what constitutes environmental excellence. The standard, however, remains a moving target. We expect more from good companies today than we expected five years ago. In fact, the standard is defined by those companies that continue to move their program to the front of the pack.

Will Rogers once said, "Even if you are on the right track, you can get run over if you are not moving fast enough." For companies that want to pursue environmental excellence, benchmarking can provide a critical tool that can help them assess where they are with respect to the train.

13

MEASURING ENVIRONMENTAL SUCCESS

Richard P. Wells, Mark N. Hochman, Stephen D. Hochman, and Patricia A. O'Connell

Process improvement, environmental results, and customer satisfaction all can—and need to—be measured in order to achieve total quality environmental management. This article details why and how to take such measures, with examples of leading company practices.

"In everything there lieth measure"
— Geoffrey Chaucer, *Troylus and Crysede*, 1375

Assuring customer-driven quality requires measurement of the customer values signifying that quality has been delivered. The usefulness of effective measures is recognized in the Baldrige National Quality Award criteria, which give heavy weight to "the scope, validity, use, and management of data and information that underlie the company's total quality management system."

Total quality environmental management (TQEM) systems are no less dependent on measurement. Yet, many environmental managers struggle with the choice of appropriate metrics, mostly because the managers need experience in using measures based on customer values. It is not that we lack the data. Rather, we have limited experience

Richard P. Wells *is vice president and director of Abt Associates' corporate environmental consulting practice in Cambridge, Massachusetts.* ***Mark N. Hochman*** *is director of Abt Associates' quality and strategy consulting practice, and* ***Stephen D. Hochman*** *is an associate at the firm.* ***Patricia A. O'Connell*** *is now with Xerox in Rochester, New York.*

in collecting and organizing environmental data that connect environmental performance to customer values.

Success measures that truly reflect environmental performance

- Create internal incentives for enhanced environmental performance,
- Set in motion a process of continuous environmental improvement that yields customer satisfaction, and
- Provide an effective means to communicate with your customers.

Poorly conceived measures can fundamentally misdirect your environmental program and mislead your customers. (See **Exhibit 1**.)

CUSTOMER REQUIREMENTS DRIVE ENVIRONMENTAL MEASUREMENT

We do not measure for the sake of measuring; we measure because the customers we serve—internal customers, end customers, host communities, regulators, or stockholders—demand environmental performance. Frequently, our customers may not have the technical expertise to measure our environmental performance. Meeting customer requirements requires *anticipating* customer requirements and *communicating* your achievements to customers.

Exhibit 1

Measurement: A Cautionary Tale

It is said of the former Soviet Union that when central planners measured success by number of units produced, nail producers delivered huge numbers of very small tacks. When success was measured by production volume, they delivered many fewer but very large spikes.

What central planners forgot, and producers had no incentive to learn, was that success must be measured in terms that are relevant to customers. How you measure environmental performance will determine the kind of performance you get. The measures you select must reflect the demands of internal and external customers for a corporate environmental policy.

Xerox Corporation is a recognized leader in customer-driven environmental measurement. Xerox has devoted several years to building the perceived requirements of internal and external customers into its environmental management systems. Moreover, the company is directing more and more of its external customer research to the development of environmental success measures.

As discussed later in this article, the formation of the Asset Management Program at Xerox is one of industry's most successful examples of a customer-driven investment in environmental quality. Using existing and *latent* customer environmental requirements as a baseline, Xerox has developed intermediate process, environmental, and customer satisfaction measures to insure that those requirements are met.

THREE PERSPECTIVES ON
ENVIRONMENTAL MEASUREMENT

Effective environmental measurement systems look at measurement from three linked perspectives: (1) process improvements, (2) environmental results, and (3) customer satisfaction (see **Exhibit 2**).

Process measures evaluate (generally, through management audits) how effectively your environmental management systems are working. They are a leading indicator of environmental results because you can tell whether appropriate management systems are in place before you can see whether those systems are having the desired effect. *Results measures* look at whether programs have in fact affected environmental and bottom-line performance. *Customer satisfaction* measures determine if customers appreciate improvements in performance and translate that recognition into changes in purchasing behavior.

No one of the three types of measures gives a complete picture of the success of environmental programs.

- Process success measures are meaningless unless the process outcome is shown to connect to environmental results.
- Environmental results, though important, will be difficult to sustain internally unless their effect on the corporate bottom line can be documented in terms of customer satisfaction and cost savings.
- Customer satisfaction calculations by themselves do not necessarily point to the strategies for addressing them.

Exhibit 2

Customer Requirements Drive
Environmental Measurement

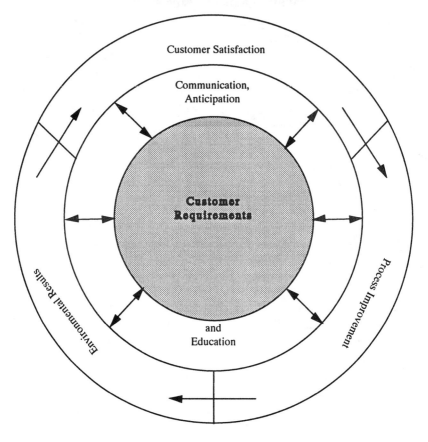

Companies that lack an understanding of the processes for achieving customer satisfaction have a tendency to drive satisfaction without looking at results. Often the result is programs that emphasize public relations over performance. Ultimately, such programs fail as increasingly sophisticated customers see through "green" programs that are not backed by performance.

Taken together, the three perspectives on measurement are a useful diagnostic tool. (See **Exhibit 3**.) If measures of process improvements do not lead to environmental results, look more closely at whether your management systems are working effectively. If you are getting the results you want, but customer satisfaction measures do

Exhibit 3

Three Perspectives on Environmental Measurement

Processes
- What systems are in place?
- Do these systems ensure compliance with applicable permit requirements?
- Do they create incentives to move beyond compliance?
- Do they minimize potential environmental liabilities?
- Do corporate materials and cost accounting systems accurately reflect environmental concerns?
- Are environmental management systems fully deployed throughout the company?

Environmental Results
- What is the company's impact on the environment?
- How is this impact changing over time?
- Are the company's releases of environmental contaminants per unit of production increasing or decreasing over time?
- Is the company improving its efficiency in using natural resources?

Customer Satisfaction
- Are your company's key internal and external customers satisfied?
- How important is this performance to each set of customers?
- What are its most important performance aspects?
- How would customers like to see the company improve?
- What customer needs will the company have to anticipate and satisfy in the future?

not show improvements, you may be measuring aspects of environmental performance that your customers do not care about, or you may be communicating your success ineffectively.

If all three sets of measures interact, you can have confidence that you have the drivers necessary for continuous improvement process that is at the heart of TQEM.

PROCESS MEASURES ARE A
LEADING INDICATOR OF RESULTS

Effective environmental management systems drive environmental results. (See the Baldrige criteria in **Exhibit 4**.) Process measures assess whether the management systems that anticipate problems and ensure outstanding performance are in place and operating effectively. Be sure that process measures assess whether management systems

- Are systematic and incorporate processes that enable you to "do it right the first time";
- Anticipate customer requirements;
- Incorporate the discipline to trace problems to their root causes...and avoid responding to symptoms;
- Make use of materials and cost accounting systems that create incentives for environmentally sound behavior; and
- Are in place throughout the company.

Recently, a number of important initiatives have introduced systematic methods to ensure that appropriate management processes are in place. The Global Environmental Management Initiative (GEMI), for example, has introduced its Environmental Self-Assessment Program (ESAP) that provides a checklist of program elements targeted at principles of the International Chamber of Commerce's Business Charter for Sustainable Development. The scoring system built into the ESAP provides a quantitative method for companies to assess their environmental programs in key areas necessary to meet the guidelines established by the International Chamber of Commerce. Standards associations, such as the Canadian and British Standards Associations, are also developing environmental program guidelines to incorporate environmental management into the International Organization for Standardization (ISO) 9000 series of Guidelines on Quality Management.

Often, management audits are used to measure processes. The nature and focus of management audits often need, however, to be

Exhibit 4

Malcolm Baldrige National Quality Award Criteria

Management systems and methods drive environmental performance. One way to assess the adequacy of management systems is to look at the evaluation criteria of the major national quality award—the Malcolm Baldrige Quality Award. Use these criteria to measure the effectiveness of your environmental quality system.

Total quality analyses:

- Is it prevention based?
- Are the tools, techniques, and methods effective?
- Is it systematically integrated and applied?
- Does the approach include scheduled evaluations that drive continuous improvement?
- Is the evaluation based on objective and reliable information?

Systematic deployment:

- Is the approach appropriate and effective to all product and service characteristics, transactions, and interactions with

   — customers?
   — suppliers of goods and services?
   — the public?
   — employees?

- Are all internal processes, activities and faculties aware of their roles and trained to perform?

extended to reflect the requirements of TQEM programs. It is not enough to ensure that management systems ensure regulatory compliance and prevent industrial accidents and superfund liabilities; they must also create incentives to move beyond compliance.

Auditing for Compliance Is Only the Beginning

Companies have developed various measures to ensure that management systems are in place companywide. Auditing is the most common technique used to monitor companywide compliance. Traditional environmental compliance audit programs have utilized a checklist approach. Facility procedures and documentation are compared against federal and state environmental regulatory requirements. Deviations from these requirements are identified and expected to be fixed. Fixes are generally achieved utilizing "band-aid" solutions. Furthermore, this symptom-focused approach tends to be reinforced by regulatory agencies' approaches to inspecting facilities.

AT&T changed from this traditional environmental compliance approach when it became evident that desired results were not achieved. The "find and fix" approach did not prevent deficiencies from reoccurring. The emphasis was on deficiencies rather than on the causes. Most importantly, continuous improvement never entered the equation. Upon audit process evaluation, they concluded that the primary problems were that their approach was too negative, focused only on the symptoms of weak systems, and lacked adequate follow-up.

- **Too negative.** Since the audit team approached facility audits in a regulatory inspection mode, only negative issues were emphasized. Program strengths were not evaluated. This gave the appearance to the facility management that the environmental department was not doing their job. Consequently, the environmental personnel felt that audits were an evaluation of job performance. This served to create resistance to the audit program at the facility level with a resentment toward the audit team.
- **Focused only on symptoms.** Emphasizing deficiencies served to place focus on symptoms rather than on the causes—"find and fix" instead of continuous improvement. Permanence was not addressed as a necessary component of an action plan. Therefore, the fixes that were implemented were generally reactive, short-term, stop-gap-type measures. Without man-

agement structural changes or a continuous improvement methodology, the same deficiencies were perpetuated.

- **Lacked adequate follow-up.** The audit team was not adequately staffed to perform follow-up action plan effectiveness evaluations. A deficiency report was left at the facility following a closing meeting, and the team would not revisit it for another four to five years.

To address these program problems, a new approach is being implemented to evaluate environmental program strengths and weaknesses. AT&T now views compliance deficiencies as indicators of systemic problems. They work with facility personnel to identify root causes and recommend more permanent structural changes. If necessary, they will assist the facility in implementing the required actions. Program effectiveness will be re-evaluated in subsequent audits every two years.

Cost/Materials Accounting Conventions
Are Disincentives to Quality

Cost accounting and materials accounting systems, which are not typically examined in management audits, need to be evaluated as part of process measures. Perhaps the single largest obstacle to effective corporate environmental management is the absence of cost accounting systems that accurately reflect the true costs of quality. If environmental costs of quality are not recognized by corporate accounting systems and allocated to the processes that give rise to the costs, process managers will have neither an incentive to minimize environmental impacts nor a reward for successful environmental management.

Similarly, materials accounting systems also create important management incentives when they are integrated with cost accounting systems. AT&T is in the process of implementing a materials tracking/accounting system at an electronics manufacturing facility. Their goal is to account both physically and economically for all materials (including energy) at the process step level. The system will account for all process inputs (raw materials and intermediate products) and all outputs (products and material losses).

This system, when fully deployed, will provide the *integrated* information necessary to realize the economic benefits of reducing environmental releases. For example, the following groups will benefit from the system outputs:

- **Environmental**—Generate regulatory reports, monitor compliance, track progress toward environmental goals.
- **Manufacturing engineers**—Monitor process efficiencies, identify potential cost reduction targets, measure economic and environmental impact of process changes, more accurate materials planning for anticipated production level changes.
- **Inventory control**—Order materials on a just-in-time basis, reduce inventory cost, and minimize losses due to shelf-life exceedances.
- **Cost accounting**—More accurate product costing (including environmental costs) and reduced overhead accounts.
- **Quality**—Provide the basis for incorporating environmental into total quality management program.

ENVIRONMENTAL RESULTS
BUILD CUSTOMER SATISFACTION

The environmental results you obtain are the way you measure whether your performance will meet your customer's expectations. (For illustrative measures, see **Exhibit 5**.) They are also what you communicate to your customers to demonstrate continuous improvement.

Paradoxically, much less effort has gone into measuring results than has gone into establishing that processes to obtain results are in place. In part, the absence of results measures reflects the complexity of the task of measuring environmental results. In part, it also reflects reluctance to ask hard questions. Generally accepted systematic methods to measure environmental results do not exist. Instead, companies use one or more of the measures listed in Exhibit 5 to track progress. Few companies have methods in place to assess their environmental results across the multiple dimensions of environmental performance.

In monitoring and communicating your performance, keep in mind a few basic principles:

- **Be customer-oriented**. Develop measures that address key customer requirements and demonstrate your success in improving your performance in areas of concern to your customers.
- **Focus on continuous improvements in your own performance**. It is very difficult to make company-to-company comparisons. It is much easier and more credible to document improvement in your own performance.

Exhibit 5

A Few Measures of Environmental Results

MEASURE	WHAT IT MEASURES	ADVANTAGES	DISADVANTAGES
Permit Compliance	Compliance with applicable permits expressed as exceedances of permit limits.	An essential measure—customers will look first to your compliance with permits.	Taken alone, a narrow measure indicating that you are doing only what is required.
Toxic Release Inventory (TRI) Chemical Releases	Over 300 chemicals subject to release annual reporting requirements under SARA Section 313.	Information on releases is widely available to the public. An effective way to communicate performance.	Does not cover all important chemicals or industries; focuses on release volume without accounting for differences in toxicity.
"30/50" Chemicals	A subset of 17 of the TRI chemicals identified by EPA as priority candidates for voluntary reductions in releases by industry.	A more refined list of chemicals than TRI; companies participating in the 33/50 program and meeting goals will receive public credit.	Leaves out many important chemicals. Not clear that a company not participating in the 33/50 program will receive special credit for these reductions.
Clean Air Act Toxics	189 chemicals listed in the Clean Air Act as "air toxics" subject to maximum achievable control technology (MACT) standards.	MACT standares will be extremely costly to meet. By reducing or eliminating releases, you avoid very high future costs.	Taken alone, like TRI, not a full measure of environmental performance. Focuses only on air; creates risk of shifting problem from air to other media.
Risk-Weighted Releases	Toxic chemicals weighted by their relative toxicity: • weightings • toxicity categories	A more realistic depiction of health and environmental effects than unweighted releases.	Toxicity data are frequently highly uncertain. To date risk-weighted approach has not been generally accepted by key customers—EPA, environmental groups.
Waste Per Unit of Production	Percent of production lost as waste; generally measured on a waste weight to production weight basis.	A very broadly applicable measure that incorporates efficiency in use of resources as well as contaminant releases to the environment.	No priority established in terms of types of wastes; absent other measures, creates an incentive to focus on high-volume low-toxicity wastes.
Energy Use	Total energy use by all aspects of corporate operations; can be expressed also as CO2 releases.	A comprehensive measure that focuses attention on efficiency in use of a key resource. Anticipates possible global warming concern; readily communicated to customer.	Energy efficiency is important, but not the only basis on which to evaluate environmental performance. Need other measures as well.
Solid Waste Generation	Total solid waste going to landfills or other disposal facilities.	An important measure in the public mind due to publicity surrounding landfill capacity shortage; often reflects efficiency in resource use.	A very narrow measure of environmental performance; often misinterpreted as the most important criterion to judge performance.
Product Life Cycle	The total impact of a product on the environment from raw materials sourcing through production use and ultimate disposal.	The most comprehensive measure of product level impact. A meaningful goal to strive for in resource use efficiency and pollution prevention.	Extremely complex to implement. Methodologies are not commonly accepted. Claims based on product-life cycle analysis are frequently treated with skepticism. Difficult to apply at a corporate or unit level.

- **Keep it simple**. Although the underlying calculations may be complex, the final indicator should be simple and "catchy."
- **Avoid commitments that you cannot keep**. In the long run, sustained improvements in performance are more credible, and more valid environmentally, than dramatic gestures.
- **Be flexible**. Rigid formulas may cause company units to focus on meeting the formula rather than the customer's needs.
- **Use multiple measures**. No single measure captures a company's total environmental performance. A well-selected set of measures can give a more complete profile. Exhibit 5 illustrates the advantages and disadvantages of a few measures you may want to consider.

Polaroid and 3M measure environmental results in different ways, but both focus on measuring continuous improvements in performance in a manner that can be readily communicated to the public.

Polaroid responded to a strong corporate commitment to environmental stewardship and to external customers—local communities, state regulators, and advocacy groups—who made reductions in the use of toxic chemicals a high priority. The company established a risk-weighted program for measuring progress in toxic chemical use.

Under the program, the company assigns all its materials to five categories that range from Categories I and II (carcinogens and other high-priority toxics) through Category V (nontoxic solid waste) and sets 10 percent per year goals for reductions in the use (Categories I and II) or the waste generation (Categories III-V) of materials in each category. This approach ensures that progress is made across all categories of materials, avoiding a focus on high-volume, low-toxicity wastes where progress is often more easily attained.

3M also started from a strong tradition of commitment to environmental stewardship. Extending the groundwork laid by its Pollution Prevention Pays program, 3M established a corporate goal of a 7-percent annual reduction in waste per unit volume.

Using a materials accounting approach, 3M compares the weight of inputs to the production process to the weight of products shipped to customers. Any loss in weight during the production process is considered a waste. The strength of the waste-per-unit-volume-shipped method is its simplicity; it provides a single metric that can be applied throughout the company. This simplicity was important to develop a consistent approach across 3M's extremely varied operations.

By focusing on total waste, this approach also emphasizes efficiency in the use of resources. The disadvantage of the waste per unit volume approach is that it encourages operating units to emphasize areas where they can obtain the greatest reductions in waste volume. 3M avoids the possible misdirection of waste reduction efforts away from low-volume, high-toxicity wastes by focusing on high-toxicity wastes.

Financial results must always be kept in mind as you measure the results of your environmental programs. (See **Exhibit 6**.) Typically, corporate accounting systems recognize only direct cost savings as returns on environmental expenditures. Avoided costs are sometimes considered, but often very narrowly. For example, accounting systems may only see avoided compliance costs as benefits of environmental expenditures, ignoring materials savings and dramatically increasing

Exhibit 6

How One Company Subsidized
an Environmental Problem

A major consumer-products company told us that one of its units produced two similar products: One used a solvent and the other was solvent-free. The two products were supplied based on a marketing assumption that customers differentiated between the two products. In fact, market research indicated that customers would be satisfied with the solvent-free product, and many customers preferred the solvent-free product based on its superior performance.

The company found that it was charging the operating unit the same amount per ton for waste disposal associated with production of the solvent-containing product as it was for the disposal of the solvent-free product, even though the company's cost was considerably higher.

In effect, the corporate accounting system was subsidizing the cost of producing the solvent-containing product. By changing their accounting system to reflect environmental costs more fully, and by recognizing that market research showed no customer advantage in providing a solvent-containing product, the company shifted production to the solvent-free product.

environmental costs. Or systems may subsidize some wasteful practices by not charging the operating unit the full cost that their wastes impose on the company.

CUSTOMER SATISFACTION IS THE KEY MEASURE OF SUCCESS

Ultimately the success of environmental programs will be measured by whether the programs' internal and external customers are satisfied. Customer satisfaction is the core of quality programs—the Baldrige award criteria assign 300 out of 1,000 points to ways of achieving and measuring customer satisfaction. Most significantly, quality of any output exists only when a customer values it. Measures of environmental program quality are different only in that they tend to require analyses of more customers than might exist for many products or services.

Yet, in many companies measurement of environmental program customers' satisfaction tends to lag well behind the companies' efforts for other functions. Corporate marketing groups frequently gather data on end customers' environmentally motivated purchasing behavior. The measures, however, have concentrated on "green" products and packaging—outputs that reflect only a small, very downstream portion of your efforts.

Environmental managers have multiple customers. End customers are important. But to satisfy them you first must meet the needs of internal customers—process managers, engineers, and others on whom you depend to implement your programs. Additionally, you may serve a variety of intermediate customers such as regulators, legislators, community groups, and others who have a strong influence on the allocation of your company's environmental management resources.

Accurate measurement of each of these customers' requirements can help you anticipate critical issues for guiding your efforts. Most important, customer satisfaction measures are critical because they

- **Provide a single independent and comprehensive measure of success.** Over the long run the satisfaction of multiple customer groups with corporate environmental programs is the best indicator that these programs are meeting their goals. By concentrating on customer satisfaction, we keep our efforts focused.
- **Bring environmental programs into the corporate mainstream.** In the past, corporate environmental programs have been considered exclusively a matter of regulatory compli-

ance. By recognizing that environmental programs support customer-oriented business objectives, customer satisfaction measures integrate environmental programs into corporate strategy.

- **Build the case for environmental programs internally.** Information about customers' values can be a powerful tool for gaining the attention of the stakeholders in your company whose support you need to take action.

Recently, there has been a recognition of the very substantial cost savings that can be attained by applying TQEM techniques. Customer satisfaction measures also recognize that TQEM programs can improve revenues and lower costs. Programs that fully acknowledge the associated cost savings and revenues are more likely to be sustained over the long term than programs that are undertaken for compliance.

One reason customer satisfaction measures are not widely used is that we are unaccustomed to

- thinking that we can measure something as abstract as satisfaction with environmental programs and we usually do not
- consider that measures of the satisfaction of all our internal and intermediate customers can promote effective management.

However, our experience shows satisfaction measures are fairly easily developed and, over and over again, are excellent bellwethers of corporate strength. Our studies in numbers of industries show that satisfied internal and intermediate customers are strong supports for end customers' satisfaction.

How Do You Measure Customer Satisfaction?

Useful measures of customer satisfaction can be made qualitatively as a result of conversations with your customers. Or, generally more credible data are developed as a result of surveys and similar quantitative approaches.

In either case, the questions about satisfaction with your existing efforts can begin with very general queries about "how satisfied are you with X?" Responses should be aided with a scale of answers (e.g., very satisfied, performance was as expected, not satisfied). The responses by themselves will provide little direction for taking actions to satisfy your customer. However, by following the general question with specific inquiries about whether customers agree or disagree with *specific characteristics* of your process's performance, you can determine which characteristics are the most supportive of your customers' satisfaction.

For example, you might ask line process managers to rate their overall level of satisfaction with your support to their efforts. You could follow with requests for them to rate such characteristics of your support as

- "Lack of conflicting guidelines your department provided to help them implement a new process"
- "Timeliness of your contribution to their efforts to identify alternative processes for hazardous substances"
- "Your ability to help them forecast the environmental consequences of a new process"

Your analyses of the data will show you which of your line process manager "customers" is most or least satisfied and which of the characteristics of your efforts correlate with the satisfaction you have produced. Then you will be in a much better position to take action on specific characteristics that are the greatest detriment to customer satisfaction.

Frequently, you will need to ask earlier, open-ended questions to know which process characteristics to ask about. Focus groups of customers can provide you with some very helpful insights because you benefit from the discussions between participants. When group discussions are not feasible, face-to-face interviews can offer the appropriate forum. Whichever approach you use, the key to gaining good information is to have a prepared list of open-ended questions about the ways in which the participants understand or use your process. Questions that begin with, "What do you think about…" or "Why?," followed by "Can you give an example?," are appropriate.

In quantitative research, the responses to the questions about characteristics can be statistically correlated with the general answers. Then multivariate regression analyses can be employed to build fairly precise models that

- Predict how specific characteristics lead to customer satisfaction;
- Tell you which characteristics deserve the greatest attention for you to have the most significant effect on satisfaction; and
- Direct you to steps that will contribute most to lowering costs or increasing revenues.

Go Beyond Satisfaction Measures...
Identify Your Non-Value-Added Activities

Using either qualitative or quantitative methods, you should expect to take an important step beyond measuring customer satisfaction; satisfaction only tells you about your existing process. To gain full value from your research, you should also establish customers' valuation of the relative importance of your existing process characteristics. Not infrequently, you will find that some of your activities are much more valuable to you than to your customer. These "non-value-added" activities are often ripe for elimination in favor of whole new steps that could anticipate customers' *latent* requirements.

Anticipating Customers' *Latent* Requirements at Xerox

Xerox Corporation has established itself as one of the leaders in anticipating the environmental needs of its internal and external customers. The key to meeting customer needs has been to follow one of the company's basic quality maxims:

We will understand our customers' existing and latent requirements.

Several years ago, senior management responded to the heightened visibility of environmental issues by creating an environmental leadership committee, which would concentrate on integrating *all* company functions into the company's environmental activities. While acting as a vehicle for internal communication of environmental successes, the leadership committee was also responsible for integrating the expected environmental needs of internal and external customers into the company's overall strategy. The committee sometimes conducts customer research through surveys and focus groups to determine customer environmental requirements.

Included in the committee are representatives from all major functional groups and operating divisions within the company. This ensured inclusion of every customer voice in long-range environmental plans. To facilitate information-sharing across functions and to foster innovation, the committee has developed a corporate electronic network that allows environmental process-improvement teams to communicate trends in customer environmental requirement and any newly discovered technical solutions to meeting those requirements.

Identifying Customer Trends

One trend identified by the leadership committee through recent surveys has been an increasing demand among end customers for maximum product recyclability. The company has augmented its environmental policy accordingly:

- The company is committed to the continual improvement of its performance in environmental protection and *resource conservation*, both in company operations and in product *design*.
- The company is committed to

  — designing its products for optimal recyclability and reuse and
  — taking every opportunity to recycle or reuse waste materials generated by its operations.

A Customer Concern: What's the Right Thing To Do?

Thus far, the end customer and regulatory responses have been overwhelmingly in favor of product recyclability, but there is some concern that these various customer groups do not know exactly what they want. More specifically, customers are not sure what *aspect* of product recycling is most important to them. Some possibilities include

- Products and parts repaired and reused
- Plastic crushed and reincorporated in raw material
- Programs for product recycling at local landfills

Translating Vague Customer Demands into Process Specifications

Many customers do not understand the subtle differences between some of these technical issues. As a result, the company has no scientific means for understanding the details of *existing* customer preferences. In this case, the general enthusiasm that customers have shown for recycling indicated their general understanding that *more recycling is better*. The feedback, therefore, translated to specific directions from top management. States the vice president of asset management, "We decided that the message customers were giving was 'recycle everything.'"

As a result, part of the company's design charter includes a requirement for *maximum recyclability*. Because of this, the corporate asset-management team has set as a target the reuse of all product materials. At the same time, the company has been educating end customers about the environmental attributes of its products. By informing customers about the subtleties of product recycling and remanufacturing, the company actually has begun to influence customer preferences. In effect, the company has been developing the ability both to monitor and control the market for its products.

Measuring the Benefits of End Customer Satisfaction

To estimate revenue-related financial benefits, the marketing staff on the design teams is responsible for projecting the *market-share* gains associated with specific product environmental attributes. Although it is known that the benefits are substantial, the company is still in the early stages of developing an accurate *metric* for customer response data. One of the asset-management subteams is currently refining the financial component of its measurement system.

CONCLUSION: "DOING THE RIGHT THING" IS STRATEGICALLY SOUND

As demonstrated by Xerox's success, there is no law that says that doing the right thing has to be bad for business. In the company's quarterly journal, Abhay Bhushan, coordinator of the company's Environmental Leadership Program, puts it this way:

"When we make decisions, we evaluate them according to five criteria: *Environment*—how does it affect resources and pollution? *Ecology*—how does it impact the relationship between people and other living things? *Economy*—does it involve optimum use of resources? And finally, *Health* and *Happiness*. In most good decisions, all five vectors are in the right direction."

The principles of the asset-management program dovetail with the company's corporate philosophy. The program has the powerful effect of driving toward one of the most notable criterion for project success: the customer satisfaction that has produced marked gains in market share and profitability. The company has substantially benefited by its years-ago commitment to "do the right thing."

14

SELECTING MEASURES FOR CORPORATE ENVIRONMENTAL QUALITY: EXAMPLES FROM TQEM COMPANIES

Chris FitzGerald

Companies undertaking TQEM programs must decide how to measure continuous improvement in the environmental field at the outset of their implementation activities. In the past three years, the leading TQEM companies have made these tough choices and have begun to share their findings with the larger professional community. The author proposes a model for classifying environmental measurement data and presents examples of approaches adopted by TQEM companies.

THE CHALLENGE OF APPROPRIATE MEASURES

Identifying appropriate measures of quality has been one of the principal challenges for companies applying total quality management (TQM) principles to their environmental programs. TQM systems rely in part on appropriate statistical procedures applied to appropriate, accurate measurements, yet at the program level most of the environmental manager's professional practice tools are almost exclusively qualitative rather than quantitative. Selection of appropriate measures is critical, because systems tend to optimize around their key measures. Inappropriate measures will produce inappropriate results; in other

Chris FitzGerald *is the editor-in-chief of the quarterly journal,* Total Quality Environmental Management, *and president of Environmental Management Information Systems in Oakland, California.*

words, watch out, because you might get what you ask for. In TQM terms the traditional site compliance audit is a qualitative, after-the-fact inspection for defects. There are reams of qualitative data items produced for reports mandated by regulations, but meaningful measures tend to get obscured rather than enlightened by production of these huge quantities of data points.

Computers are not helpful in selecting *what* to measure. The availability of large databases can be a temptation to substitute volume for meaning, much as vague requests for proposal (RFP) specifications for big projects can lead to consultant proposals that are intended to be weighed rather than read. Environmental professionals more often serve their information systems than are served by them. Deming Prize-winner Florida Power & Light (FPL) recognized this by "banning" the term *environmental information management systems*, because that term reflected the need to service these potential data-hungry monster systems. Information systems must demonstrate and justify their value to the management goal at FPL, where the acceptable term is *environmental management information systems (EMIS)*.

Who Is Measuring What?—
Classifying Environmental Information Functions

What measures are meaningful in our TQEM program? The answer will vary according to who is doing the measuring. In general, the selection of an appropriate measure will be more straightforward as you get closer to the *task-level engineering function* (See **Exhibit 1**). If your job is to run a water treatment plant (source monitoring), you know that timely reporting and minimizing the concentrations and quantities of target pollutants are likely to be among your principal measures of quality and continuous improvement potential. There are many data points (results), but the parameters are consistent and comparable.

For the manager with *plant-level, cross-media* responsibilities, there are many more data sources and more complex data relationships involved. Reduction of stack or wastewater emissions is no longer a pure benefit if it increases shipment of wastes to landfills; the full life cycle of hazardous components within the plant must be identified and to some extent quantified. Although dedicated environmental emissions databases are useful for source monitoring, at the material management level data must be captured from a wide range of operational sources, such as purchasing, distribution, personnel, material planning, process management, and shipping. The meaning-

Exbibit 1

A Hierarchy of Environmental Management Information Requirements

Responsibility	Orientation	Typical Data Sources	Data Characteristics
Environmental Performance; Compliance/Risk Management	Corporate Environmental Policy & Programs Internal Compliance	Auditing Permit Management Facility Reports Surveys	Highest Integration Summary & Exception Relatively Lower Volume
Materials Management	Plant-Level Processes	Chemical Inventory Waste Tracking Material & Emissions Balances	High Integration High Volume
Source Monitoring	Engineering Task	Air & Water Reporting Tank Testing Exposure Monitoring Groundwater & Soils	Low Integration High Volume

ful integration of these data in a timely and cost-effective manner is a significant challenge at this level, and without prioritizing key measures it is impossible to identify performance levels and opportunities for continuous improvement.

At the *corporate or divisional program level,* it becomes even more difficult to identify quantitative measures that associate program goals with hard, measurable data. If the source management and material management level data collection analysis is being done properly and consistently, there are many millions of data points available, but which measures are meaningful within the context of a corporate-level program? On one level there is a need to assure that the functions are being carried out properly, and compliance-oriented measures are an obvious choice. These measures typically focus on the number and timeliness of audits conducted, reports submitted, and notice of violations, releases, incidences, and noncompliance occurrences. But compliance in itself is assumed to be a basic performance standard for TQEM firms and not much of a rallying cry for excellence and continuous improvement. What other quantitative measures are being applied to corporate environmental performance?

REPORTS FROM THE MEASUREMENT FRONT

This discussion will focus on the attempts to create measurement systems to be employed and promoted companywide to help implement corporate environmental policy statements. All of the TQEM firms discussed here also employ a variety of other measurement systems to track improvement at other function levels (e.g., source management and materials management).

Apart from a few pioneering companies, most firms are still in the first few years of implementing TQEM programs. Measurement systems rely on several years' data to become meaningful, because TQEM measures gauge progress rather than absolute levels of quality. TQEM companies are still devising, implementing, or calibrating their corporate measurement systems, but are now beginning to share their findings in the environmental management community. At two recent TQEM conferences, twenty speakers addressed measurement strategies in their presentations. The Total Quality Environmental Management Conference was held in San Francisco on March 9-10, 1992, and was sponsored by Executive Enterprises. The Corporate Quality Environmental Management II: Measurements and Communications Conference took place on March 16-18, 1992, in Arlington, VA, and was sponsored by GEMI: The Global Environmental Management Initiative. We will summarize eight of the measurement programs that represent the different approaches presented here (see **Exhibit 2**). In referring to the papers presented, we will abbreviate the conferences as TQEM-SF and GEMI '92.

AT&T/Intel Joint Benchmarking[1]

In 1991 AT&T and Intel joined forces to identify the "best-in-class" corporate pollution prevention (PP) programs and develop benchmarks for targeting their own firms' efforts at continuous improvement in PP. The proposed benchmarks were needed to serve PP participants by (1) encouraging them to "look outside the box" of existing practices for new PP opportunities; (2) providing comparative data to help convince management of the need for improvement; and (3) developing momentum for the PP efforts at every level of the company.

The project team used scoring systems to weigh PP quality parameters, select the best-in-class companies, and again to weight the factors that would determine level of PP quality. Quality parameters

Exhibit 2

Selected TQEM Measurement Systems

Company	Purpose of Measures	Parameters
AT&T/Intel Joint Project	Develop benchmarks for corporate pollution prevention (PP) programs.	• Weightings of program elements • Evaluation of "best of class" • Design of generic PP program • Gap analysis
Sandoz Corporation	Plant and corporate S & E (safety and environmental) performance	Key indices reported at all facilities: • Lost time & workday accident rates • Totals: energy, water, waste • S & E investments, expenses, personnel • Total production, personnel
Niagara Mohawk	Track effectiveness of corporate environmental protection programs	• Weighted index comprised of — Compliance incidents (NOVs etc.) — Emissions and wastes — Enhancements (dollar value)
Green Environment	Track effectiveness of corporate environmental protection programs	Score sheet of program implementation: 25 questions, 0-2 pts. each. Categories: • PLAN • DO • ACT • CHECK
Xerox Corporation	Integrate environmental issues to core company values	Economic Incentives • Gain market share via positioning • Cost savings reporting • Reduce risks, future costs
3M Company	Track continuous improvement in Pollution Prevention Pays (3P) and production efficiency	Waste quantities reflect 3P, efficiency • Absolute values • Reductions over time • As percentage of inputs
U.S. EPA	• Publicize polluters • Economic incentives • Recognize "good citizens"	• SARA 313/TRIS • Clean Air Act 1990 pollution market • 33/50 • Green Lights

were selected in brainstorming sessions in which environmental and safety work areas were categorized (i.e., Superfund management, audit process, smoke detection, paper recycling, etc.) and then scored on the basis of relative importance and self-evaluation of their own company's progress and process status:

- Importance   1= Very important   to   5 = Not important
- Self-Grading   A = Excellent   to   F = Poor
- Process Status   E = Emerging   or   M = Mature

After voting on scores, the team created a weighted evaluation template, brainstormed a list of potential best-of-class companies, then conducted high-level searches to provide data for scoring companies on the weighted template. This process narrowed the list to eight companies for evaluation, five of which were visited for face-to-face structured interviews. After the interviews the team assembled to evaluate which program elements of successful PP systems were (1) critical, (2) important (3) nice to do, or (4) not relevant.

As a result of the research, the team developed a "generic pollution prevention program" synthesizing the weighted program elements and performed gap analyses to determine what their own companies needed to do to implement the generic program.

Sandoz Corporation[2]

Sandoz Corporation decided that relatively simple, straightforward parameters were the best choice from the standpoint of comparability and easy access to data, allowing for immediate implementation. All of Sandoz's 350 facilities worldwide now report these ten safety and environmental data items on a regular basis:

1. Lost time accident rate
2. Lost workday rate
3. Total energy consumption
4. Total water consumption
5. Total liquid and solid waste
6. Total S & E investments
7. Total S & E expenses
8. Total S & E personnel
9. Total production
10. Total personnel

Another advantage of this approach is that almost all of the data items can be provided from existing data sources. Items 1 and 2 are already required for US OSHA reporting, and the remaining items can be summarized from existing production and personnel systems. The measures are primarily useful for comparisons over time for individual facilities, but additional inter-plant comparisons can be made for similar operations by creating ratios, such as waste per ton of product.

Xerox Corporation[3]

Although Xerox Corporation employs many other measurement

systems to monitor environmental quality, economic indicators are emerging as key incentives to integrate environmental values with the corporation's core values. Laws and regulations, which were originally the driving forces for environmental improvements, are external drivers. By identifying environmental improvement with values of internal customers (employees, customers, and management), TQEM can become an integral aspect of company operations. While maintaining other environmental quality measurement systems, Xerox is emphasizing data that illustrate opportunities to

- Gain market share by positioning environmental quality as an aspect of total quality management;
- Treat pollution at the source via redesign; and
- Reduce risks and future costs.

Even though Xerox has implemented and maintains many other qualitative and quantitative measures of environmental progress, Xerox will emphasize its commitment to environmental leadership by explicitly stating the economic benefits of each program element. Thus proactive compliance is justified as an opportunity to reduce future costs; packaging reuse produces both cost savings and cost avoidance; and energy programs are quantified both as conservation improvement and cost savings. In every instance, the environmental initiatives produce results that are visible on balance sheets in the company's mainstream financial reporting, rather than just in special environmental reports.

Niagara Mohawk Power Corporation (NMPC)[4]

At Niagara Mohawk an interdisciplinary task force was formed to develop an index to measure progress in achieving a new corporate policy for environmental protection. Five options were considered:

1. A compliance-oriented index modeled on another utility's environmental index.
2. External benchmarking of selected utilities.
3. A three-category "weighting and rating" index.
4. An index based on air emissions.
5. A social welfare index based on weighting emissions and waste parameters.

The task force selected the third option and developed parameters to measure and weigh corporate environmental performance based on compliance, waste/emissions, and environmental enhancements. Benchmarks for current performance are being established, and future performance will be weighed on a -2 to +2 scale representing lower or higher performance against the benchmark.

The *compliance* parameters weigh notices of violations and fine paid the highest, followed by audits performed and then nonconforming discharges and emissions. The *emissions and wastes* parameters apply half the weight to emissions/MWhr of SO_2, NOx, and CO_2, and the remainder to solid wastes, hazardous wastes, LLRW, and discharges of heavy metals. *Environmental enhancements* are rated based on NMPC's dollar investment in each enhancement. Niagara Mohawk recognizes that the index is measuring widely disparate parameters, and doesn't assign significance to the actual score on the index. The real value of the index is to measure relative improvement over time.

Green Environment, Inc.[5]

Environmental consultant Mark Green has developed an ambitious tool for measuring corporate environmental, called TQEMPE: total quality environmental management performance evaluations. TQEMPE is patterned on the Baldrige Award criteria and reflects aspects of the Deming, Crosby, Juran, and Harwood methodologies. Green identifies seven essential criteria for an evaluation tool:

1. Instrument must be accurate.
2. Instrument must be precise.
3. Measurement must be powerful.
4. Instrument cost and cost of measurement must be economical.
5. Instrument must be adaptable.
6. Instrument must be simple to use.
7. Instrument must be effective.

TQEMPE attempts to meet these criteria through a twenty-five question evaluation tool in which each question can be scored from zero to two, for a potential perfect score of fifty (nonapplicable questions are scored two). The questionnaire is divided into four topical areas: PLAN (five questions); DO (seven questions); CHECK (seven questions); and ACT (four questions). A sample question from the DO section asks

...Are all levels of management involved in and accountable for achieving environmental objectives?

- All levels of company management have a role in and are accountable for achieving company environmental objectives. (2 points)
- Some levels of company management have a role in and are accountable for achieving company environmental objectives. (1 point)
- Company management roles for achieving company environmental objectives are not defined, or an accountability mechanism does not exist. (0 points)

TQEMPE can be applied as an assessment tool at the plant, division, and/or corporate level. Green stresses that the tool is intended to provide a common language and metric system for comparison over time and between operations, and that the scores are not intended as absolute values for one-time ratings.

3M Company[6]

3M Company's pioneering and influential *Pollution Prevention Pays* (3P) program employs the simplest measurement approach of all: absolute data for waste produced are reported companywide and are expected to show improvement each year. Every plant measures all of the wastes being generated from that facility, including all facility wastes that go into the air or water, or are generated as hazardous or solid wastes. Waste measurements are taken before the wastes are subjected to any treatment measures, to assure that any reductions that are achieved have been accomplished by pure pollution prevention rather than by improvements in pollution control efficiency. These waste values are normalized to production levels so that increases or decreases in production levels are removed from the evaluation.

Tom Zosel, manager of 3M's pollution prevention program, says that this approach to measuring improvement is consistent with 3M's engineering orientation and commitment to placing responsibility for 3P in the operating divisions:

> If we really look at what we are measuring, it is the efficiency in our total use in raw materials. We believe that 3M is one of the first companies that can quantitatively determine on a percentage basis exactly how much of our raw materials goes into product, how much goes into productive recycling or secondary uses, and how much ends up as waste. This takes into account all materials used at product facilities including packaging supplies, quality control materials, maintenance materials, and clean-up supplies.

The success of 3P is well-documented. Established in 1975, the program has reduced 3M's pollution by an estimated 50 percent and has saved the company over $500 million.

U.S. EPA

We'll ask you to suspend skepticism for a moment and look at recent EPA program initiatives as efforts to serve the corporate customer sector by providing simpler, comparable measures as both carrots and sticks. On the stick side, the SARA 313 Form R can be seen as a reporting burden and a community embarrassment when TRIS reports make the local front pages. But many firms also report that the Form R reports have provided operational data that they never had available before, allowing comparisons both among plants within a company and between companies utilizing comparable production processes. In his address to the GEMI conference, EPA Administrator William Reilly posed TRIS-type disclosure as the single most effective first step Eastern European countries can take in the effort to clean up the massive pollution legacies of the old Eastern bloc regimes:

> My answer is to begin with the disclosure of emissions, that the data be published in local newspapers. They support a healthy nongovernmental, environmental movement. At that point a fascinating dynamic will begin to occur: The community will interact with plant managers, workers, and government to reduce pollution levels. Such is the power of information.[7]

On the carrot side, the 33/50 and Green Light programs offer industry quantitative goals, quantitative information on progress, and the opportunity for companies to demonstrate leadership and good citizenship. Although the Clean Air Act Amendments have many proscriptive provisions, they also encourage continuous improvement by developing benchmarks for emissions per unit of production for many processes and rewarding the top 12.5 percent of companies for performance in this arena. Finally, by encouraging the development of markets for surplus emission credits, EPA and regional agencies such as California's South Coast Air Quality Management District are supporting the coin of the realm (dollars) as the most basic, comparable measure of improvement.

CONCLUSION

Although even the pioneering companies described here will caution that the development of measurement systems is still in its infancy, a number of consistent trends are emerging:

- Measurement systems are essential to give meaning to corporate environmental policy statements; without measures they are platitudes.
- No measurement system has value as a one-time exercise; meaning emerges only as data are reported over time to track improvement.
- Deciding what to measure is only one aspect of the measurement challenge. Measurement programs must be implemented to encourage ownership and provide useful feedback at the levels where improvement can be implemented.
- You can't keep the measures in the corporate closet; results must be widely distributed in order to be effective. Documenting accomplishments is critical to encouraging pride of ownership and momentum to the people who are ultimately accomplishing continuous improvement.
- The right measures will draw data from mainstream business data systems rather than exclusively from specialized, isolated environmental applications. The better the measure reflects the core values and goals of the company, the more the environmental functions will be integrated into everyone's job.
- Make the measures as lean and clean as possible. The more complex, fuzzy, and data-hungry the measure, the less likely you will be to achieve wide-scale, meaningful reporting. There is a definite need for qualitative evaluation as well as quantitative measures, but people understand and respond to success that can be plotted.

Finally, the degree of cooperation and open information sharing in the measurements field is remarkable. There are strong disincentives to sharing company information about pollution issues with other companies, and one can imagine that a lot of corporate counsel time has been engaged in examining how much can be disclosed. But the constructive, open disclosure of methods and the devotion of time to intercompany benchmarking, publishing, and speaking reflect the real enthusiasm and value that the leading TQEM firms are deriving from seeing the results of measurement systems.

Notes

1. GEMI '92: Klafter, Brenda A. (AT&T), "Case Study: AT&T and Intel Pollution Prevention Benchmarking."

2. GEMI '92: Ankers, Ray, "Measuring Safety and Environmental Performance and Risk."

3.   TQEM-SF: Bhushan, Abhay K. (Xerox Corporation), "Economic Incentives for TQEM: How Will It Improve Your Bottom Line?"

4.   GEMI-92: Miakisz, Joseph A., "Developing A Composite Index for Measuring and Communicating Environmental Performance."

5.   TQEM-SF: Green, Mark (Green Environment, Inc.), "Total Quality Environmental Management Performance Evaluations Using TQEMPE."

6.   TQEM-SF: Zosel, Thomas W., "Pollution Prevention from a TQM Perspective."

7.   GEMI '92 Reilly, William K., "The Power of Information."

15

TQM AND THE COST OF ENVIRONMENTAL QUALITY

Richard S. Greenberg and Cynthia A. Unger

Because management is driven largely by financial concerns, determining the cost of environmental quality is a critical step in developing an environmental TQM program for which management will actively demonstrate commitment and support. Costs of environmental quality can be grouped into three categories: failure, prevention, and appraisal. The total cost of environmental quality can be used as a benchmark to monitor the level of environmental quality and to justify the redirection of resources.

The Total Quality Management (TQM) philosophy is being viewed with widespread interest by American industry. In its attempt to remain competitive, industry has embraced TQM's common sense and customer-oriented principles. Many companies can point to significant benefits in terms of increased revenue and profits, fewer customer complaints, and a more motivated work force.

Another factor in the movement to remain competitive is business' demonstration of environmental responsibility and quality. Companies are beginning to recognize the relationship between environmental quality and opportunities for economic growth. Determining the total cost of environmental quality is key to implementing a successful TQM program.

There are many obstacles to the initiation of a companywide environmental TQM program, however. The most formidable obstacles are twofold: Top management is usually interested in results,

Richard S. Greenberg *is director, Environmental Consulting Practice, for Coopers & Lybrand, Denver.* ***Cynthia A. Unger*** *is a senior associate in Coopers & Lybrand's Environmental Consulting Practice.*

not means, and it is difficult to identify and quantify benefits associated with introducing quality into the organization. Management usually will ask two questions before agreeing to initiate an environmental TQM program:

- Will it result in an increase in sales?
- Will it result in a decrease in operating costs?

LEVELS OF ENVIRONMENTAL QUALITY AND MATURITY

Every organization is situated somewhere along the quality maturity spectrum shown in **Figure 1**. This quality maturity spectrum ranges from "innocence" to "excellence." At any given time, every organization demonstrates a quality maturity level for key organizational characteristics: management approach, role of top management, quality responsibility, management process, government/public rela-

Figure 1

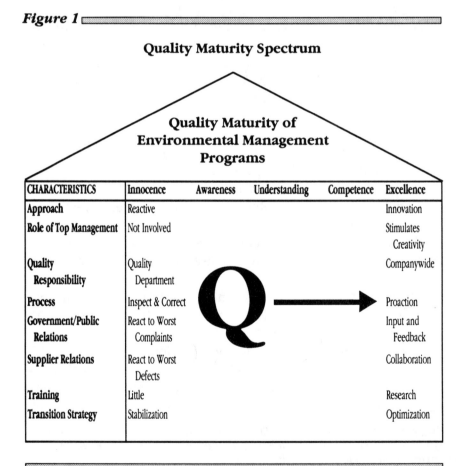

Quality Maturity Spectrum

Quality Maturity of Environmental Management Programs

CHARACTERISTICS	Innocence	Awareness	Understanding	Competence	Excellence
Approach	Reactive				Innovation
Role of Top Management	Not Involved				Stimulates Creativity
Quality Responsibility	Quality Department				Companywide
Process	Inspect & Correct				Proaction
Government/Public Relations	React to Worst Complaints				Input and Feedback
Supplier Relations	React to Worst Defects				Collaboration
Training	Little				Research
Transition Strategy	Stabilization				Optimization

tions, supplier relations, training, and transition strategy. The goal of a TQM program is to move the organization along the quality maturity spectrum from a state of innocence to a state of excellence. Before an organization can progress, management must first assess where it is situated along the spectrum. Some organizational characteristics may be further along than others.

Viewing environmental management programs through the TQM perspective calls for examining the quality maturity level in a more specific, narrower context. The level of maturity demonstrated by mere compliance could represent the baseline of environmental commitment for a quality-driven organization. Going beyond this level of maturity can increase the level of quality of an environmental organization if management commits to the investment of resources and long-term cultural changes.

Each position along the quality maturity spectrum is associated with a certain cost. As related to an environmental management program, this cost is the company's total cost of environmental quality.

TOTAL COST OF ENVIRONMENTAL QUALITY

A company's total cost of environmental quality consists of all costs associated with maintaining its existing level of environmental quality. Environmental costs are not limited to only those costs incurred by the "environmental department," but may also include costs incurred by other departments (for example, legal, insurance, operations, and so on). These costs include all resources expended in resolving environmental issues—financial, personnel, and goodwill.

Because management is driven largely by financial concerns, determining the cost of environmental quality is a critical step in developing an environmental TQM program for which management will actively demonstrate commitment and support. In general, determining the total cost of environmental quality means identifying all direct environmental expenditures, accounting for all personnel time devoted to environmental activities, and estimating implied costs (for example, lost sales). After these costs are identified, they can be tracked to provide management with valuable data to evaluate the change in quality and identify areas for improvement, consequential cost reduction, and ultimate savings.

The cost of environmental quality can serve as a benchmark against which improvements can be measured. Because a company's level of environmental quality is correlated to its environmental compliance record, management will find that as the company's level of environmental quality and regulatory compliance increase, the cost of envir-onmental quality will decrease over the long term. As shown in **Figure 2**, an inverse relationship exists between the level of environmental quality/regulatory compliance and the cost. This total cost of environmental quality concept is a persuasive tool to gain management support for introducing a TQM program for environmental management into an organization.

BREAKING DOWN COSTS

Costs of environmental quality can be grouped into three categories: (1) failure, (2) prevention, and (3) appraisal.

Figure 2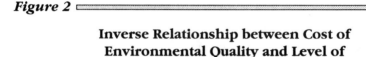

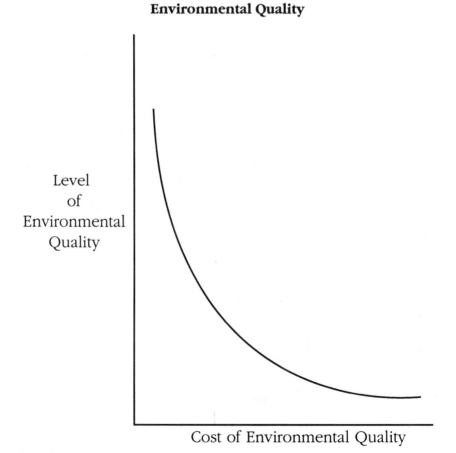

Inverse Relationship between Cost of Environmental Quality and Level of Environmental Quality

Level of Environmental Quality

Cost of Environmental Quality

Failure Costs

Costs of *failure* can be either internal or external. *Internal failure* costs are those costs associated with evaluating, testing, analyzing, correcting, reworking, repairing, and scrapping failed products, materials, or components—all detected before the customer receives the product. Examples of internal failure costs are those costs associated with reprocessing and remanufacturing catalytic converters that fail to meet U.S. Environmental Protection Agency (EPA) requirements.

External failure costs are those associated with customer-detected failures in products, materials, or services. These types of costs are nonvalue-added. Examples of external failure costs are those expenses associated with the recall and repair of catalytic converters that fail to meet EPA requirements. Other examples include environmental fines, penalties, and cleanups. External failure costs represent opportunity costs, that is, sales lost because of lack of quality. Consumer boycotts due to perceived acts of corporate environmental irresponsibility can result in significant and long-term losses in revenue.

Prevention Costs

Prevention costs cover those costs associated with nonvalue-added support activities that prevent the recurrence of product or process failures. Examples of prevention costs may include those costs associated with waste minimization and pollution prevention programs, use of double-hulled oil tankers, and product testing. Some companies have experienced significant cost savings by redesigning processes to avoid generating pollution, rather than incurring future expenditures associated with cleaning it up.

Appraisal Costs

Appraisal costs include those costs associated with evaluating, measuring, inspecting, and auditing products, processes, components, and materials to ensure conformance with requirements/expectations and specifications. Examples of appraisal costs may include those costs associated with environmental auditing programs, monitoring equipment, and government reporting requirements. Appraisal costs are most apparent to management when they estimate the total cost of environmental quality.

Every company must determine its total cost of environmental quality. This cost necessitates an in-depth examination of the organization's operations, cost accounting systems, environmental liabilities, and risk management procedures. Categories of expenses that an organization may include in its determination are

- Payroll and direct expenses associated with the environmental compliance program;
- Environmental audits and environmental testing;
- Purchasing, calibrating, and operating environmental monitoring equipment;
- Purchasing, calibrating, and operating environmental control equipment;
- Environmental fines, penalties, and cleanup costs;
- Environmental liability insurance premiums;
- Waste disposal costs;
- Reserves set aside for contingent environmental liabilities; and
- Revenue loss because of negative public relations.

The cost cycle for environmental quality is a closed loop that contains an element of continuous improvement (see **Figure 3**). If failure costs are identified, direct actions can be taken to reduce failures. These actions may be investments in prevention activities;

Figure 3

Environmental Quality Cost Cycle

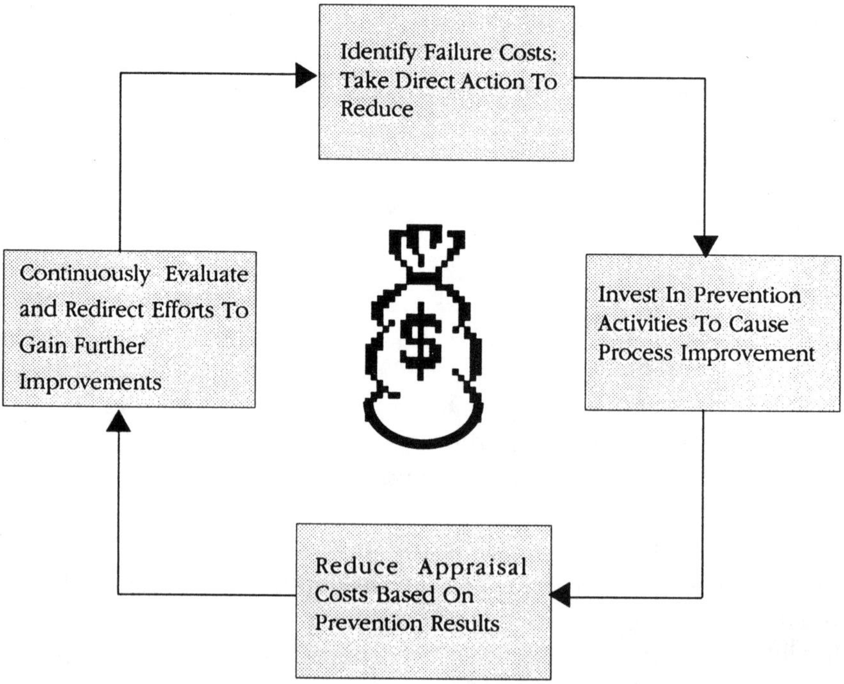

therefore, appraisal costs should be reduced. Evaluation and redirection of efforts should be undertaken continuously to gain further improvements.

The total cost of environmental quality is important to management because it can be used as a benchmark to monitor the level of environmental quality and to justify the redirection of resources.

DETERMINING COST ON A PRODUCT/SERVICE BASIS

In the present competitive economy it is important for management to be aware of the cost of environmental quality for each service and product. For example, a company located in California may need to know which of its products is associated with higher environmental costs. This knowledge may enable management to decide to produce those products in another location with less stringent environmental regulations or not to produce that product at all. Determining the cost of environmental quality on a product/service basis will allow management to make decisions with respect to product/service mix that reflect changing market conditions.

A significant environmental expense that is not always adequately accounted for on a product/service basis is the payroll expense associated with personnel involved in the "environmental department." In many companies the environmental department is treated as a general support function. In these companies, personnel are charging time to an undifferentiated general/administrative or overhead account that does not identify specific tasks. In determining the total cost of environmental quality related to producing a particular product or service, management must be able to identify and calculate the direct production costs and to determine the specific environmentally-related labor costs associated with the activity.

A product's costs include not only the cost of factory resources to convert raw materials and purchased components to finished items, but also the costs of resources devoted to ensuring that all environmental requirements associated with the life cycle of that product are met. For example, all costs associated with the generation, transportation, and disposal of wastes in the production of a widget must be considered and calculated as the cost of that widget. In those cost accounting systems that allocate environmental overhead as a function of direct labor, specific environmental costs cannot be ascertained.

One approach to better understand all real costs associated with producing a particular product or service is Activity-Based Costing. Activity-Based Costing accumulates and reports costs by activity or process, rather than by traditional budget categories (for example, environmental overhead salaries). Environmental overhead costs are rarely linked to a product or service. Furthermore, traditional cost systems do not permit the identification of environmental costs to the activity (for example, producing the widget) they support. In fact, the typical measures commonly found today conflict with the continuous improvement philosophy inherent in TQM. It is becoming more widely recognized that activities consume resources (for example, environmental overhead) and that products consume activities. A key to continuous improvement is to understand the activities and the resources they consume.

Because Activity-Based Costing reveals the linkage between performing particular activities and the demands those activities make on a company's resources, it can give managers a clear picture of how products, brands, facilities, and regions generate revenues and consume resources. With an Activity-Based Costing system management can readily determine which of the company's products are "environmentally expensive."

Although developing and implementing an Activity-Based Costing system may seem to impose additional and tedious administrative and accounting burdens, in the long run it is a necessary foundation for a successful TQM program.

Once the costs of environmental quality for the company and for each product/service are determined, they can be used as valuable management tools to

- Indicate financial significance of poor environmental quality;
- Identify production/service areas of poorest quality;
- Allow wise allocation of capital and professional resources;
- Allow the establishment of quality goals and budgets; and
- Show cost reduction results of improvement efforts.

CONCLUSION

Over time, management will be able to see that the introduction of TQM into an environmental management program can result in cost savings. TQM requires a quantitative baseline that reflects the cost of existing environmental quality. An effective approach to establishing this quantitative baseline is determining the total cost of environmental quality for the company and for each product and service. This can be best accomplished through Activity-Based Costing.

▬▬▬**16**▬▬▬

GETTING ORGANIZATIONAL BUY-IN FOR BENCHMARKING: ENVIRONMENTAL MANAGEMENT AT WEYERHAEUSER

Kenneth M. Karch

Benchmarking is a process companies use to identify and evaluate the best practices, both inside and outside their industry, in their field of interest. The goal is to identify gaps between their performance and the benchmarks so that they can find ways to improve their performance. This article describes an early benchmarking effort in the environmental management area of the Weyerhaeuser Company.

Public expectations, community concerns, environmental group pressures, and federal, state, and local legislative and regulatory activities were constantly and rapidly changing during the 1980s. As a result, firms in the private sector realized that they could no longer merely respond to these changes; they had to learn how to anticipate change and adopt new ways of conducting business.

During this volatile period, the Weyerhaeuser Company, a *Fortune 100* forest products company with 1991 sales of $8.7 billion, recognized the need for continuous improvement in its environmental management efforts. Although the company enjoyed the top spot in environmental management for its industry segment in *Fortune's*

Kenneth M. Karch, P.E., is director of corporate quality for the Weyerhaeuser Company, Tacoma, Washington.

annual "most admired companies" survey, its management realized that there was much that the firm could learn from others. Therefore, in mid-1987 it began a benchmarking effort to determine what improvements the company could make in its environmental management.

The mission of the environmental group, which was established during a companywide redesign in 1983-84, was to provide environmental policy for the company and to help business units manage their significant environmental issues. Specifically, the group established environmental policy; identified emerging issues; analyzed the impact of environmental issues on the corporation and its operating units; developed environmental issue management plans; tracked and responded to federal and state environmental laws and regulations; handled association management; interpreted environmental laws and regulations for businesses and operations; and provided direct services to operations, such as training, auditing, negotiations, and permit acquisition.

Customers for the environmental group's products and services included investors, the board of directors, the CEO, the COO, the holding company of which the group was a part, individual businesses and operations, and employees, as well as a variety of external groups. The expectations of these various customers included compliance assurance, public perception/image, financial impact awareness, major and emerging issue management, environmental policy management, permit negotiation, technology transfer, legislation and regulation interpretation, and training.

News of the use of benchmarking was beginning to spread throughout U.S. industry by mid-1987, largely through the efforts of Xerox. Nonetheless, little was available in the public domain to explain how to benchmark. Robert Camp's seminal book, *Benchmarking,* was still two years away; few articles had been written; and consultants with significant experience were rare. Weyerhaeuser was, thus, forced to develop its own process.

STARTING OFF WITH A 33-STEP PROCESS

Figure 1 shows the 33-step process that the company devised to carry out its benchmarking effort. The process was devised to fit a PDCA (Plan, Do, Check, Adjust) cycle and to start earlier and end later than much of the current literature on benchmarking suggests. Benchmarking is considered here to be only one of many ways to achieve performance improvement, in competition with others for

Figure 1

Steps in Benchmarking Effort

1. Decision to benchmark for an organization or function
2. Top management selection of the organization or function
3. Top management selection of the team and leader
4. First team meeting; self-organization
5. Education/training plan development
6. Education/training of team
7. Selection of activities to benchmark
8. Selection of criteria by which to judge
9. Identification of "best of the best" in the field
10. Query outside for "best of the best"
11. Selection of "best" outside companies
12. Preparation of request to "best" companies
13. Preparation of questionnaire
14. Preparation of own answers to questionnaire
15. Contacting the "best" companies and securing cooperation
16. Arranging visits to "best" companies
17. Selection of interviewers
18. Preparation of interviewers
19. Visits to "best" companies
20. Preparation of individual reports on visits
21. Distribution to team of individual reports on visits
22. Individual analysis of individual reports
23. Meeting of full team to review results
    - analysis of individual reports
    - selection of critical lessons
    - analysis of critical lessons
    - application of critical lessons to the group
    - identification of general areas for recommendations
    - assignments
    - consideration of other factors
      - corporate vision
      - group vision
      - employee attitude surveys
      - work process analysis
      - customer identification
      - customer needs feedback
24. Preparation of interim report on benchmarking effort
25. Team review of interim report
26. Preparation for management review presentation
27. Presentation to management for review
28. Adjustment of recommendations per management feedback
29. Preparation of final report on benchmarking effort
30. Presentation of final report on benchmarking effort to management
31. Securing commitment on management actions
32. Tracking progress on management action commitments
33. Instituting corrections to actions

attention and resources; thus, a management decision must be made to undertake a benchmarking effort. In addition, the benchmarking process is not considered to be complete without a management presentation, a process for tracking progress on action commitments, and a process for standardizing and continually improving the benchmarked area. In short, it is not enough to complete the analysis and put it on the shelf. Among the key points to consider in the benchmarking process are

Leadership—Top management of the unit must provide leadership to the benchmarking effort. **Figure 2** shows some of the roles and responsibilities of leadership for benchmarking.

Education—An education module is necessary for benchmarking; such a module should identify

- The need for benchmarking
- The extent to which it is being done elsewhere
- The benefits expected
- The elements of the process itself, including means of selecting the key functions to benchmark, the variables to measure, the

Figure 2

Roles and Responsibilities of Leadership

1. Emphasizing the need and setting the expectations
2. Selecting members of the team and a leader (if he or she does not directly lead the activity)
3. Providing the necessary resources, time, and support to the team members to allow them to do a quality job
4. Setting the boundaries within which the benchmarking effort is to take place
5. Ensuring that adequate education and training are provided to the benchmarking team members to allow them to carry out the activity
6. Making necessary contacts with other companies (because of the weight that the leadership position carries)
7. Receiving the results/recommendations with an open mind, and making every effort to implement the most important of them
8. Recognizing and rewarding the team members for their contributions.

means of selecting the "best of the best" in the field, the process for comparing the "best of the best" processes with your own, and the means for selecting improvements to your own program.

The environmental team was provided with some explanatory material at the time the team was selected, the team members reviewed it, and discussed it at length. Throughout the process, questions continued to be raised about the nature of the process and the expected product. There was a strong predisposition toward viewing benchmarking as a "project" with an end point and implementable results that, once carried out, would solve the "problem," rather than as a process for creating a climate for continuous improvement. More "going-in" education was necessary than the company initially provided.

Teamwork—Teamwork is critical because of the varying knowledge and values that each member brings to the effort. Upon assignment, the team met, organized itself (that is, set rules about meeting norms), underwent the (limited) education module, and committed itself to the task.

What To Benchmark—The team identified which functions it would benchmark against. The environmental team identified twelve

Figure 3

Selected Success Factors for Environmental Management

1. Corporate philosophy and policy
2. Structure of the organization
3. Communications flow
4. Prioritization procedures
5. Emerging environmental issues
6. Resource availability
7. Internal tracking and information systems
8. External communications (except regulatory agencies)
9. External relationships with regulatory agencies
10. Trade association involvement
11. Dispute resolution
12. Key activities

categories of "success factors" (see **Figure 3**). Other groups will have different success factors to benchmark against. The company also decided to ask its benchmarking partners about their perceptions of their own success and opportunities for improvement.

What and How To Measure—The team identified the key variables to be measured. This turned out to be an extraordinarily difficult task, as quantitative data were desired. The environmental team agreed that some hard data could be collected (number of employees, dollars spent on pollution control, sales, earnings, and so on), but that many of the kinds of questions about key functions would solicit answers that were "yes/no" or qualitative (high to low; A through F; 10 to 1) in nature. In fact, it was clear that most of the answers obtained would be qualitative.

The Questionnaire—The team developed a questionnaire around the key variables; it then developed the Weyerhaeuser "answers" to each of the questions. Answering the questions for Weyerhaeuser enabled the team to understand and appreciate the process that the firm's benchmarking partners would go through, and to add, drop, and fine-tune specific questions. The company used its best judgment in stating the questions to avoid biasing the answers; professional polling help was not used. The final questionnaire was fifteen pages long, with 118 questions.

Whom To Benchmark—As seasoned professionals with considerable experience, the team members had their own views on which were the best companies in the field. The company also decided to seek the advice of outside groups who were in a position to evaluate company environmental programs. It asked local, state, and national regulatory agencies, environmental groups, and national trade associations for their assessment of the "best of the best." For the most part, these outsiders were willing to provide their judgments (with anonymity promised), and generally volunteered that Weyerhaeuser enjoyed a reputation among the best. The team took all the input and selected three companies (one in the industry and two outside) for initial contact; a second tier of three was selected in case any of the companies that were initially selected did not cooperate.

How To Get Cooperation—The team members developed a telephone script and letter to go to the selected companies seeking their cooperation. They were prepared to offer a copy of Weyerhaeuser's "answers" in return for cooperation as well as a condensed summary of the findings of the entire benchmarking effort, if necessary. The vice president for environmental, energy, and regulatory affairs (EERAG) was asked to provide the entrée to the companies. All three "first choice" companies agreed to cooperate, without the team having to offer them the complete summary. The team later followed up with the second tier of three companies, with complete cooperation.

Company Visits—Weyerhaeuser's plan was to visit a company for a day and remain in town that evening to complete the report on the company the next day while the information was still fresh in mind. Two EERAG representatives visited each of the three companies (three EERAG representatives were involved; each visited two companies). Preliminary reports were prepared for each company. Each benchmarking team member who participated in an interview prepared his or her own summary of the total experience. The data were entered into a simple computerized file management program and a summary table was generated to allow comparison of the company-by-company responses to each question. The completed summary table consisted of forty-five pages.

Acquiring Independent Data—Independent business data on benchmarking partners can be gathered from such sources as the Dow Jones News Retrieval Service and other on-line data bases, as well as from a variety of business periodicals. These data can help put the companies' business performance and outlook in perspective and generate some benchmarks.

PUTTING TOGETHER THE RESULTS

A special meeting of the entire EERAG team was held to discuss the results that had been provided to each team member several weeks earlier. At the meeting, the team conducted a brainstorming session to identify

- The key things they learned from the companies (they ended up with thirty-four; some are given in **Figure 4**)
- The apparent degree of importance attached to each of those items by each of the companies (on a scale of high/medium/low)
- The degree of importance attached to each by the Weyerhaeuser environmental team (also on a scale of high/medium/low)
- The degree to which the EERAG team felt that Weyerhaeuser met the criteria (on a scale of adequate/inadequate)

Exhibit 4

Selected Findings of
Environmental Benchmarking Effort

1. Proactive process for identifying and managing emerging key issues
2. Compliance with laws and regulations part of your competitive edge
3. Audits critical
4. Waste minimization/elimination
5. Strong environmental policy
6. Formal process for setting priorities
7. Top-level awareness/commitment
8. Communication of top management commitment
9. Internal education/training on environmental issues
10. Compliance responsibility at facility level

This exercise allowed the firm to compare its own views with those of the best companies, to compare its performance against an "ideal," and to prioritize the areas on which it wished to focus.

The EERAG team prepared a report of the major lessons learned that contained a series of recommended mid-course corrections to the Weyerhaeuser environmental program. That report was presented to top management. The EERAG team realized that the benchmarking effort could not be done in a vacuum, that its results must be consistent with the firm's vision of the future, the limitations of the present, and the ability to make the changes. Thus, the team realized it had to review its mid-course and long-term recommendations in light of the (then) new vision statement, the department's existing vision statement and mission, a view of current employee attitudes and work processes, the views of its customers, and constraints imposed by external forces beyond its control (for example, corporate policies that might conflict with team recommendations and changes in laws and regulations).

The benchmarking team eventually worked with a total of six benchmarking partners, identified thirty-four key findings, analyzed these key findings against a set of criteria, and identified seven short-term items and a number of long-term items to address.

Some of the easier-to-tackle, short-term items were implemented immediately; some of the long-term items requiring significant organizational changes have been implemented only recently. For example, on April 20, 1992, Jack Creighton, the company's CEO, unveiled his senior management team's set of five key environmental expectations for Weyerhaeuser:

1. Operating in full compliance with all state and federal regulations;

2. Establishing specific targets, milestones, and long-range business plans to keep the company in full compliance and provide it with a competitive advantage;

3. Educating and training every employee about the requirements of regulations and audit standards within the next two years;

4. Managing the company's environmental challenges to create competitive advantage by developing products with minimal impact on the environment, limiting use of and exposure to toxic materials, maximizing recycling and reuse, and minimizing waste; and

5. Better understanding the concerns of the company's communities and neighbors, participating effectively in public policy forums, adapting quickly to evolving expectations, and communicating openly.

Here are some of the key lessons learned in this early benchmarking effort:

- *Top management commitment and participation are necessary from the beginning and throughout the process.* The necessary time commitment by team members will almost certainly be underestimated.
- *Individual team members will have "going-in" biases.* These will influence the kinds of questions that are generated and asked, and how the answers are interpreted. Therefore, considerable effort is required in designing the questions, answering the questions for your own company, getting answers from your benchmarking partners, summarizing the answers, and drawing conclusions from them in an objective manner.
- *Team approaches are absolutely critical.* Brainstorming, nominal group, and other techniques and tools must be used to help eliminate going-in biases, broaden viewpoints, and secure buy-in and commitment to the process and its results.
- *The process cannot be rushed.* People need time to consider the new ideas that will be generated and the challenges to their ways of thinking engendered by others' views. Even though

only sixty-five person-days of effort were required to bench-mark the first three companies, no less than four to six months of calendar time were necessary to get to that point.

- *An education and training session/module is critical.* Individual team members will have tough questions about the need for the benchmarking effort, what is expected to result, how they will be able to find the time necessary to do the job, and how to do it.

- *The activity is resource-intensive.* Management must be willing to commit the resources to the effort if it wants good results. Each individual team member who makes the actual visits will have to commit to spending no less than fifteen person-days of effort to get the first three companies. Nonvisiting team members will have to commit about ten person-days each to the initial start-up effort. The total person-day commitment by the company to get to this point for a five-member team (three of whom take part in the visits) is about sixty-five. Thereafter, about twelve person-days per company benchmarked (assuming two interviewers per company and a five-member review team) are required.

- *Efforts to secure answers to all questions must be rigorous.* Failure to make such efforts will bias the results and leave information gaps. Interviewers must probe deeply to understand subtle differences between partner strategies, organizational structure, resource allocations, and so on.

- *There are huge opportunities for breaking old paradigms even in the absence of quantitative data.* Defining questions for which quantitative data is available can be extraordinarily difficult. As a first effort, a company should do the best it can with qualitative data when quantitative data is not available, then move toward quantitative data as it improves its process. Some of these lessons have already been applied in the Weyerhaeuser benchmarking efforts listed in **Figure 5**.

GETTING STARTED WITH BENCHMARKING

Today, companies that want to understand and implement benchmarking have a variety of means at their disposal: There are a number of excellent texts available; numerous articles have been written on the subject; benchmarking conferences detail what others have done; and many consultants are available to educate and help interested companies through the process. In addition, there are organizations such as

Figure 5

Selected Areas that Have Been Benchmarked

1. Environmental Management
2. Communications (Environment, Total Quality, Organizational Change)
3. Total Quality Education
4. Capital Project Management
5. Human Resource Management Practices
6. Organization System Change
7. Employment Security
8. Transportation
9. Financial Systems
10. Investor Relations
11. Multiple Technical/Operational Support Areas

the International Benchmarking Clearinghouse in Houston, Texas, designed to provide a variety of information and other services to novices, intermediate benchmarkers, and experts alike. Basically, any company interested in benchmarking will have to take the following ten steps:

1. ***Provide leadership***—Begin by having your top managers become knowledgeable about benchmarking and committed to and supportive of it. Get them to communicate their support throughout the organization and to provide clear expectations and necessary resources. Perhaps get them involved in a benchmarking project of their own, on an issue that is their direct responsibility.

2. ***Adopt a new philosophy***—To be successful in benchmarking, a company must shed the "not invented here" syndrome. It must get rid of such notions as "We can't learn anything from others," We're as good as you can get," "There's no one outstanding in this field," "We're a commodity business—we have to work on price," and "Our work is different—it can't be measured against the work of others." Instead, the company must adopt a philosophy of continuous learning and improvement, along with such attitudes as "We'll borrow shamelessly," "We can learn something from anyone," "We don't have all the answers," and "We'll do it this way only until something better comes along."

3. ***Create a steering committee***—Assemble a top-level group

with credibility in the company to oversee the benchmarking effort. Get the group members excited and educate them about benchmarking. Have them develop a benchmarking plan for the company, including a way to compile and disseminate best practices throughout the company.

4. *Create a support structure*—Create a benchmarking group to promote benchmarking, educate and train those wishing to move ahead, assist in the development of benchmarking plans, compile and disseminate information and success stories, and celebrate successes.

5. *Find the champions/pioneers and support them*—Encourage them from the top. Communicate their successes, and recognize and reward them.

6. *Educate people*—Incorporate benchmarking into your core total quality education module. Develop benchmarking education plans as part of the overall benchmarking plan.

7. *Communicate*—Develop a communication plan around benchmarking. Get your top management to personally communicate the value of benchmarking and to set clear expectations.

8. *Make benchmarking part of your planning process*—Build benchmarking into the company's strategic and business planning processes. Develop a reliable benchmarking process and promote its use in the organization.

9. *Find and use success stories*—Develop processes for securing information on best practices from within and outside the organization, as well as from benchmarking studies the company has done, and for disseminating this information throughout the company. Share success stories widely, particularly the improvement that has resulted.

10. *Recognize and reward successful benchmarking efforts*—Use a variety of techniques to celebrate, recognize, and reward successful benchmarking efforts. Provide public recognition. Establish "Benchmarking Days." Send teams to competitions and conferences.

Benchmarking is a powerful tool for identifying improvement opportunities, but that is only one of it virtues. Benchmarking findings may lead to breakthroughs and innovation. By providing better ways of supplying products and services, it will enhance customer satisfaction. Through its participative nature, it can promote employee empowerment. It will almost certainly stimulate new ways of thinking about, and looking at, current ways of doing things. The process of consciously searching out better ways of doing things is the essence of productivity improvement and of the learning process itself.

Section V

AUDITING FOR ENVIRONMENTAL TOTAL QUALITY

17

BUILDING AUDITS INTO TQEM MEASUREMENT SYSTEMS AT P&G

Michael T. Fisher

This article discusses an approach to building environmental compliance audits into an effective TQEM measurement system. With this approach, companies can move their existing programs from just "meeting the law" to being viewed as "leaders in environmental excellence." The benefit of this change is that local communities are more likely to allow their environmental leaders the operating flexibility that minimizes cost and the necessary permits for expansion.

During the past ten years, the federal government has essentially doubled the amount of regulations governing the environmental area. In addition, there have been similar rates of growth in the states and throughout the rest of the world. Looking to the future, it is expected that similar growth will continue, particularly considering the implications of the new Clean Air Act in the United States and the regulatory efforts presently underway in the European Community. To handle this growth, many companies have instituted environmental compliance audits in order to keep up with the rapidly expanding enforcement activity.

Unfortunately, such audits are often not viewed positively by the sites on the receiving end, and the staff personnel conducting such audits are not viewed as helping the business. Needless to say,

Michael T. Fisher *is associate director of the Procter & Gamble Company's Environmental Control Department. This department provides environmental, technical, and regulatory support for P&G's 150-plus worldwide operating facilities. This article is based on a paper presented at the 1992 Global Environmental Management Initiative (GEMI) Conference.*

corporate environmental staffs do not find this very effective and often want a better way to improve performance. Environmental auditing should be a positive experience—one that unites the auditors and the people at the operating sites to jointly learn and plan for continuous improvements. Total quality audits represent such an approach.

Total quality audits focus on system evaluation and identification of improvement opportunities—not just on compliance. For example, instead of conducting a detailed review of how drum labels are filled out, a total quality audit would assess the overall drum management system and identify methods to improve it.

THE PDCA CYCLE

Implementing a total quality environmental system audit process goes beyond completing an audit checklist and issuing a report, as is often the case with compliance audits. These system audits involve a total process (see **Exhibit 1**) best described in the following four elements of the plan-do-check-act (PDCA) cycle.

- **Plan:**   Obtain customer commitment and alignment.
- **Do:**   Identify key performance factors and rating criteria.

Exhibit 1

Environmental System Audit PDCA Cycle

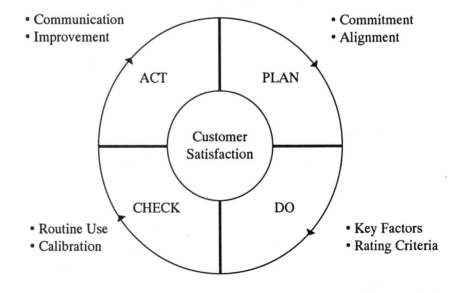

- Communication
- Improvement

- Commitment
- Alignment

ACT   PLAN

Customer
Satisfaction

CHECK   DO

- Routine Use
- Calibration

- Key Factors
- Rating Criteria

- **Check:** Ensure consistent use of the audits and ratings.
- **Act:** Communicate results and identify improvement plans.

With this as general background, the following will now describe each of these steps in more detail.

STEP 1: *PLAN* FOR TOTAL QUALITY SYSTEM AUDITS

This step involves obtaining customer commitment and alignment on this new approach. To accomplish this end, you must first identify who your customers are and understand their needs. These customers must be committed to a program of on-going measurement and system improvement. They must also assure that the required resources will be made available. Without such commitment, this approach will not produce the desired long-term system improvement, and alternate approaches such as compliance audits may be more appropriate.

Once you have commitment from your customers, it is important to obtain their alignment on a performance target. Performance targets can be

- Reactive—postponed until an agency inspects the site and issues a compliance order.
- Responsive—conducted as compliance audits followed by issue resolution.
- Proactive—in other words, evaluate management systems via audits and and identify continuous improvement plans. For a long-term system audit program to be successful there must be customer alignment to a proactive performance target.

With customer commitment and alignment in place, the next step involves developing a method to effectively measure the capability of the management systems that will achieve the desired performance target.

STEP 2: *DO* TOTAL QUALITY SYSTEM AUDITS

One effective way to "do" such management system capability evaluations or audits involves identification of the key factors that are consistent with the desired performance target. For example, if your personal performance target is to get and stay physically healthy, possible key factors could include routine visits to the doctor, weight control, exercise, modifying smoking and drinking behaviors, and stress management.

The specific environmental system key factors should vary to match the needs of the individual company implementing the process. Typical key factors to meet a performance target of cost-effective maintenance of long-term compliance could include

- **Regulatory and Policy Compliance Capability**
  - Does the site use total quality measurement tools and procedures to manage its compliance with the law?
  - Are all issues expeditiously resolved?
  - Does the site have a robust method to keep Resource Conservation Recovery Act (RCRA) recordkeeping up-to-date?
  - Are all applicable regulations and permit limitations understood?

- **Personnel Capability**
  - Does the site have the appropriate amount of environmental staffing?
  - Has the environmental leader been properly trained?
  - Do the line personnel own their environmental behavior?

- **Equipment Capability**
  - Does the site have robust operating procedures and proactive maintenance capability to ensure reliable environmental equipment performance?
  - Are the equipment systems in statistical control, and do they have robust capacity?

- **Other Key Factors**
  - Environmental cost management
  - Environment issue management
  - Relationship with community
  - Community outreach
  - Pollution prevention

Once appropriate key factors are selected, rating criteria must be established. This means that for each key factor you need to define a rating scale, identify the appropriate descriptors for each performance level, and assign the appropriate weighting to each key factor. A rating scale can involve a number of different choices. For example, you could assign a value of 1 for reactive performance, 2 for responsive performance, and 3 for proactive performance. An alternate rating scale approach could be to have these same items, but rate on a continuous spectrum from 0 to 10.

Next, specific descriptors need to be identified for each level of performance. For example, in the case of personnel capability you could identify weak environmental staff as reactive, adequate environmental staff as responsive, and strong environmental staff as proactive. Under this key factor, similar descriptors would also be developed for the environmental leader's training and the level of site line ownership for their environmental performance.

Finally, a decision must be made on how the key factors should be individually weighted. Key factor weighting recognizes that certain system elements, such as regulatory compliance, are more important than others, such as community outreach, to achieve the desired result. In Procter & Gamble's case, the twelve management environmental key factors have each been weighted from a minimum of 5 percent up to a maximum of 20 percent. Specifically, five key factors represent 65 percent of the total score, and the other seven key factors represent the remaining 35 percent of the score.

In any case, it is critical to note that the selection of key factors, rating scale, performance descriptors, and weightings, though somewhat arbitrary, must always be focused on meeting the desired needs (targets) of each individual company. Otherwise, this process could show improvements that do not mean real value to the business.

STEP 3: *CHECK* TOTAL QUALITY SYSTEM AUDITS

Once the key factors and rating criteria have been selected, the next PDCA step involves ensuring consistent use of these measures. The ability to produce consistent results from audit to audit is critical to identify improvements that will really make a difference. Ensuring consistent use of these measures involves (1) making sure that site and staff personnel are appropriately trained on the use of the key factors and rating criteria and (2) establishing a routine measurement process, such as an annual audit.

Procter & Gamble's environmental system audit process involves several important elements, including

- A minimum audit frequency of once a year with staff involvement every two to three years;
- Pre-work that encompasses identifying audit teams, scheduling necessary resources, and ensuring that an environmental pre-work questionnaire is completed;

- A two-day, on-site audit visit during which data on management systems is collected, systems are rated, and improvement plans are identified; and
- Follow-up, which involves a standardized audit report and a six-month review of all audit action plans.

STEP 4: *ACT* ON TOTAL QUALITY SYSTEM AUDITS

This last step in the PDCA cycle involves communicating performance results and ensuring that improvement plans are developed. The ability to sustain progress toward any performance target depends on routine and effective communication of the results to your customers so that they can respond appropriately. In addition, it is necessary to ensure that these results are properly analyzed and appropriate process improvements identified, including new performance target(s).

Two communication and improvement tools used by Procter & Gamble include an audit report and an annual environmental review. In the case of each environmental system audit, a report is developed using a common report format that includes an executive summary, specific rating data, and improvement action plans. At the end of each fiscal year, an internal environmental report to company hierarchy and line management is developed. This annual review includes data on specific systems status as well as other important environmental outcome measures, such as number of incidents and pounds of releases to the environment. Each of these internal reports focuses on what will be required to improve system performance in the future and achieve a realignment with our customers on the targets (Step 1, repeated).

CONCLUSION

With each of these four total quality process steps in place, you have the capability of making significant long-term improvement to your systems. However, there are several factors that you need to be aware of as you implement a total quality system audit process:

- An excellent rating does not mean the absence of risk. For example, a highly rated but complex chemical plant handling large quantities of hazardous materials will have much more risk of an upset or accident than a similarly rated low-complexity operation, such as a food packing facility.
- Be careful of system indicators that look good on the surface

but do not deliver results. If a plant is always in crisis mode of operation but they have an excellent management systems rating, you may want to reevaluate the key factors or the auditors' calibration: Will the key factors as defined deliver the desired results? Have the auditors been properly trained?

* The legal liability for everyone involved in audits is considerable. Don't do audits unless you are committed to fixing the problems and shortcomings they identify. If you are not committed to improving performance, system audits will only document the lack of progress.

The rapid increase in environmental regulations and enforcement is causing many companies to consider more proactive management capability. One effective method that will achieve this end involves moving from compliance audits to a total quality system audit process. This process involves continuous improvement of key factor measures and can be used to drive an existing program from reactive to proactive, thus reducing long-term costs.

18

CONTINUOUS IMPROVEMENT THROUGH ENVIRONMENTAL AUDITING

Ann C. Smith

Environmental auditing evolved as a means of providing assurance to top management that its health, safety, and environmental responsibilities were being adequately discharged and that no significant noncompliances existed. The author takes an in-depth look at the HSE audit program developed at AlliedSignal to permit continuous improvement of environmental management systems.

AlliedSignal Inc. developed its environmental auditing program in the 1970s to provide top management and the Board of Directors with independent information on the status of health, safety, and environmental (HSE) programs at its operations. Over 500 audits have been conducted since then at AlliedSignal's more than 240 facilities worldwide.

The program has a dedicated staff of three full-time professionals, one of whom leads each audit team. In addition to the team leader, teams include an independent third-party auditor and many also include from one to three HSE professionals from other operations. Each audit lasts three to five days and features a standard approach controlled by a written protocol, interviews with key personnel,

Ann C. Smith heads AlliedSignal Environmental Services Inc.'s worldwide consulting practice. She currently chairs the Environmental Auditing Roundtable, the international professional society of environmental auditing.

documentation review, visual observation of plant features, and a final audit report distributed to appropriate parties.

DEFINING THE ENVIRONMENTAL AUDIT

There are a number of activities conducted under the term "environmental auditing":

- Remediation investigation/feasibility studies (RI/FS) conducted in support of RCRA corrective actions or CERCLA (Superfund) cleanups;
- Assessments of environmental liability associated with real property transfers;
- Quality or product safety audits;
- Environmental impact studies;
- Hydrogeological studies;
- Meteorological studies; and
- Audits designed to assess an operation's status of compliance relative to specific environmental statutes and other criteria.

It is the last of these that this article addresses, as the objective of AlliedSignal's audit program is verification of compliance with the law and with corporate policies and procedures, and assurance that systems are in place to ensure continued compliance.

HSE AUDIT PROGRAM OVERVIEW

AlliedSignal Inc. is organized into three sectors: Automotive, Aerospace, and Engineered Materials, each of which operates with considerable autonomy.

The vice president, Corporate Health, Safety and Environmental Sciences Department, reports to the chief operating officer of the corporation. The department has sixteen full-time staff in Pollution Control, Product Safety, Occupational Health, Loss Prevention, and Environmental Auditing.

Each function is headed by a director, who is responsible for overall coordination of and guidance to the sectors and operating companies, program monitoring, and regulatory affairs interaction.

The three sectors also have environmental, health, and safety staff structured similarly to that of the corporate staff (but without an audit function), with day-to-day responsibility for compliance. The sector director reports at a high level and has staff commensurate with the risks inherent in the sector industries. A functional reporting relationship exists with corporate counterparts. Personnel assigned to specific facilities are likewise tied in functionally to sector HSE staff.

Corporate Policy

AlliedSignal's health, safety, and environmental policy commits the corporation to establish regulatory compliance programs and to adopt its own standards when laws and regulations may not be ade-quately protective or do not exist. The policy is supported by written corporate guidelines. To supplement the corporate guidelines, sectors, compa-nies, and individual facilities also have written operating pro-cedures that address environmental concerns specific to the individual busi-nesses.

Organization and Staffing

A number of criteria were established when AlliedSignal Inc. considered an approach to organizing and staffing the audit program, including

- Independence of the audit teams from those responsible for managing corporate and sector environmental programs, but with organizational proximity to facilitate communication and resolution of problems and conflicts.
- Minimizing the full-time staffing commitment to the audit program, yet having a readily available supply of competent, objective team members, continuity in the conduct of reviews, and long-term accountability for the program.

With those objectives, several options were considered, such as using external auditors; establishing an independent internal group housed within the corporate audit department or the corporate health, safety, and environmental sciences department; or using task forces made up of persons drawn from throughout the corporation. Each option was viewed as having advantages and disadvantages. For example:

- An external auditor would not require the addition of any full-time employees and would have a high degree of indepen-dence; however, there could be substantial barriers to coordi-nation and communication. Also, this approach would involve relatively higher total costs.
- An independent group within the corporate audit department

would have a high degree of independence from health, safety, and environmental program management, but would not have the needed understanding of subject matter.

- A separate, independent group of full-time auditors within the HSE department would afford a good opportunity for communication with health, safety, and environmental management, but its independence might be questioned.
- A task force would have broad participation, high flexibility, and relatively low cost, but carry the potential for loss of continuity and disruption of regular functions.

In order to achieve as many of these objectives as possible, the audit program was established within the corporate HSE department and is staffed by three full-time professionals. To ensure continuity and accountability, the team leader for each audit is one of those three professionals. The remainder of the audit team (which varies from two to five people depending on the review scope and size of facility) is comprised of corporate, sector, or division HSE professionals familiar with the review subject, but not directly involved in the programs being reviewed, and an outside consultant who provides the advantages of an external auditor.

AUDIT SCOPE AND FOCUS

All of AlliedSignal's facilities worldwide fall within the scope of the audit program, with operations assessed as having lower health, safety, and environmental risk receiving less attention than those assessed as high-risk operations. The functional scope of the program includes

- Air pollution control
- Water pollution control and spill prevention
- Solid and hazardous waste disposal
- Occupational health and medical programs
- Safety and loss prevention
- Product safety and integrity
- Special focus audits

The compliance scope includes all legal requirements, corporate policies and procedures, and good health, safety, and environmental practices.

With some 240 locations and seven functional areas, a comprehensive review of all subjects at all locations would be a formidable task.

Therefore, most audits are limited to only one of the functional areas listed above (for example, air pollution control only) in order to maximize the amount of in-depth review in the time available. Thus, although the program covers a variety of topics, the scope of a specific audit is narrow.

AUDIT SELECTION PROCESS

Approximately fifty audits are conducted annually. Thus, the program reviews only a relatively small sample of the corporation's facilities each year. The selection process uses a fairly sophisticated approach to choose locations that represent a cross-section of AlliedSignal's business interests and health, safety, and environmental concerns where potential risks are high. Audits are apportioned evenly among the various functional areas.

At the beginning of each year, the audit schedule for the year is sent to corporate and sector health, safety, and environmental staff. Two months prior to the review, the team leader sends a letter to the facility manager, with copies to the appropriate sector and corporate environmental staff, identifying the type of audit to be conducted, which is not revealed until this time.

Audit Methodology

The HSE audit program employs a number of tools and techniques such as formal internal control questionnaires, formal audit protocols (or guides), informal interviews with facility personnel, physical observations, documentation review, testing, and verification.

A written audit protocol covering each functional area of the review reflects the objectives of the audit, facility characteristics, and time constraints. The protocol methodically guides the auditor to an understanding of requirements affecting the facility and the facility's management system, the conduct of tests to confirm that the system is working, and the determination of specific deficiencies. Auditors carefully document the accomplishment and results of each audit protocol step in their audit working papers.

The audit process can be analyzed in four phases:

Phase I: Preparation

Among the pre-audit activities conducted by the audit team leader are the confirmation of review dates and organization of the audit team based on the functional scope of the review. Corporate files are screened to obtain and review information on the facility and its processes (for example, process flow diagrams, plant layout diagrams, policies and procedures, operating manuals, permits, required reports to the corporate office). Regulations applicable to the facility are also studied.

Phase II: On-Site Review

The on-site review commences with a meeting of the audit team, the facility manager, and appropriate facility personnel. During this meeting, the team leader discusses the objectives of the audit program and the review scope. Facility personnel present an overview of the facility's operations—products, processes, facility organization, and so on. The team is then given a tour by facility staff to gain a general understanding of plant characteristics.

Following the tour, the review team and appropriate facility environmental staff meet to complete an internal controls questionnaire. This questionnaire, administered by the audit team leader, aids the auditors in developing an initial understanding of facility operations, processes, personnel responsibilities, and environmental management controls.

Working from the audit protocol, with major sections apportioned among team members, each auditor gathers system information and performs relevant tests. In the course of the review, the auditor must use sampling techniques and exercise professional judgment in selecting the type and size of samples to be used to verify that the key controls in the system under review are in place and working. Testing is not done until the system is well understood and a carefully reasoned plan of testing is worked out. This understanding may come from interviews with facility staff, review of facility operating procedures and systems, observation of physical features of control systems, and so forth.

Testing of the systems can take a variety of forms. For example, verification testing for water pollution control can include

- Visual observation downstream from an outfall;
- Comparison of analytical results with contaminant reports required to be filed with regulatory authorities;
- Review of programs to assure the reliability of treatment or monitoring equipment; and
- Determination that composite samplers, effluent flow measuring devices, and in-place monitoring devices are properly maintained and calibrated.

Each auditor carefully documents all testing plans and test results, sharing observations and information on deficiencies found throughout the audit with team members and facility staff. Also, time is set aside at the end of each day to exchange information and share any concerns that have developed during the day's work. The audit team continuously feeds back impressions about the system's compliance with established criteria to plant personnel. This continuous feedback is intended to

- Eliminate misconceptions and false trails for the team member who may have misunderstood the initial description;
- Encourage team members to organize their thoughts;
- Give facility personnel an opportunity to participate in the audit process; and
- Maintain the audit as an open process among team members and between the team and facility staff.

Significant findings are compiled by the team leader on a summary sheet that is used as the basis for discussion with plant management at a close-out meeting.

Phase III: Reporting and Record Preservation

The purpose of the written report is to provide information to top management (sector presidents) on the more significant findings of the audit. The written report states the auditor's opinion as to whether or not the facility is in substantive compliance and lists any observed exceptions. The report is based on findings listed on the audit findings summary form.

A standardized four-part format for the written report has evolved:

- Section I provides details on the place, date, scope, and personnel involved in the audit.
- Section II addresses compliance with legal requirements (federal, state/provincial, regional, and local).
- Section III covers compliance with AlliedSignal's policies and procedures (corporate, sector, or facility).
- Section IV indicates deficiencies in the facility control systems that would make continued compliance with the law or company policy questionable (such as record retention, documentation, clear assignment of environmental responsibilities, and so on).

The length of the report depends on the number of findings; typically it is four to five pages.

Report Distribution

The written audit report is issued in draft form by the team leader to the involved line and staff personnel at both the operating company and corporate levels, the facility manager, and the audit team. Comments on this draft report are requested within two weeks of its issuance. When comments necessitate significant revision of the first draft, a second draft of the report may be prepared and circulated for review.

The final written report is issued to the sector president six to eight weeks after the review, with copies to appropriate facility, business, legal, and environmental management. The final report is accompanied by a request that the operating company provide a written corrective action plan.

Records Retention

A formal records retention policy for all audit documents exists to help keep the records' volume at a manageable level and to ensure that all audit records are retained for a period of time consistent with their utility in the program and with applicable federal regulations. Thus, audit working papers are retained for three years. Audit reports and action plans are retained for ten years or longer when subject to specific records' retention requirements.

Other Reporting

In addition to the formal written report for individual reviews to the sector president, the Board Corporate Responsibility Committee receives regular reports on audit program activities at least twice a year. These reports, both oral and written, are given by the audit program director to the Board Committee. A representative of the program's consulting firm is also present to respond to board requests for independent information on the status of compliance programs and the audit program. The purpose of reporting to the board is to confirm that the audit program is functioning and to provide assurance that concerns material to the corporation have been identified.

Phase IV: Company Action

The job of the audit team ends with the submission and management's understanding of the final report. The review *process,* however, continues until responsible management prepares and executes an action plan for correcting the identified deficiencies.

Once the action plan is developed by facility personnel and received by the audit director, the audit team leader reviews it to confirm that the final report has been understood and that the plan is responsive to the findings of the report.

Action plans are typically received within two to three months of the issuance of the final written report. The plan reports on corrective actions already taken as well as those that are planned. Operating management then assumes responsibility for follow-up and monitoring of the corrective actions. The audit group performs follow-up reviews to confirm the completion of approximately 20 percent of these action plans.

The corporation's environmental assurance system also includes other formal procedures for follow-up and corrective action on all environmental, health, and safety deficiencies.

Program Benefits

AlliedSignal has noted a number of benefits throughout the corporation resulting from the audit program. Among them are

- For top management and the Board of Directors, the program provides independent verification that operations are in compliance with applicable requirements of environmental law and the corporation's environmental policy.
- For environmental management, the program serves as another source of information on the status of operations and the individual deficiencies and patterns of deficiencies that may occur.
- For line management, there is added incentive for much closer self-evaluation to confirm that operations are in compliance. The program has stimulated line management to become more familiar with the detailed implications of environmental requirements. The program has also identified problems in their operations that require corrective action, or, more frequently, it has confirmed that environmental requirements were being met.
- For business management, improved understanding of health, safety, and environmental liabilities can improve planning and budgeting.

CONTINUOUS IMPROVEMENT IN ENVIRONMENTAL MANAGEMENT

Environmental auditing developed as a means of providing assurance to top management that its health, safety, and environmental responsibilities were being adequately discharged and that no significant noncompliances existed. The concept and application were taken virtually wholesale from the financial audit field, where

> audits evolved as a means of verifying compliance with bookkeeping practices. They were created basically to uncover cheating—which, of course, is still a prime audit application. The intent of compliance auditing is to identify operations where standards aren't being adhered to and to then force changes in practices—or people—to make sure that standards are met. A standard might be a specification, law, policy, procedure, contractual agreement, or the auditee's own documents.[1]

Auditing will have no value, however, if the deficiencies it uncovers are not corrected. It is therefore a fundamental tenet that management be committed to fixing what is found.

The environmental management process can be viewed as diagrammed in **Figure 1**.

In this scheme, each goal is planned for, acted on, checked, and modified. The modification is actually a new plan, so the process is

Figure 1

Simplified Environmental Management Continuous Improvement Process

Plan to Meet Compliance Goals

Report Audit Results to Management

Implement Compliance Plan

Collect Data: Audit Compliance

circular, as diagrammed, and continuous. Note that the "check" step is actually auditing. So the process of auditing supplies the feedback loop to permit continuous improvement of environmental management systems. In most cases, the audit is not the only source of such information; regulatory agency inspections, insurance carrier audits, customer audits, and many other activities can also supply valuable inputs to improve management schemes.

Because environmental auditing is itself a component of the environmental management system, it too should be subject to continual evaluation and feedback to enhance its functioning.

At AlliedSignal, we solicit feedback from all organizational levels of HSE management and from other parties affected by the audit program as a means of improving the program. Recent improvements have involved modifications to the audit selection process, reporting frequencies and methods, and audit field work.

There are a number of other quality assurance steps taken in Allied Signal's audit program. For example, a member of the audit staff leads each audit to assure program consistency. The team leader's role includes supervision of team members to assure completion of all assigned tasks. In addition, the team leader takes pains to encourage open and full communication among the team and plant personnel.

Allied's audit protocols provide a structured framework to guide the auditors through a series of steps designed to create an understanding of the system under review, conduct appropriate tests to confirm that the system is working, and determine specific deficiencies.

Another quality measure relates to the audit working papers. The credibility of the audit depends on the thoroughness of the review and its documentation. Each team member must prepare working papers that document the information gathered, tests performed, and conclusions reached. At the end of each audit, the team leader reviews the working papers, which serve as support for the audit report and a way of evaluating the performance of each team member.

The program is guided by written procedures describing such things as site selection, documentation, record retention, training, audit conduct, and so on. Standard forms are likewise used to the extent possible in order to assure consistency of approach.

Finally, AlliedSignal's outside consultant provides an additional quality control check. A representative of the consulting firm participates in each review. All audit reports are reviewed by the consultant to ensure accurate and consistent audit reporting. The consultant periodically reviews working paper files at corporate headquarters to assure their quality.

ACHIEVING TOTAL QUALITY

The argument is frequently made that total quality is not achievable. Whereas *perfection* might be unattainable, aggressively and assiduously pursuing a continuous improvement process can be synonymous with achieving total quality. The argument will no doubt continue. While it does, let me assert that achieving total quality demands that certain fundamentals be in place:

- Adequate training of personnel to assure that they know how to meet requirements;
- Personal and organizational commitment, or wanting to do the job right every time;
- Doing the job;
- Having the humility to know that mistakes will be made; and
- Correcting and redoing the process in response to the mistakes and their implicit lessons.

An environmental audit can serve as a catalyst for gearing up programs in a continuous improvement mode, rather than simply as an analysis for deficiency. It develops information on the current compliance status. Properly used, this information permits process and program changes that improve HSE management. Re-audits then evaluate the effectiveness of corrective actions, permitting even more refined modifications. Over the years, AlliedSignal's environmental auditing program has proven its value as an effective tool for continuous improvement of the management of the corporation's health, safety, and environmental responsibilities.

Note
1.   Aquino, "Improvement vs. Compliance: A New Look at Auditing," *Quality Progress*, October 1990.

19

POLAROID'S ENVIRONMENTAL ACCOUNTING AND REPORTING SYSTEM: BENEFITS AND LIMITATIONS OF A TQEM MEASUREMENT TOOL

Jennifer Nash, Karen Nutt, James Maxwell,
and John Ehrenfeld

*Polaroid Corporation has established an ambitious pollution pre-
vention program that calls for reducing chemical use and waste by
10 percent per unit per year during the period 1988 to 1993. A notable
aspect of Polaroid's efforts is the environmental accounting and
reporting system (EARS) it has developed to measure progress toward
this goal. EARS is a Total Quality Environmental Management tool with
applicability in similar industries.*

T otal quality environmental management (TQEM) can be defined as an approach for continuously improving the

Jennifer Nash *is a research associate with the Technology, Business, and Environment Program at the Massachusetts Institute of Technology. Her background is in
environmental planning and pollution prevention studies.* ***Karen Nutt*** *is a student of
environmental engineering.* ***James Maxwell*** *is program co-director and* ***John
Ehrenfeld*** *is director of the MIT Technology, Business and Environment Program. The
authors wish to thank Harry Fatkin, James Ahearn, and Bob Loring of Polaroid
Corporation, as well as Joanne Kauffman and Yiorgos Mylonadis of MIT, for their
invaluable assistance.*

environmental quality of processes and products through the participation of all levels and functions in an organization. Polaroid did not design its environmental accounting and reporting system (EARS) with TQEM in mind. Nevertheless, EARS functions as a TQEM tool in two respects: It provides Polaroid employees with rapid, accurate feedback about the environmental quality of their operation, and it rewards those who contribute to the company's environmental goals, thereby encouraging continual environmental improvement.

EARS has helped Polaroid reduce the amount of toxic chemicals it used and the waste it generated for the period 1988 to 1991 by approximately 20 percent. It has reduced the burden of government environmental reporting requirements and improved Polaroid's relationships with environmental advocacy groups. Implementing EARS, however, has not been without difficulties. Some at Polaroid have been resistant, disagreeing with the philosophy behind the system and objecting to the amount of work involved in keeping it up to date. The problems Polaroid has encountered offer some insights to firms that are developing and implementing TQEM programs.

EVOLUTION OF POLAROID'S PREVENTION PROGRAM

Founded in 1937, Polaroid Corporation, with over 11,400 employees and net sales in 1991 of more than $2.07 billion, is in the business of designing, manufacturing, and marketing instant photographic and imaging products such as cameras, film, light polarizing filters, and lenses. It manufactures a large variety of chemical, optical, and commercial products, many of which produce large amounts of hazardous waste as by-products.[1]

The evolution of Polaroid's environmental activities was characterized by increasing production of specialty chemicals throughout the 1970s and 1980s. Polaroid has moved from a reliance on waste disposal (primarily incineration) to an emphasis upon waste reuse, recycling, and ultimately, prevention. This evolution has been spurred by government's continued tightening of environmental regulations as well as by pressure from environmental advocacy groups.

Polaroid began manufacturing specialty chemicals in the 1970s to support its production of photographic film that developed instantly. Manufacture of these chemicals in-house caused a "quantum leap in generation" of wastes.[2] In 1970, as part of this internal scale-up, the company built a hazardous waste incinerator at its Waltham, Massachusetts site with capacity to burn 500,000 gallons of liquid waste a year. The company added a second incinerator in 1973 with five times the capacity of the first, and by 1979 nearly three million gallons of waste were burned annually in Polaroid incinerators.

In the early 1980s, Polaroid's manufacture and use of chemicals expanded rapidly with the introduction of additional new products. The focus of its waste management program began to move from incineration to waste reuse and recycling, primarily due to the limited availability and high cost of off-site contract hazardous waste treatment and disposal facilities. Of the chemical waste Polaroid treated on-site at that time (about half of the total generated), the company reused or recycled approximately 75 percent.[3] The volume of liquid waste incinerated dropped off, and in 1982 the company dismantled its larger incinerator. But in 1985 Polaroid installed a new vapor incinerator to burn organic vapors produced in the manufacture of photographic positive coatings. Incineration of the vapors was necessary to meet tightening environmental regulations.

First Director of Health, Safety, and the Environment

To address the growing body of environmental regulations promulgated during the 1970s, Polaroid created the position of director of health, safety, and the environment in 1974. The company chose Harry Fatkin, who had previously served in manufacturing and management positions in the company, to fill the job. An initial em-phasis for Fatkin was company compliance with environmental regulations. But Fatkin found compliance an elusive goal that required continually "running hard to stay in place."[4] Federal and Massachusetts state environmental regulations kept changing, and the two levels of government did not always agree. Fatkin and others began to feel that "compliance was a losing strategy."

Fatkin looked around for alternative ways to manage the company's environmental issues. In 1984 he was invited to join a panel advising the U.S. Office of Technology Assessment (OTA) in a study of source reduction. The OTA study, issued in 1986,[5] recommended that companies set the goal of reducing waste by 10 percent a year for five years and that they base reduction calculations on waste generated per unit of production.

Fatkin tested Polaroid's receptiveness to source reduction. First, he asked plant managers how difficult they would find reducing waste by 25 percent, 50 percent, and 75 percent. He put source reduction on the agenda of the Health, Safety and Environment Affairs Steering Committee numerous times, initiating dialogue around the issue. Fatkin argued that by "redefining the problem" from controlling pollution to preventing it in the first place, Polaroid could avoid being trapped by the "regulatory rotary." James Ahearn, senior manager of environmental programs in Polaroid's Research Division, has made this point even more emphatically. The goal of source reduction efforts, he explained, "was to be in a position to never have to worry about regulation again."[6]

Source reduction would also help protect the company from liability associated with waste disposal. The Environmental Protection Agency (EPA) had identified Polaroid as a "potentially responsible party" in three hazardous waste sites included in the Superfund National Priority Listing. Fatkin reasoned that another benefit of cutting waste production would be to reduce Polaroid's liability in the future.

Confronting Negative Publicity

In 1986 two events brought the futility of the "regulatory rotary" to the forefront. First, EPA found Polaroid in violation for emissions from its photographic coatings operation. Second, the environmental advocacy group Greenpeace attacked the company for its environmental practices. It issued a report titled "Polaroid—Instant Pollution: #1 in Toxic Waste" and hung a banner outside the company's Waltham facility, on a bridge over well-traveled Route 128, proclaiming the company the biggest polluter in Massachusetts.

According to Fatkin, Polaroid groped for a way to address the consequences of these events, which some felt portrayed the company as a callous polluter. In the spring of 1987 Polaroid's chief executive officer announced the Toxic Use and Waste Reduction (TUWR) Program based, in part, on OTA's recommendations.[7] Polaroid set the OTA reduction goal of 10 percent per unit every year for the next five years, for a total reduction of 41 percent. According to Fatkin, this goal was established as a "stretch goal" that seemed "doable" in view of the OTA work. Polaroid did not base the goal on any detailed analysis of its own. Polaroid's program, however, went beyond the OTA recommendations in that it included all materials the company handled, as well as a strategy to reduce the company's use of toxic chemicals. Polaroid's CEO intended the numerical goal and the structure of Polaroid's TUWR program as a challenge to the company. What it would take to meet this challenge, and what the implications would be for the company, were largely unknown.

POLAROID'S ENVIRONMENTAL ACCOUNTING AND REPORTING SYSTEM

EARS is the tool Polaroid has developed to measure progress

toward TUWR goals. EARS is a centralized database that allows Polaroid to track virtually every one of the 1,400 materials the company uses, from office paper to chlorinated solvents. Materials are categorized on the basis of toxicity. Every material is assigned to one of five categories (see **Exhibit 1**) to reflect the degree of potential environmental harm it poses. Polaroid reviews the categorization quarterly, adding new chemicals and incorporating new evidence on chemical toxicity.

With EARS, Polaroid records the quantities and treatment methods of materials in all five categories at several points along the process line: at the input stage (usage is recorded for all Category I and II chemicals), at the end of the process line before abatement (amounts of all by-products are recorded), during abatement (abatement techniques are recorded for all by-products), and after abatement (quantities and emission destinations are recorded for all wastes).

Use, waste, and by-products are measured and recorded per unit

Exhibit 1

Environmental Accounting and Reporting System Categorization of Chemicals

Category	Number of Chemicals	Environmental Impact	Examples	Reduction Emphasis
I & II	Category I—38 Category II—65	Most severe environmental impact; highly toxic; human carcinogens	Ammonia, benzene, CFCs	Minimize use
III	279	Moderately toxic; corrosive; suspected animal carcinogens	Acetic acid, pyridine, styrene	Recover and reuse on-site
IV	Remaining chemicals Polaroid uses	Least impact on the environment	Acetone, butanol	Reuse on-site following on- or off-site recycling
V		Deplete natural resources during manufacture, disposal	Cardboard, paper, and plastic from offices and manufacturing plants	Maximize recycling and reuse on-site

of production. Before the TUWR program was put into place, Polaroid management asked every division to determine a unit of production for its processes. The Camera Division decided to use the number of cameras it produces as its unit of production, the Chemical Operations Division decided to use kilograms of chemicals manufactured, and the Research Division selected a standard number of labor hours. Polaroid felt this standardization technique was necessary "to emphasize process improvements and to minimize the impact of production schedule variations."[8] Thus, it would be possible for EARS per-unit numbers to *decrease* while the actual pounds of chemicals used and waste generated remained the same or even *increased*. This could occur if production volume increased significantly relative to the amount of chemicals used and waste generated. Conversely, if releases declined because of production decreases, the EARS numbers would not decline unless there were also reductions from pollution prevention.

Incentives for waste reduction are built into the system. Category I and II materials are judged to be the most hazardous that Polaroid uses. Managers and divisions can receive EARS credit towards TUWR goals by reducing their *use* of these chemicals. Category III materials are of a lower hazard, but their transport could pose significant risk. To receive EARS credit, therefore, these materials must be *recycled and reused on-site*. Category IV and V materials are the least hazardous in the Polaroid hierarchy; EARS credit can be earned if they are *treated off-site, provided they come back to Polaroid for reuse*. For example, the Chemical Operations Division cannot receive EARS per-unit credit for xylene (a category IV material), which it sends for reuse by another corporation. To receive credit, the xylene can be treated off-site, but it must come back to Polaroid for use within the company.

Polaroid does not award EARS per-unit credit for improved abatement techniques. This is a key distinguishing feature of Polaroid's program. Most firms strive to improve environmental performance by installing advanced pollution control equipment that reduces emissions. Polaroid believes that pollution prevention must be focused at the point of generation. Emissions reductions are recognized by EARS only if they are achieved through reduced use of Category I and II chemicals, reduced generation rates, or through recycling and reuse of Category III, IV, and V materials, as described above.

Using the EARS data base, Polaroid produces reports that are available to the public. It produces a corporate index report that shows the company's progress toward achieving TUWR goals. In addition, the company produces a "hierarchy report" that shows how all Polaroid waste (Categories I through V) is managed: how much is reused, recycled, incinerated, and landfilled.[9]

EARS AS A TQEM TOOL

EARS provides the information Polaroid workers need to assess the environmental quality of their actions. It provides incentives for making continual improvements in environmental performance. It is an effective TQEM tool, fulfilling several different functions throughout the company.

EARS allows Polaroid employees to predict the environmental impact of new chemicals before the company makes a commitment to their use. People working in Polaroid's Chemicals Division have developed a spreadsheet template that allows engineers to estimate and compare the amounts of pollution that would be created by different chemicals used in the manufacturing process. They use this information to determine the "efficacy" of a particular chemical—to answer the question, "Is this chemical the best choice for the intended use?" Chemicals are selected to minimize use of Category I and II materials and maximize recycle and reuse for Categories III and IV.[10] By inputting the various chemical choices to the spreadsheet, engineers can anticipate, for example, that manufacture of a product using chemical X will produce one hundred pounds of waste per unit of production, whereas chemical Y will produce fifty pounds.

Helping To Understand Processes

Those working in the company's manufacturing divisions say that EARS's rigorous data requirements have forced them to increase their understanding of their processes and have provided a mechanism by which to measure environmental quality progress. Bob Loring, environmental manager for Polaroid's Coatings Division, explains that EARS reporting initially required him to devote "quality time" to thinking about the question, "What are all of the waste streams that these plants generate?" He has gained a "detailed overview of the plants," as well as increased sensitivity to where and how chemicals are used. Before people were expected to account for every pound of chemical they used, as required under EARS, small losses went unnoticed, such as, for example, the amount of chemical left at the bottom of a certain reaction vessel after the vessel had been emptied. Now Polaroid employees have developed a device to scrape out the vessel so that virtually every drop of chemical can be used. EARS has forced Loring and others to challenge the assumptions about chemical use. Loring was surprised to discover, for example, that the spray cans his division used to clean slides emitted more chlorofluorocarbons (CFCs) than did the chillers.

EARS translates complex environmental data into a simple index that has meaning throughout the company. It gives weight to environmental considerations, allowing Polaroid to move toward continuous reductions in chemical use and waste generation. Loring explains that EARS has given his manufacturing division leverage to "push" on the Research Division for environmentally sound products. Loring cites the example of a proposal he received from the Research Division to use a particular Category I or II chemical. According to Loring, his division was able to "say 'no, we're not going to use it.' " The Research Division then came back with a Category III chemical that served the same purpose.

EARS also gives weight to environmental quality concerns in trade-offs against concerns about costs and scheduling. On several occasions the company's vice president has called together managers from research, manufacturing, and business divisions to discuss the EARS impact of a new product. According to Loring, usually the simple act of sitting down together has been sufficient to develop a consensus for an environmentally sound alternative.

Polaroid employees know that their job performance will be assessed, in part, on the basis of their ability to meet TUWR goals, as reflected in EARS numbers. This knowledge encourages them to keep environmental concerns in mind and helps them to achieve continuous improvement. Timely progress toward meeting TUWR goals helps to determine managers' material rewards and opportunities for advancement. Division managers are evaluated annually in terms of their performance in seven areas: cost, quality, meeting schedule, inventory, diversity of employees, safety, and environment. According to Fatkin, if division heads fall behind in meeting the TUWR goals as reflected in the EARS numbers, "this is a factor in their performance review." Fatkin notes that the vice president of worldwide manufacturing has made it clear that environmental performance is equal in importance to the other areas in which performance is assessed. Fatkin explains, "there is no formula that says, 'you're behind in this area, so you get such and such a penalty.' But if someone's having a problem, I'm confident it's reflected in the performance review."

According to Fatkin, EARS reporting has "energized" all Polaroid employees to think of ways they can contribute to waste reduction.

Fatkin cites the example of paper recycling. In order to receive EARS credit, collecting paper and sending it to a recycling facility is not sufficient; recycled paper must also be used by Polaroid offices. The waste paper that Polaroid employees collect now goes to paper companies that use it to manufacture toilet tissue and hand towels. These are purchased by Polaroid and used in company restrooms. Fatkin says that if he had "gotten up on a soapbox" and told everyone "you must recycle," few would have acted. But because EARS simply "shows people the story in a nonpunitive way," they want to help. EARS lets people see the benefits of their environmental efforts. Explains Ahearn, waste reduction "takes on the elements of a contest, even if it's just a contest with yourself." As a result, "people are interested in it."

PROBLEMS IN IMPLEMENTATION

The Toxic Use and Waste Reduction Program was developed by Fatkin and his staff. According to Fatkin, "agreement around TUWR and the initial architecture of EARS was a senior corporate issue." As Fatkin worked to build support for the program among Polaroid employees, he encountered some resistance. Some objected to the program because they were comfortable with the company's historic strategy of pollution control and had difficulty grasping the direct linkage between process waste and pollution. According to Fatkin, people who had "grown up with the old paradigm, which has been reinforced by the part per million, compliance mentality" were resistant when asked to change. Source reduction required people to "completely redefine their way of looking at environmental issues." Many employees felt that the "end-of-pipe" approach was the quickest and surest way to achieve compliance with environmental laws. It had the additional advantage of not disrupting the manufacturing process.

Internal Resistance

Early complaints about the program show how hard it was for people to shift from thinking in terms of waste management to waste prevention. Some people objected to Polaroid's definition of waste. Under the program, waste is anything the company produces that is not product. Many felt that this definition was too broad. Waste should mean materials *without value*. They argued that recycled materials and the chemicals Polaroid sends off-site for treatment should not count as waste.

People with training in engineering and science, particularly in

Polaroid's Chemical Operations Division, felt that the TUWR program and the categories established in EARS would diminish their authority. They were suspicious that the program was being developed to appease environmental groups and to get government off the company's back and that it would substitute for their own judgment and thinking. A team of Polaroid's toxicologists and chemists established the initial I-through-V categorization scheme used in EARS. The categories are not based solely on risk; for example, flammability is not a criterion. CFCs do not have high toxicity, but were assigned to Categories I or II because of their ability to harm the earth's ozone layer. Before the assignment of chemicals to categories was finalized, Fatkin had the scheme reviewed by a group of leading environmentalists. According to Fatkin, as a result of the meeting some chemicals were moved into more restrictive categories. Some Polaroid employees felt that categorizations were just plain wrong and resented "being forced" to abide by them.

For example, some chemists objected to the company's assignment of the chemical dimethyl sulfate to Category I. Dimethyl sulfate is an acutely toxic methylating agent and is lethal in small amounts. But because of the chemical's high boiling point and low volatility, it is relatively easy to handle. Chemists reviewing their choices under EARS felt the company was telling them not to use dimethyl sulfate—an extremely useful and controllable chemical. They complained that the hazards from alternative methylating agents were greater.

Problems in Data Collection and Manipulation

Polaroid experienced major problems as it tried to implement the EARS framework Fatkin had conceptualized. "For one thing," recalls James Ahearn, "no one had ever thought about such a system before; there was a total lack of knowledge of the entire process. No one knew where the data were going to come from or how they were going to be collected." According to Ahearn, the detailed monitoring of waste necessary for EARS requires intricate knowledge of the amounts of materials used, products manufactured, and by-products created, as well as where the by-product is disposed of and how it gets there. This is no easy task, especially because at Polaroid emissions data are not from continuous processes, and manufacturing processes use bulk materials stored in large tanks whose contents can sometimes be difficult to measure accurately.

For the first year of implementation, 1988, Polaroid required divisions to report only by categories, as this was the underlying structure of the TUWR program. Divisions had to consolidate all of their chemical-specific information and input only chemical use and waste generation numbers for each category as a whole. This was soon seen to create a weakness in the system, especially when attempts were made to link EARS data to regulatory information needs, such as SARA Title 313,[11] that are chemical-specific. So in 1989 all divisions were required to report on a chemical-by-chemical basis. When the 1989 data were compared to the 1988 data, some divisions were able to recognize inaccuracies in early data submissions. Says Ahearn, "some chemicals were forgotten and others were counted two or three times." Revisions had to be made to the original 1988 data because they were to be used as the base data for future years.

The original computer software used for EARS was not user friendly. Along with being extremely slow, it was impossible to review or modify any information once it had been input, making it very difficult to change data if a mistake was made.

MEANS OF OVERCOMING RESISTANCE

How did Polaroid manage to get the program on its feet if some division managers were not clear about what they were supposed to be doing or how they were to do it? Corporate management was firmly committed to the program and was its driving force.[12] According to James Ahearn, management told the people in the divisions responsible for collecting the EARS data to "just do it."

The effectiveness of this authoritative approach was enhanced by the fact that the program was introduced in accordance with Polaroid's somewhat unusual corporate structure. The primary unit of organization in the company is the division. Polaroid's corporate environmental affairs department is small, consisting of just twelve people. Most of the corporate functions are carried out in conjunction with the corporate office by divisions or by cross-functional committees and teams. Each division appoints its own people to handle environmental affairs. These individuals report directly to their operating divisions and not directly to the corporate environmental group. Polaroid gave division environmental staff responsibility for EARS. The fact that division staff were already accustomed to dealing with the processes and products helped to ease the program more easily into place and improved the accuracy and credibility of the EARS data being collected.[13]

Polaroid undertook an environmental campaign of "relentless information" throughout the company to explain the reasoning behind its program. Says Ahearn, "Two of the primary tactics employed were education and communication." Fatkin told people who felt Polaroid was essentially banning the use of Category I and II chemicals that although the company now required people to account for their use of these chemicals, it did not prohibit their use. For example, Fatkin told people who were concerned that they would no longer be allowed to use dimethyl sulfate, the hazardous but controllable methylating agent, to "use their judgment." He said to people, "if this is the best chemical for the use, go ahead."

Complaints about the amount of time involved in EARS data collection, voiced frequently when the program began, have begun to diminish as people have seen benefits from their hard work. According to Ahearn, EARS data allow people to estimate waste costs of certain projects, identify division by-products for reuse in other divisions, and assess their own progress toward TUWR goals. Soon Polaroid employees should be able to use the data to prepare reports required under SARA Title 313 (after certain adjustments are made for definitional differences) and Massachusetts air pollution reports.

PERSISTENT ISSUES

Although Polaroid has been able to correct some of the early problems with implementing EARS, other problems persist. People still complain that EARS data requirements take too much time and that it is cumbersome to use. Each division assigns two or three people responsibility for maintaining the EARS database. According to Loring, those responsible for EARS data entry in the Chemical Operations Division (which produces most of Polaroid's waste) spend one week or more inputting numbers each quarter.

Accuracy is also a concern. People responsible for computing EARS numbers and recording the data have varying levels of skill. According to Ahearn, chemical engineers usually input the data correctly because they are familiar with the chemicals, but other people devote less energy to obtaining precise numbers. In some cases the person collecting the data is not the same as the one entering the data into the corporate computer system, which can also lead to errors. Despite these problems, Ahearn feels that at this stage EARS data are about "85 to 90 percent accurate," which, he says, is "a very good degree of precision."

The EARS computer system does not link with the company's financial system. When the EARS system was in its initial planning stages, Harry Fatkin made it clear that he did not want the reduction program to be financially based. Says Ahearn, "Harry wanted the main goal of the system to be source reduction. He felt that the economic benefits would follow naturally because both yields and efficiency would increase." The need for linked environmental and financial accounting systems, however, would be useful. Polaroid (and other companies) would benefit from being able to assess readily the financial benefits of environmental improvements.

PROGRAM OUTCOMES

Polaroid instituted EARS and the TUWR program in order to achieve several objectives: to reduce toxic use and waste generation 10 percent per unit per year, escape the "regulatory rotary," and strengthen the company's relationships with outside groups. Has the company achieved these objectives?

In the period 1988 to 1990, Polaroid met its targets for achieving overall TUWR goals. (See **Exhibit 2**, columns headed "TOTAL Category I-IV" and "Category V.") Polaroid reduced the amount of chemicals it used or generated as waste to 80 percent of 1988 levels, per unit of production. Nearly all of this reduction was in Category III and IV materials, those Polaroid considers only moderately toxic to the environment, rather than Category I and II materials, those the company considers highly toxic and whose use is discouraged under EARS.

In 1991 Polaroid began to see reductions in its use of Category I and II chemicals. It took Polaroid three years to achieve progress in reducing these chemicals. Ahearn explains that reductions in chemical

Exhibit 2

TUWR Index Performance 1988-1991

Year	Category I and II	Category III	Category IV	TOTAL Category I-IV	Category V
1988	1.00	1.00	1.00	1.00	1.00
1989	0.95	0.80	0.87	0.87	0.87
1990	0.98	0.68	0.79	0.80	0.81
1991	0.85	0.71	0.78	0.78	0.83

Source: Polaroid Corporation, 1992

use have been relatively slow because they require wholesale changes in the way products are manufactured or in the products themselves. Changes to the manufacturing process require two to four years, from concept to implementation, according to Ahearn.

Despite these reductions, in 1991 Polaroid's rate of progress achieving its overall TUWR goals slowed. The company saw increases in Category III and V over 1990 levels. According to Ahearn, in the initial years of the program, reductions in these categories were achieved primarily through greater employee attention to issues like conservation and efficiency. Ahearn now cautions that achieving 10-percent-per-unit reductions in the years ahead will almost certainly depend upon the company replacing more of its solvent-based coating systems with aqueous-based systems. Approximately 25 percent of the by-product in Category III and IV comes from Polaroid's coating operation. Polaroid's recent attempts to introduce additional aqueous-based processes have failed. Ahearn still hopes for a breakthrough in this area. He says that people are working hard to come up with additional processes, but he cannot be certain about the outcome.

Fatkin and Ahearn have both expressed some concern about the rate of change reported in the amount of trash it produces (Category V). Fatkin cautions, however, that the recent increase in the Category V index may be misleading. "Quarter-by-quarter, year-by-year readings don't necessarily tell the whole story," explains Fatkin. Fatkin says that the increase may be due to production scheduling, start-up of new products, or a combination of factors that have little to do with environmental performance. "The EARS numbers tell me that I need to start asking 'Why is this happening?' " says Fatkin. "To conclude that we are headed in the wrong direction on the basis of a small increase in the index would be overly simplistic," given the size and complexity of the database behind a single number.

The TUWR program and the EARS reports that support it have perhaps been more successful in helping Polaroid reduce its environmental regulatory burden. For example, because the company is producing less waste, it cancelled plans to build a new incinerator at its Waltham, Massachusetts, site, thereby avoiding the extensive environmental permitting that would have been required for siting and operation. The company is better prepared to submit environmental performance reports required under SARA Title 313 and Massachusetts' Toxic Use Reduction Act (TURA), which requires companies to report the chemicals they use, the amount of by-products they generate, treatment methods, and emissions. Although EARS data must be adapted to comply with differing SARA and TURA definitions, most of the necessary information is on hand. Polaroid is attempting to use a preventive approach to minimize the impact of new regulatory requirements. For example, if the company can reduce emissions from particular processes to below regulatory thresholds, requirements for additional end-of-pipe treatment may be eliminated.

A Mixed Review

EARS may also have helped to improve the way environmental groups view Polaroid, although that result has not yet been achieved in all cases. In 1987 Greenpeace wrote the following about the company:

> Polaroid is the worst toxic polluter of Boston Harbor. Polaroid generated more hazardous waste than any other corporation in Massachusetts during 1986. Polaroid is the only company in Massachusetts which uses the dangerous practice of on-site burning for its wastes. It may face the largest toxic cleanup bill in Massachusetts history.[14]

Today, Kenny Bruno,[15] formerly Greenpeace's Northeast toxics campaigner and now the group's director of hazardous exports prevention, has this to say:

> Polaroid's toxic use reduction program addresses the root of the problem. They are addressing the very materials that are the basis of their business. Polaroid is not just complying with regulations, is not just treating the waste end. The company has prioritized chemicals on the basis of toxicity and is working to eliminate the worst chemicals—the ozone depleters and the carcinogens. Polaroid's understanding of the problems is more sophisticated than many chemical companies, and their message has gotten out.
>
> On the other hand, Polaroid remains fundamentally reliant on chemicals that are not friendly to the environment and human health...If Polaroid wants Greenpeace to say its program is effective, then we would need more information, process-by-process information...
>
> We are not satisfied with what the company has done.

An important unanticipated benefit of the TUWR program and EARS is financial. Ahearn estimates that EARS costs approximately $1 million to develop and $100,000 annually to operate. But overall, the net financial impact of EARS has been positive. According to

Ahearn, "everything we have done has saved money." Polaroid does not directly link EARS with the financial impacts of the program. The program was designed for environmental, not financial reasons. But Ahearn says that "for most chemical processes, our experience is that the minimum waste process is usually the minimum net cost process."[16]

CONCLUSION

Systems for measuring environmental quality and fostering continuous improvement are essential to successful TQEM. Polaroid's EARS is an example of one firm's approach to achieving these objectives. A number of features make EARS unique. It measures virtually every material Polaroid uses. It categorizes materials on the basis of risk. It is an exacting program, allowing divisions to claim credit for chemical use and waste reduction measures only if they meet a rigorous set of environmental criteria. Improvements in pollution controls are not recognized by EARS.

Polaroid employees use EARS for a number of purposes. Those in Polaroid's operating divisions use EARS to predict the environmental impact of new chemicals. They have used the system to learn where and how their processes affect the environment. EARS has provided leverage for those within the company to argue on behalf of continuous environmental improvements. Because "environment" can now be measured, environmental considerations carry more weight. EARS serves as a vehicle for communication and negotiation on environmental issues among divisions, and top-level managers use EARS to assess and reward the performance of division managers.

Polaroid's use of EARS has yielded important benefits, including substantial reductions in chemical use and waste. Perhaps the greatest benefits from EARS were achieved during the design of the database and its initial implementation. The detail that EARS requires helped Polaroid workers to understand the problems in their processes and ways to implement countermeasures. Polaroid employees at many levels began to think about their work in new ways. Were the chemicals they used hazardous to the environment? Where was waste being produced, and why? Many of the countermeasures implemented actually saved money rather than adding to the costs of production.

Continuing Challenges

Polaroid has found, however, that obtaining continual progress in reducing waste is not always predictable. EARS numbers show the company moving towards its overall TUWR goal, but progress is not consistent. In order for Polaroid to meet its environmental goals, Polaroid's Research Division must develop the technology to replace its solvent-based coating systems, which, so far, it has been unable to do. The problems Polaroid is facing are not restricted to the difficulty associated with developing new, environmentally sound technologies, however. Reducing the generation of Category V materials—cardboard, paper, and plastic—has also proved challenging.

The fact that the primary architects of the TUWR program and EARS were people within the corporate office may be an obstacle to implementation. Harry Fatkin and his staff wanted to develop a program that was consistent with the anticipated goals of government and environmental advocates. But approval from these outside interests is not a major concern of most Polaroid employees. EARS feels cumbersome to many at the company. Only a few people fully understand the complexities of the system. The fact that EARS is not integrated with financial data management systems may also reduce its strength.

Companies need tools like EARS to help workers identify environmental and associated production problems. Problem solving based on these TQEM tools can lead to improvements in production efficiency, quality, and environmental performance. The Polaroid case shows that successful systems for measuring environmental quality and achieving continuous improvement must be understood and accepted by all those involved. Companies committed to TQEM face the fundamental dilemma of balancing the complexity of assessing environmental impacts against the need to develop tools that workers can easily understand and use.

Notes

1.   Corporate database.

2.   Robert Reid, "Polaroid Focuses on Hazardous Waste Control," *Occupational Hazards*, September 1986, pp. 39-43.

3.   Id.

4.   Comments from Harry Fatkin included in this case study were obtained during an interview with Jennifer Nash and Joanne Kauffman, Cambridge, MA, June 12, 1991.

5.   Office of Technology Assessment, *Serious Reduction of Hazardous Waste*, U.S. Government Printing Office, September 1986.

6.   Comments from James Ahearn included in this case study were obtained during an interview with Jennifer Nash and Karen Nutt, Cambridge, MA, July 16, 1991.

7.   Polaroid's Toxic Use and Waste Reduction (TUWR) program is a key aspect of its three-part environmental program. The other two elements are compliance and community outreach.

8.   James Ahearn, Harry Fatkin, and William Schwalm, "Polaroid's Systematic Approach to Waste Minimization," *Pollution Prevention Review* (Summer 1991), pp. 257-71.

9.   James Ahearn, "Polaroid's Environmental Accounting and Reporting System (EARS)," June 18, 1991.

10.   Ahearn et al. (cited in note 8).

11.   Title III, Section 313 of the 1986 Superfund Amendments and Reauthorization Act (SARA) requires many companies, including Polaroid, to report releases of more than 300 chemicals.

12.   Ahearn et al. (cited in note 8).

13.   Id.

14.   Greenpeace, "Polaroid: Instant Pollution—#1 in Toxic Waste," 1987.

15.   Bruno helped write the Greenpeace report, "Polaroid: Instant Pollution—#1 in Toxic Waste" and led the group's campaign against Polaroid's environmental practices during the late 1980s.

16.   Ahearn et al. (cited in note 8).

20

EVALUATING MANAGEMENT SYSTEMS AS PART OF ENVIRONMENTAL AUDITS

Lawrence B. Cahill

Evaluating management systems is a crucial component of any environmental audit. Evolving regulations and directives acknowledge this importance. Remedying management deficiencies can result in long-term, lasting improvements in environmental compliance with external requirements and internal policies. This article presents ideas and examples from leading companies on how environmental audits can be designed to enhance TQEM systems.

For the past few years, there has been much discussion in the environmental auditing profession about evaluating management systems as part of a facility audit. Some have gone so far as to say that the management systems evaluation should be the *principal* objective of an environmental audit. It is probably fair to say that many people, though they espouse this approach, are not quite sure what it means.

Within the last two years, there has been considerable legislative and policy activity that needs to be considered in any decision to modify current internal environmental audit programs. Congress has

Lawrence B. Cahill *is a vice president with McLaren/Hart Environmental Engineering Corporation, a subsidiary of Sandoz Corporation, in Lester, Pennsylvania. He is the principal author and editor of* Environmental Audits, *6th Edition, Government Institutes, Inc., Washington, DC, 1989.*

proposed several bills that require audits, or in some way define how they should be carried out. The Department of Justice has provided guidelines on what it would value in deciding if a violation of environmental law should receive prosecutorial leniency. These proposals and guidelines do not focus on auditing for regulatory compliance verification as much as on auditing for the presence of management systems that can assure a high level of compliance. Interest in environmental systems is also expressed in two other efforts; the European Community (EC) Eco Audit regulation and the Environmental Protection Agency's proposed Environmental Excellence program. The EC program contains management standards that an operating site must meet in order to be eligible for an Eco label. The site prepares a public statement on its status with regard to these standards, its targeted level of management, and how long it will take to reach that level. This statement is then certified by an independent auditor for accuracy. The EPA Environmental Excellence program, though not fully developed, is similar in concept. Companies meeting a very high level of environ-mental program criteria would be invited to join the program and receive the benefit of being recognized by the agency and the public as a facility that goes beyond compliance. In addition, the British Standards Institute has published an Environmental Management Systems Specification that provides guidance on what effective systems should look like and how to evaluate them.[1]

Even with all this activity, one might still ask the question: Does this "management systems" approach add value to an audit? It most assuredly does! Focusing on management systems allows one to identify the underlying causes, as opposed to the symptoms, that are typically at the heart of noncompliance at a site.

For example, if an auditor were to observe something as simple as a label missing from a waste solvent drum, the resultant finding could be described as just that—"a drum had a missing label." Surely the next action would be that the site staff would immediately place a label on the drum, and the matter would be considered closed. However, if that same site were to be audited a year later, it is likely that *at least* one drum would be missing labels. Why?

The auditor failed to address the underlying cause of the problem and, nine times out of ten, this is likely to be the breakdown of a management system. In the case of the problem drum, the label could be missing for a variety of reasons, including

- The person responsible for drum storage and management has not been trained properly.
- It is unclear who maintains responsibility for the drum as it moves to various locations on the site, from accumulation near the point of generation, to a ninety-day accumulation pad, to a permitted storage facility.
- The drum has been sitting around for quite a while and no one is sure of its contents. A sample has been sent out for analysis and the decision has been made to not label the drum until the results are known.
- The purchasing department bought "cheap" labels and they cannot withstand the rigors of outdoor storage. They keep falling off the drums.
- The site inadvertently ran out of labels and the normal purchasing process for resupply takes two weeks.

Now, as we look at the problem, it takes on a different light. Maybe the solution is more complicated than simply placing a label on the drum. Maybe, for example, the site's training programs are not including the right people, or job position responsibilities are unclear, and so on. Thus, the corrective actions can now focus on underlying causes. They might, for instance, state that the site needs to train its operators better, or assign drum management responsibilities more clearly, or do something as simple as incorporating minimum quality specifications into the label purchasing process. By identifying and remedying the true problem, it is more likely that when the next audit takes place a year later, there will be no repeat occurrence. In this way, focusing on management systems can result in long-term environmental compliance improvements, not quick fixes.

WHAT IS A MANAGEMENT SYSTEM?

One can define an environmental audit as a verification of the existence and use of appropriate on-site management systems. As such, an audit is not meant to substitute for good site environmental management. "Good" management implies that there are systems in place on-site to assure compliance on an ongoing basis. These systems can be defined as "the organizational structure, responsibilities, practices, procedures, processes and resources for implementing environmental management"[2] at an operating site.

"The environmental management system should be designed so

that emphasis is placed on the prevention of adverse environmental effects, rather than on detection and amelioration after occurrence. It should

- Identify and assess the environmental effects arising from the organization's existing or proposed activities, products, or services;
- Identify and assess the environmental effects arising from incidents, accidents, and potential emergency situations;
- Identify the relevant regulatory requirements;
- Enable priorities to be identified and pertinent environmental objectives and targets to be set;
- Facilitate planning, control, monitoring, auditing and review activities to ensure both that the policy is complied with, and that it remains relevant; and
- Be capable of evolution to suit changing circumstances."[3]

Although the above elements should be at the core of a site's environmental management system, they are often difficult to audit against because a site's programs frequently are not structured that way. More typically, the site's environmental management system is the sum total of separate programs that would include most, if not all, of the following:

- Specific programs designed to address corporate environmental policies and procedures;
- Employee training and statements of job accountabilities;
- Regulatory tracking system;
- Environmental review of new activities;
- Waste minimization planning;
- Release prevention/emergency response planning;
- Environmental auditing, including noncompliance follow-up and reporting;
- Community outreach program/complaint management;
- Product stewardship;
- On-site contractor reviews and evaluations; and
- Off-site contractor reviews and evaluations.

These are the *auditable* program elements of a site's environmental management system.

HOW DO YOU DO IT?

To conduct an audit of a management system, an auditor needs to select those programs that are to be evaluated and to audit the following components of each of the selected programs:

- Organization
- Administrative procedures
- Staff assignments
- Documentation, reports, and records
- Implementation

These components would be evaluated against the standards set by regulations or corporate policy. For example, if a site is required to have an emergency response plan, it could be because of contingency plan requirements under the Resource Conservation and Recovery Act, spill prevention control and countermeasure requirements under the Clean Water Act, hazardous materials response requirements under OSHA's Hazardous Waste Operations rule, or under a mandated corporate procedure. The auditor would first have to determine which of these requirements apply and then evaluate the program organization, procedures, documentation, and implementation against those requirements.

When a facility falls under more than one set of requirements in one program area, the auditor would have to determine if the site has been responsive to each requirement and if the overall program is workable. For example, in the emergency response area some sites will attempt to develop one site emergency response plan addressing all applicable regulatory requirements. The advantage of this approach is that the site management does not have to determine what kind of incident has occurred before initiating the actions recommended by the plan. On the other hand, having an individual plan developed for each set of requirements simplifies the regulatory response and allows for a more direct assurance to agency inspectors and others that the regulatory requirements have been met. Yet, this approach, though valid, can create response time problems when an incident does occur. In either case, the workability criterion becomes paramount.

Much of the organization and procedural review of management systems can be conducted through interviews and evaluations of the programs' documentation. And if the systems can be identified ahead of time, protocols or checklists can be developed to guide the auditors in their investigations.

One of the most important aspects of the audit, however, is to assure that written procedures are, in fact, carried out effectively. This can best be explained by way of example. Take again, for instance, emergency response planning. One can review the organization and planning documents designed to respond to an emergency and find that they respond well to regulatory requirements. The real test of effectiveness, however, is in the implementation. In practice, this effectiveness can be tested either through evaluations of the response to actual emergencies or through drills or simulations. Thus, the auditor can determine that the system is effective only if there are assurances that it is tested or evaluated on a routine basis. In other words, any audit of management systems should include an evaluation of actual practices as well as documented procedures.

WHY IS IT SO HARD?

Many companies have considerable experience in assessing management systems on environmental audits. Yet, observation of numerous audits suggests that even those with experience have difficulties in applying consistent review techniques. The reasons for this include

- **Performance Appraisal.** An audit of management systems is truly an indicator of personnel performance, and therefore, it will always have a performance appraisal flavor to it. This means that interviews will have an additional tension that must be dealt with by the auditor.
- **Underlying Causes.** Identifying the root causes of a problem requires extra digging and investigation by the auditor. This will take even a very experienced auditor additional time. Such luxuries may not be available to the team.
- **Lack of Standards.** There will be many requirements placed on an organization (e.g., increased environmental awareness) that will have no standards against which they can be evaluated.
- **Cross-Cutting Programs.** Assessing management systems is difficult because responsibilities typically cut across media, and, therefore, necessary review techniques would be counter to the more traditional approaches.

In addition, developing management systems findings on an audit is just plain difficult. Building the case for a management breakdown requires a certain mind-set that has to be learned. For example, an auditor might conclude that the "hazardous waste management system at the site is inadequate." Immediately, staff personnel will justifiably ask the question, "Why do you feel that way?" And the response is all too often, "Well, I'm not sure, but I just wasn't comfortable after looking at the records and talking with a few of the staff." This is an insufficient evaluation.

The above conclusion related to the hazardous waste management system may, in fact, be correct. But the conclusion must be verified and substantiated with evidence. Accordingly, a deficiency statement or conclusion should have the following structure:

The hazardous waste management program at the site is not completely responsive to Corporative Directive HW-100. Deficiencies include

1. Five drums at the accumulation point had no labels.
2. Accumulation point inspection logs had not been completed for the past month.
3. Two of the maintenance staff had not received their annual training.

Developing findings in this fashion begins to build a strong case that the system is breaking down and needs rebuilding.

EXPERIENCE AT WORK

The following examples illustrate how two leading companies view the auditing process and are working to implement more comprehensive audits of their TQEM programs.

Conoco

Conoco has conducted environmental audits of its operations since 1980 under an Environmental Quality Assurance Program (EQAP). This program was developed to assure compliance with environmental laws, regulations, and corporate policies. Each business focused inwardly to satisfy its own need, and the environmental audits primarily emphasized compliance checking via the traditional "snapshot" approach.

The growing importance of environmental auditing and its impact on the thinking of the regulatory community and public stakeholders has brought a more outward focus on the purpose of all environmental programs at Conoco. As a result, the company is currently restructuring the EQAP by building a stronger process to evaluate environmental management systems. This new approach recognizes that a deeper look into the management systems within operations is needed to complement the more traditional compliance status "snapshots."

These changes have been challenging. Adopting management system evaluations into the traditional compliance-check audits is not a simple process. This is a relatively new concept and Conoco is now beginning to understand what environmental management systems really are and how to audit them. Without this understanding, it is sometimes difficult to accept what is perceived as criticism of management performance.

Limited audit staff and time needed to conduct quality compliance-check audits also impede reviews of environmental management systems. These two conditions are self-reinforcing. Compliance checks require more audits to assure that each and every facility is in compliance. This takes more time and drains audit resources. Conversely, the need for numerous compliance checks is reduced when strong management systems are in place to minimize the risk of noncompliance.

The Conoco Environmental Quality Assurance Program is a dynamic process. The company is committed to further improvement by increasing the focus on the management systems as a strong compliment to the compliance checks that are the backbone of the program. Conoco is convinced this focus will bring more assurance that it is meeting its compliance responsibilities in a cost-effective way. Conoco believes that these benefits will be observable, and over time will facilitate implementation throughout the organization.

Rohm and Haas

Using internal audits to measure environmental performance has been a management tool at Rohm and Haas since the late 1970s. In 1986, a revised compliance verification program was implemented. More emphasis is placed on training of internal auditors, providing current protocols, and strengthening the follow-up system to assure audit findings are corrected quickly. This process works well for the company. Operating sites use audit results to raise compliance levels and improve the quality of their management systems.

ALTERNATIVE PATHS

Redefining current audit programs to accommodate measurement of environmental management can take several paths. One is to determine the fault in a management system that caused noncompliance, and then correct it. Although this approach strengthens the system, it is time-consuming and creates inconsistent approaches to managing environmental issues throughout an organization. A second approach would audit against a management standard such as the British Standards Institutes 7750 or the standards developed by the Canadian Standards Institute or the International Standards Organization's environmental management standards currently under development. This latter approach allows the site to install a standard system rather than build one based on failure feedback. It also allows for consistency in management systems throughout an organization.

Regardless of which approach is taken, an element of compliance verification must be retained in the audit process to ensure that these systems are fully implemented.

Notes

1. "Specification for Environmental Management Systems," British Standard BS 7750:1992, ISBN 0 580 20644 0, March 16, 1992.

2. Id., p. 4.

3. Id., Annex, p. 9.

21

ENVIRONMENTAL HEALTH AND SAFETY MANAGEMENT AT VULCAN CHEMICALS: TOTAL QUALITY AND AUDITING

W.T. Parrott

At Vulcan Chemicals, total quality requires auditing and auditing ensures total quality. This article details the continuing integration of the two processes and describes some of the audits—and their measured regulate.

I n 1987, Vulcan Chemicals, a division of Vulcan Materials Company, embarked on its quality program. The phrase "Take the Journey" was coined to identify this process, which involved the concept of continuous improvement. Every employee was trained using the Deming curricula, and we all became Deming disciples.

As Vulcan's employees started to accept this new process, the company formed a Division Quality Council. In its initial meeting, the council determined that the environmental, health, and safety areas were of key importance to the long-term survival of the company's Chemicals Division. As a result, in early 1988, Vulcan organized the Environmental, Health, and Safety (EHS) Quality Team, which was composed of representatives from the legal, public affairs, marketing

W.T. Parrott is environmental, health, and safety director at Vulcan Chemicals, in Birmingham, Alabama.

and sales, technical service, manufacturing, and EHS organization functions.

To begin implementing a quality management approach for EHS, the quality team developed the following mission statement to provide guidance and vision:

> The mission of the Environmental, Health, and Safety Quality Team is to evaluate, on a continuing basis, the Chemicals Division's EHS Management System; to develop and communicate recommendations that will improve that System; and to monitor the System to assure that the Division establishes and implements the policies and practices that will
>
> - Protect our employees, the environment, and the public;
> - Develop and foster EHS awareness among employees, customers, and suppliers;
> - Promote public acceptance of the Chemicals Division's operations; and
> - Anticipate and proactively address potential EHS risk.

With the development of the mission statement and the realization that the EHS management system was a macro-process, the quality team began using brainstorming and grouping techniques to define the subprocesses (**Exhibit 1**) that would make up the system. In doing so, it identified the inputs (including proposed and/or existing legislation and regulation, projects, and risk) and outputs (compliance, controlled risk and liability, and effective communications) of these subprocesses or transformation subsystems.

Exbibit 1

Environmental, Health and Safety "Macro" Process

INPUTS	SUBPROCESSES	OUTPUTS
— Proposed Leg./Reg.	* Regulatory	+ Compliance
— Existing Leg./Reg.	* Marketing	+ Controlled Risk
— Plant & Division Projects	* Manufacturing	and Liability
— Liability	* Permitting	+ Effective
— Risk	* Risk Management	Communications
— Public Concern	* Public Relations/ Communications	
	* EHS Assurance	

It quickly became evident that the EHS assurance/auditing subprocess was the feedback loop in the overall system. This function came to be viewed as the quality check on the system that would play a key role in signaling the need to improve the process and assure quality outputs. Because providing internal feedback for the system was critical, this process was thoroughly analyzed for potential improvement. This article describes some of those recent improvements, their tie to our total quality management process, and a discussion of some of the results.

OVERVIEW

Under the "Environmental Responsibility" portion of Vulcan Chemicals' Total Quality Commitment (**Exhibit 2**), we have clearly stated our intent to

- Continually improve EHS Management functions;
- Implement strategies that will demonstrate commitment to the CMA Responsible Care® initiative and the concept of continued, never-ending improvement of EHS performance; and
- Conduct audits to provide feedback and assurance that will maximize performance and minimize risk in all EHS areas.

Along with this more present-day commitment to EHS assurance (embodied in a total quality approach) has come an evolutionary approach to all facets of the auditing function: (1) environmental, (2) health and safety, and (3) chemical product responsibility (i.e., terminals, distributors, customers, and products).

Environmental auditing has evolved since 1980 from a process in which environmental compliance reviews (ECRs) were, and still are, conducted annually at each manufacturing plant, to a point in 1986 when we began conducting detailed environmental compliance audits at our manufacturing plants. Whereas these ECRs are primarily issues reviews for management, the audits cover detailed regulatory requirements and compliance in a very comprehensive manner.

Comprehensive occupational health programs have been established since 1979 for the division. These programs consist of medical examinations, industrial hygiene monitoring, and biological monitoring. Industrial hygiene monitoring and biological monitoring are conducted on a frequent basis to identify and control possible employee exposure. Medical examinations are conducted to ensure that overexposure has not occurred. Every three years, occupational

Exhibit 2

Total Quality Commitment

health reports are compiled to audit our industrial hygiene and biological monitoring programs. The data from occupational health examinations is aggregated into exposure groups and analyzed to determine if any adverse health trends are developing in the workplace.

Annual safety audits have been conducted at our manufacturing, R&D, and transportation facilities since 1979. The focus of these audits is to review regulatory compliance and safety procedures and performance. A team with representatives from management, manufacturing, and technical is headed by a facility manager. The team spends a day at each facility reviewing procedures and records and conducting employee interviews. Discrepancies are noted and recommendations for improvement made. A follow-up on the actions taken by the facilities comes at an annual division safety review in the fall.

More recently, as part of the Division's Chemical Product Responsibility Program (CPRP), an environmental, health, and safety compliance assurance effort is underway with all of our terminals and many of our distributors. In the future this process will continue to be expanded to other distributors and customers who use our products.

As our assurance processes have evolved and with the advent of TQC, they have begun to not only provide the "classical" assurance that no significant noncompliances exist, but also are being viewed as the critical feedback loop to permit continuous improvement of our EHS management systems. This is a significant philosophical shift that should provide a much more positive, long-term outlook for auditing.

ENVIRONMENTAL AUDIT PROGRAM

In 1989 a thorough evaluation of the environmental audit process was initiated. This evaluation was completed in 1990, and comprehensive environmental audits were conducted using the revised process in 1991.

The new audit process involves the use of audit protocols provided for each major regulatory area. These protocols promote consistency between audits and also provide a resource for the facilities to use when conducting their own compliance checks. They will be updated annually to incorporate any regulatory changes or additions.

The audit team is staffed by members of the division environmental, health and safety (EHS) group. The independent nature of the audits has been strengthened through use of third-party observers, who watch audit procedures and report to the audit team leader any observations that affect the independence or accuracy of the audit.

The audit follow-up system has been improved to ensure prompt resolution of compliance concerns. Improvements include assigning an individual at each facility as audit coordinator for each audit. This individual is responsible for ensuring that action plans are developed to address each finding, and for tracking the completion status of each follow-up action. The follow-up system has also been improved by the use of the audit module of the EHS database. The audit reports are inserted into the audit module, where they can be easily updated by the facility audit coordinator. Calendar "ticklers" are used to alert the audit coordinator to important follow-up dates. The module also allows remote viewing of the audit status by designated personnel as well as preparation of audit status reports to update management (**Exhibit 3**).

Another significant improvement in the audit process has been the

Exhibit 3

Environmental Audits—Findings Resolution Time

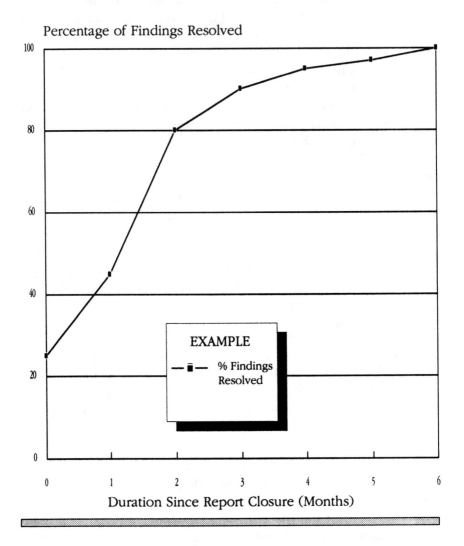

Percentage of Findings Resolved

Duration Since Report Closure (Months)

active participation of the corporate legal staff. A member of the legal department is assigned to assist the facilities and the division audit coordinator in addressing audit findings. This is valuable in reaching quick resolution of the numerous "gray" issues that arise in environmental compliance. The legal department representative also provides an additional third-party perspective to the audit process.

Program Implementation and Results

The results of the 1991 comprehensive environmental audits

conducted at the plants support the success of the new audit process. The advance planning incorporated into the new process allowed the audits to proceed smoothly with minimal interruption to the facility staff. The facility audits discovered a need for improvement in several regulatory areas. Consequently, the plants prepared an action plan to address all of the findings, which were incorporated into the final audit reports. The plants have actively been addressing the follow-up plans and in many cases have corrected issues before the final reports were released. All of the follow-up actions will be completed within six months of issuance of the final audit report. The facilities each underwent several regulatory agency inspections shortly after completion of the audits. The comprehensive nature of the audits and the quick resolution of identified issues have prevented the facilities from receiving compliance violations during these inspections. In addition to the compliance issues raised during the audit, there are numerous areas where the facilities are in excellent compliance. The audit reports noted such instances when appropriate.

HEALTH AND SAFETY AUDIT PROGRAM

Safety audits were conducted at all three plants and research and development. Audit topics included behavioral accident prevention process (BAPP), process safety management (PSM), management of change, confined space entry procedures at the plants, and hazard communication and electrical safety at R&D. Audit questionnaires that were completed prior to the physical audit were utilized. The physical audit consisted of reviewing procedures and records, employee interviews, and field inspections.

Observations and considerations as well as recommendations were documented as a result of the audits. Observations were general views, both positive and negative, that the auditor compiled during the audit. Consideration items were those that the plants and R&D should evaluate for improving their overall safety program. Of course, recommendations required formal responses and implementation plans.

After the safety audit responses were received, a division safety review was conducted to evaluate the safety audit recommendation responses. Plant managers presented implementation plans and time-tables for completion to division management. The completion status of each audit recommendation is reviewed during the next scheduled audit.

Plant goals in the safety and health areas are also communicated during the division safety review. These goals include injury/illness statistics and process safety management implementation, as well as goals in the health area including reduction in potential exposures and schedules for completion of occupational health examinations.

Program Implementation and Results
BAPP

In 1989 the chemicals division implemented the Behavioral Accident Prevention Process. The process focuses on identifying and correcting unsafe behaviors in the workplace. The theory behind the process is that an accident happens when unsafe behaviors and conditions occur at the same time. By focusing on and correcting the factors that result in unsafe behaviors, serious consequences such as lost-time accidents and fatalities can be prevented.

The mechanics of this process are based on observation, feedback, evaluation, and planning. Employees are observed at various tasks by trained observers, immediate feedback is given, areas within a facility track their observation results, and action plans are established to correct the unsafe behaviors identified in the observation process.

The implementation of this process has been reviewed during the 1990 and 1991 safety audits. Incorporation of the Behavioral Accident Prevention Process has contributed to a 30-percent reduction in our OSHA recordable incidence rate and a 70-percent reduction in our lost workday cases (**Exhibit 4**).

PSM

Process safety management systems were reviewed during the 1990 safety audit. This review was utilized as the basis for the self-evaluation questionnaire for the CMA Responsible Care® Process Safety Code of Management Practices. In 1991 process safety management implementation plans based on the 1990 audit were reviewed. The plants are continuing PSM implementation plans that include the updating of process and instrument drawings, process flow diagrams, and operating manuals. Hazard assessments of our existing processes are continuing and hazard assessments are conducted for all new or modified processes. To date, Vulcan has expended approximately 25,000 man-hours and over $2 million on updating basic data and conducting hazard assessments.

Implementation of process safety management systems has resulted in improved operations and is one of the reasons we have experienced an almost 40-percent reduction in the number of reportable releases for the division.

Exhibit 4

Vulcan Chemcials—Injury/Illness Statistics

INCIDENCE RATES

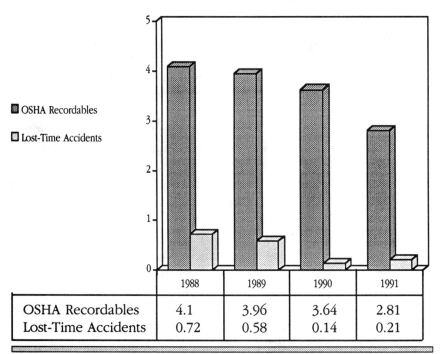

	1988	1989	1990	1991
OSHA Recordables	4.1	3.96	3.64	2.81
Lost-Time Accidents	0.72	0.58	0.14	0.21

Occupational Health

Occupational health examinations (OHE) are conducted at the plants on a triennial basis. The OHE serves as the ultimate audit function for our industrial hygiene programs and procedures. General health indices as well as chemical-specific health criteria are evaluated.

CHEMICAL PRODUCT RESPONSIBILITY PROGRAM (CPRP)

It is no longer acceptable to simply manufacture a product safely; but rather, products must be developed, manufactured, distributed, consumed, and disposed of in a manner that meets public expectations (i.e., handled properly throughout the entire life cycle). Laws and regulations are viewed as minimum standards, as our commitment to customer and public satisfaction causes us to pursue increasingly higher levels of excellence.

In response, over the past two years we have developed our

comprehensive product stewardship process called Chemical Product Responsibility Program. CPRP has been designed to comply with the developing CMA Responsible Care® Product Stewardship Code of Management Practices and, we hope, future EPA regulations. It will also give us an improved ability to aggressively manage the risks associated with our products.

CPRP is a management framework that consists of eight elements: (1) Product Development and Assessment, (2) Quality Assurance, (3) Product Educational Material, (4) Customer Care™, (5) Communications, (6) Product Recall, (7) Distribution, and (8) Legislative and Regulatory Affairs. Two of these elements that are integral to the EHS assurance process are highlighted below.

The first is the product development and assessment element, which ensures the evaluation and management of potential adverse health and environmental impacts of new and/or existing products and their end-use applications. This new process will provide a basis for life cycle assessment or auditing of all existing and new products and applications. When initiated this year, this process will require the collection/development and documentation of the information that has been outlined on a set of product review forms. Based on this information, the risk of the product and its commercial application can be characterized and an appropriate risk management plan put in place. Performing these "product use" audits will result in a more formal evaluation and management of potential product risk and a better prioritization of our risk management efforts.

The second element is Customer Care™. It is the primary focus of CPRP because it is the process that facilitates the transfer of our CPRP principles to customers' operations and is designed to motivate and assist them in attaining environmental, health, and safety excellence. In other words, Customer Care™ is what the customer will see and experience of our Chemical Product Responsibility Program.

The goal of Customer Care™ is to improve EHS performance. This will be accomplished by (1) educating our customers about our products; (2) responding to their needs and inquiries on EHS issues; (3) utilizing monitoring, inspections, and audits to identify customer needs; and finally, (4) utilizing the Customer Care™ Improvement Process (CCIP) to facilitate improvement when deficiencies are identified.

Program Implementation and Results

We piloted Customer Care™ with the Penta wood treaters in 1991.

Most of our efforts were focused on development of a training manual that was used to introduce our CPRP concepts and get the wood treaters' feedback on the design of our program. The response was phenomenal: over 70 percent of the participants indicated that the seminars were highly useful, and 85 percent wanted audits to be performed in 1991. We did not have the resources to begin in 1991, but we have completed an organizational change that will allow us to begin on-site evaluations this year.

Over the past two years, we have performed audits at over sixty distributor and terminal locations and have, with the above-mentioned organizational changes, positioned ourselves to carry out a four-year plan to audit and follow up at our distributors, company-owned and contract terminals, manufacturing facilities, and waste disposal facilities.

CONCLUSION

Implementation of auditing processes clearly requires an evolutionary approach as a company allows itself time to deal with all of the cultural, legal, management, and technical questions and concerns. A TQEM approach to implementing and executing EHS auditing, with a focus on never-ending improvement and customer satisfaction, can greatly enhance a company's eventual progress.

22

AUDITING FOR ENVIRONMENTAL EXCELLENCE AT UNION CARBIDE

Paul D. Coulter

Union Carbide formed its current Health, Safety, and Environmental Audit Program in 1985 following the Bhopal, India, tragedy in December 1984. Although our pre-Bhopal record confirmed our belief that we had an excellent program, with the help of a consulting firm we went back to the drawing board and questioned everything. We raised the bar and set as one of our goals the development and implementation of an audit program that is "second to none." This article details the specific tools being used by Union Carbide auditors to ensure environmental excellence at our numerous plant sites.

A lthough each of Union Carbide's major businesses has staff professionals who are responsible for a full range of traditional health, safety, and environmental (HS&E) functions, the Health, Safety and Environmental Audit Program reports directly to the chief executive officer and the Health, Safety, and Environmental Affairs committee of the board of directors. As an independent unit of Union Carbide, we are responsible for auditing our worldwide

Paul D. Coulter *is director of the compliance audit program at Union Carbide Corporation in Danbury, Connecticut. Since 1960, he has been particularly interested in the application of computers to solving problems. Currently, he is involved in using computers in compliance audit scheduling, classifying, deficiency analysis, report preparation, action plan tracking, and related items in the audit program. He is a member of the American Chemical Society, the American Academy for the Advancement of Science, and the Environmental Auditing Roundtable.*

companies and affiliate operations, and some suppliers. In addition to auditing against applicable regulations, we audit a location's compliance with Union Carbide's own HS&E standards that in many cases exceed legal requirements.

The objective of the compliance audit program is to provide independent assessment of line management and location performance against the following criteria: compliance with applicable internal standards and governmental requirements, and the existence of management systems that assure continued compliance.

The program is composed of the following elements:

- Standard Operating Procedures (SOPs)
- Audit protocols
- Facility profile database
- Hazard ranking model database
- Audit Timeliness Index (ATI)—site selection
- Location audits
- Performance classification
- Written reports
- Action plan reviews and response
- Action plan follow-up
- Root cause/findings analyses

PREPARING FOR THE AUDIT

We have developed a comprehensive set of standard operating procedures for compliance audits. These procedures give detailed instructions to the auditors regarding the planning, execution, and completion of the auditing process. There are general SOPs that cover the overall procedures for the department, and the purpose, scope, and key elements of the audit program. The fundamental SOPs address such items as (1) pre-audit planning, (2) audit preparation, and (3) on-site compliance audit activities such as the opening meeting, the understanding of management systems, assessing management systems, gathering audit evidence, sampling strategies (e.g., random number tables) and techniques, evaluating the audit evidence, management feedback meetings, preparing and issuing the audit reports. Also described in the SOPs are interviewing techniques, working papers requirements, and the post-audit dispute resolution process. Other SOPs cover recordkeeping retention requirements, good travel practices, emergency procedures, and security. The SOPs are regularly reviewed and updated as appropriate.

Audit Protocols

We have developed thirteen audit protocols to cover three issue areas. The three issue areas are health and safety, which includes occupational health and medicine, plant and employee safety, and operational safety events; environmental, which covers air emissions, waste management, groundwater and surface water protection, and environmental emergency preparedness; and product responsibility, including product risk assessment, product safety communications, product quality, the Toxic Substances Control Act (TSCA), and product distribution. In addition, a general protocol is used to direct the auditor review of management systems and miscellaneous issues. The protocols are regularly reviewed and updated as appropriate. Each protocol is maintained on a computer network disk. Before each audit, based on the functional areas they are to cover, the auditors print out the most recent version of the applicable protocol to take along with them.

To maximize the benefits and intent of the auditing process, sites must be selected and audited in a timely manner. Only then can management derive the maximum benefit from the program consistent with the resources employed. The principal components of Union Carbide's scheduling criteria are hazard potential, compliance potential, facility size, and past audit performance, to which we add a special site-specific component. In addition, we select a representative group of locations from all businesses and geographical areas. Because of the large number of sites covered by our program, we developed a mathematical model for prioritizing audit sites for scheduling purposes. The site data used for the model and to calculate the site's hazard ranking are contained in a facility profile database that is updated regularly by the locations and reviewed for accuracy by our auditors during an audit.

Audit Timeliness Index

The audit scheduling algorithm is shown in **Exhibit 1**. We refer to it as the Audit Timeliness Index (ATI). Each of the five components is related to one of our scheduling criteria. The hazard component is based on the location score from the hazard ranking data. The prior-audit component is based on performance classifications from the last two audits. The time-since-last-audit component is based on the number of years since the last audit. The plant-population component is proportional to the number of employees and on-site contractors at the location. The special site-specific component allows us to tune the model for site-specific factors, such as laboratories with special

Exhibit 1

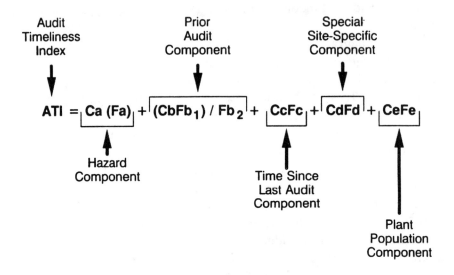

Auditing Scheduling Algorithm

$$ATI = Ca\,(Fa) + (CbFb_1)\,/\,Fb_2 + CcFc + CdFd + CeFe$$

Audit Timeliness Index

Hazard Component

Prior Audit Component

Special Site-Specific Component

Time Since Last Audit Component

Plant Population Component

considerations, new businesses, or other situations that are not adequately covered by the other four components.

The scaling constants are chosen so that sites that should be audited during the current year receive an ATI numerical score of 10 or higher. The effect of prior audit performance and hazard ranking is illustrated in **Exhibit 2**. In general, the better the prior audit performance, the longer the time interval between audits.

Information about the site, prior audits, and ATI index are consolidated on a computer printout, a page of which is shown in **Exhibit 3**. Each site has a description, a business group code, an internal audit unit number code, the total number of sites contained within that audit unit, the date of the most recent audit of the location, and the year and performance classification of the two most recent audits.

The log of the hazard ranking score is in the numerical section of the printout plus flags, such as "+," "-," or "%," that indicate whether any data are missing from either the facility profile or chemical thesaurus (used in the calculation of risk). Next come the components calculated from the hazard ranking score—classifications received in prior audits, last audit (factor proportional to the numbers of years since the last audit), any site-specific data, and the population factor—

Exhibit 2

Effect of Prior Audit Performance
and Hazard Ranking

Location A	(GM, GM)[a]	=	11
	(SM, M)	=	9
	(M, M)	=	7
Location B	(GM, GM)	=	13
	(M, M)	=	9
Location C	(X, RSI)	>	10

[a] For an explanation of these abbreviations, see Exhibit 4.

and finally, the ATI score itself. An asterisk after the ATI score indicates that an audit has been scheduled for the current year.

The use of the ATI score as a tool by an experienced audit team has allowed Union Carbide to reach its goal of making site selection more objective.

THE AUDIT PROCESS

After the audit schedule has been established, the team leader assigned to the audit issues a notification letter and requests materials for auditor review before the audit team visits the site. For non-U.S. sites and for non-owned Union Carbide facilities, notification is given thirty to forty-five days before the scheduled audit. All other locations receive a ten-day notice.

The audit team leader assigns specific functional areas to each of the team members and arranges the logistics. The team leader is also responsible for arranging a pre-audit meeting with audit management and other Union Carbide health, safety, and environmental personnel as appropriate.

Once on site, the audit is conducted in a manner that is consistent with the five-step process described in the book *Environmental Auditing: Fundamentals and Techniques* by Maryanne DiBerto, J. Ladd Greeno, and Gilbert S. Hedstrom (Cambridge, Massachusetts: Arthur D. Little, 1987), and in accordance with Union Carbide's SOPs. In approximately 25 percent of our audits, a consultant auditor

Exhibit 3

Union Carbide Audit Timeliness Report 92

DESCRIPTION	GROUP	AUD UNIT	LIN COUNT	MOST REC VISIT	MOST REC YEAR	MOST REC PERF	PREV YR	PREV PERF	LOG SRS	COMPONENT HAZARD	PRIOR AUDIT	LAST AUDIT	SITE SPEC	POP NUM	ATI
Location A	CP	183	2	MAR 89	89	GMX	87	N/A	4.1-	6.7	.0	1.5	.0	2.4	10.7*
Location B	CP	043	13	JUN 89	89	N/A	87	RSI	4.6+	7.3	.0	1.5	.0	1.8	10.6
Location C	CP	255	3	MAY 91	91	GMX	88	GMX	4.6	7.6	.0	.5	.0	2.5	10.6
Location D	CP	092	2						3.5	5.7	.0	3.5	.0	1.3	10.6
Location E	CPD	162	1	OCT 91	91	SMX	89	GMX	4.9	7.8	.0	.5	.0	2.3	10.6
Location F	MEL	005	29	JUN 91	91	SMX	90	GMX	4.6%	7.3	.0	.5	.0	2.8	10.6

participates in the audit to provide an independent assessment of our performance.

During the performance classification, we assess the current level of the location's health, safety, and environmental protection performance. Performance classification allows Union Carbide to set benchmarks for health, safety, and environmental protection objectives and to measure improvement in performance from year to year.

Several steps are taken to establish a performance classification. We develop a list of exceptions, which is used to integrate and summarize exceptions within a functional area. Performance classifications for each functional area are evaluated and the overall location performance classification determined.

For each exception, we determine whether it is of imminent concern (demands immediate management attention); priority concern (has the potential for serious adverse health, safety, environmental, or corporate impact); or other (all other situations). For each functional area, we determine whether the degree of compliance is high, substantial, general, or limited. Using the severity and compliance factors and the table shown in **Exhibit 4**, we determine the performance classification for each functional area.

Exhibit 4

Functional Area Performance Classification

	Severity Factor	
Compliance Factor	**Priority Concern**	**Other Concern**
Full	GM	M
Substantial	GM	SM
General	RSI	GM

M = Meets governmental and internal compliance requirements
SM = Substantially meets these requirements
GM = Generally meets these requirements
RSI = Requires substantial improvement to meet requirements

For an audit rating of "Meets," at least 75 percent of the functional areas must be "Meets," no functional area is "Generally Meets" or "Requires Substantial Improvement," and there is no other relevant information that suggests that the overall rating should be different from a "Meets." Similarly, we determine "Substantially Meets" and "Generally Meets." The location receives a "Requires Substantial Improvement" (RSI) classification if more than 25 percent of the functional areas are classified as RSI.

By assigning a value to the various classifications, we can develop an index for groups of audits. Visual representation of progress can be made by plotting the index versus time, as shown in **Exhibit 5**. Generally, such plots indicate an increasing improvement in a location performance classification. However, if an analysis is made based on the classification of a location on its first audit, following the second and third audits, and after four or more audits, a slightly different story emerges, as is shown in **Exhibit 6**.

Over a period of time, the results of first audits are nearly constant, whereas the results of second and third audits and four or more audits show a higher degree of improvement. Because of the progressively greater number of locations having four or more audits, the overall audit performance classification index climbs steadily. This illustrates the importance of visiting sites periodically to help them identify weaknesses. As most of the improvement occurs in the early audits and tends to plateau after repeated audits, sites that have been audited repeatedly and are showing a high degree of compliance should have less frequent audits.

Each of our auditors has a laptop computer that is used to write individual findings and, ultimately, the audit report. Each audit team carries with it a portable printer. On the evening before the closeout meeting, the team meets, merges all their findings, prioritizes them within each functional area, and prioritizes the functional areas. The audit summary is written and combined with the findings and the standard boilerplate to generate a draft report. Unless the performance classification is RSI, or the audited location requests time to respond to some of the findings, the draft report, with any minor editorial changes as necessary, becomes the final report and is left with the site.

In those unusual and special situations in which RSI is proposed as the performance classification, the report is reviewed by audit management and issue specialists in the Corporate Health, Safety, and Environment Department. When the RSI performance classification is

Exhibit 5

Illustration of Average Audit Classification

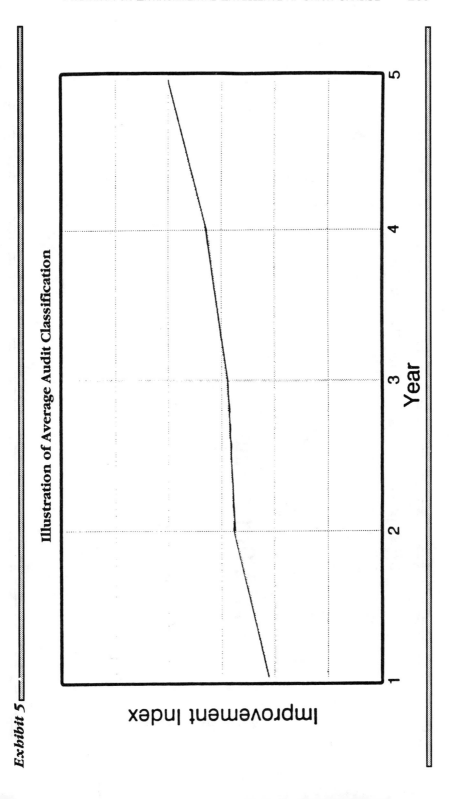

Exhibit 6

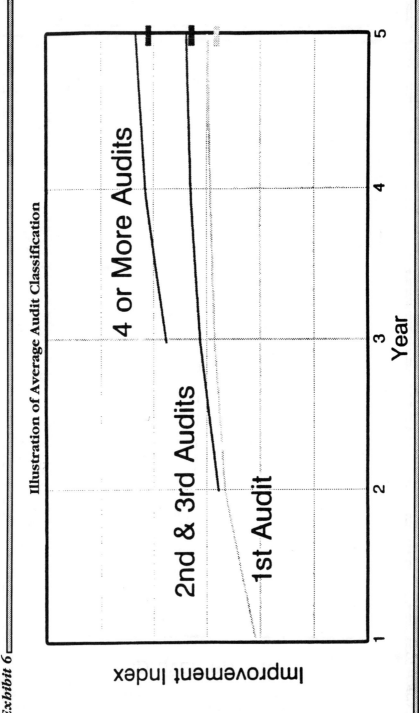

Illustration of Average Audit Classification

confirmed, the location is notified and the final report is issued to business group management.

In all cases, the final report is entered into our computer database and sent to the responsible Union Carbide managers.

AUDIT FOLLOW-UP

Within sixty days of the issuance of the final report, each audited location is required to develop a detailed action plan to correct the deficiencies noted during the audit. This action plan must reference each finding, the action being taken to correct the deficiency, the projected completion date, and the responsible person. The action plan is reviewed by health, safety, and environmental professionals in the business unit and forwarded to the accountable vice president for his or her endorsement and submittal to the audit group. All action plans are reviewed by the audit team leader. If the team leader has questions about some of the proposed actions, the action steps in question are reviewed with the appropriate issue manager within the corporate HS&E department. If it is deemed that some proposed actions are not adequate or, less commonly, overstated, the action plan is sent back to the location requesting revision.

Approximately 10 percent of the submitted action plans are subjected to an in-depth review that includes both the team leader review and a review of each item by appropriate issue managers and audit program management.

Each location is required to submit a semiannual update on its action plan until all items are completed. On repeat audits, the auditors verify that physical or system revisions noted in the action plan are complete and correct the problem.

Recently, we have improved our root cause analysis. During the preparation of the final report, each auditor makes an analysis of the root cause(s) of each exception and codes them in the audit report. We have developed a comprehensive list of factors so that we can analyze recurring weaknesses within our overall health, safety, and environmental program. We are able to analyze by business, type of plant, process, or geographical area. We believe this will allow us to continue progressing toward excellence in our health, safety, and environmental programs.

Section VI

MANUFACTURING AND INFORMATION TECHNOLOGY FOR TQEM IN THE NINETIES

23

ENVIRONMENTALLY CONSCIOUS MANUFACTURING: A TECHNOLOGY FOR THE NINETIES

Suzanne H. Weissman and
Janine C. Sekutowski

Companies embracing TQEM must evaluate and change their manufacturing processes to stay globally competitive in the nineties. This article, reprinted with permission from AT&T Technical Journal, shows how an environmentally conscious manufacturing program incorporating new approaches to waste reduction will help companies achieve their corporate-wide TQEM and strategic goals.

Environmentally conscious manufacturing involves developing and implementing manufacturing processes that minimize or eliminate hazardous chemical waste, reduce scrap, or are operationally safer. The benefits include safer and cleaner factories, reduced future costs for disposal and worker protection, reduced environmental and health risks, improved product quality at lower

Suzanne H. Weissman is supervisor of the Process Optimization and Control Division, Sandia National Laboratories, Albuquerque, New Mexico. Her group is responsible for research, development, and implementation of process monitors, process controllers, and environmental monitors, and for assessing the impact of environmental regulations on manufacturing operations. Janine C. Sekutowski is a supervisor in the Environmental and Materials Technology Department, AT&T Bell Laboratories, Princeton, New Jersey. Her group is responsible for research into reducing the environmental impact of AT&T's manufacturing operations. This article is reprinted with permission from AT&T Technical Journal, copyright © 1991 AT&T.

Panel 1

Acronyms in this Paper

BAT	best available technology
CFC	chlorofluorocarbons
CHC	chlorinated hydrocarbons
DFE	design for environment
DFX	Design for X, where X stands for downstream concerns such as manufacturability, testability, and installability
DI	deionized
DOE	Department of Energy
ECM	environmentally conscious manufacturing
EPA	Environmental Protection Agency
FT-IR	Fourier transform—infrared [spectroscopy]
IPA	isopropyl alcohol
LSF	low solids flux
MDA	methylene dianiline
PWB	printed wiring board
T_c	critical temperature
TDI	toluene diisocyanate

cost, and higher productivity. Sandia and AT&T are committed to environmentally conscious manufacturing.

INTRODUCTION

In recent years, U.S. manufacturers have been subject to increasingly stringent environmental legislation. Federal, state, and local legislation currently regulate air emissions, water discharges, occupational exposure, and treatment and disposal of various hazardous chemicals. In addition, the Montreal Protocol, an international agreement signed by the United States, regulates the production and use of halogenated organic compounds now known to deplete the Earth's ozone layer. In particular, chlorofluorocarbons (CFCs or Freons), some chlorinated hydrocarbons (CHCs), and halons are regulated. The 1990 Clean Air Act addresses urban air pollution, toxic emissions, and acid rain and emphasizes waste minimization as well as emission monitoring and reporting. The act lists 189 compounds for regulation as air toxics. Its regulations will have a serious impact on manufacturing.

Environmentally conscious manufacturing (ECM) goes beyond simple compliance with environmental regulations to drive a philosophy of pollution prevention. Sandia National Laboratories and AT&T

are committed to improving the environment, and are actively researching ways to minimize or eliminate solid, liquid, and gaseous wastes. Included in our ECM programs are steps to decrease employee exposure to hazardous chemicals.

Increasingly stringent environmental regulations correlate directly with increased waste-associated costs. Waste disposal costs are increasing at an annual rate of 10 percent. Often, stricter laws, new knowledge, or better chemical analyses redefine waste from nonhazardous to hazardous, resulting in a tenfold increase in disposal costs.

Minimizing waste can reduce these costs. Optimizing processes and procedures to more efficiently use material will reduce production and disposal costs, because one frequent component of waste is material that is not used in the final product. For example, inventory practices can be optimized to ensure that a material with a short shelf life is used before its expiration date. Processes that are not optimized produce scrap and rework because the product doesn't meet quality specifications. The result is increased materials and disposal costs.

Another component of manufacturing waste is packaging material. Supplies, components, and subassemblies come from suppliers packed in disposable material. Packaging material use should be limited to no more than is necessary to achieve basic product protection. Minimizing waste will also improve operating cost and energy efficiency. There are many hidden waste-associated costs—e.g., to track waste and hazardous materials, to obtain permits, to comply with the regulations, and to operate waste treatment facilities. Often, these costs are included in the operating overhead of a manufacturing plant and are not identified with waste management. Waste reduction can often result in significant cost reduction.

Today's manufacturing process waste minimization will affect the company's future liability. It has become apparent that even well-regulated disposal can cause environmental damage. For example, as the detection limits of chemical analyses have improved, lower pollutant levels can be detected, resulting in even stricter regulations. Many landfills, operated with what was considered the best available technology (BAT) for that time, have now become Superfund sites with the associated liability costs. (Superfund sites are hazardous waste sites especially designated by EPA for cleanup.) Reducing generated wastes should result in reduced future liability costs associated with solid waste, air emissions, and liquid effluent.

The technology developed for ECM can have ancillary benefits for manufacturers. For example, operations that minimize the number of cleaning steps can improve productivity and quality. Decreasing hazardous chemicals emissions will improve public acceptance of manufacturing operations and enable manufacturers to be perceived as good neighbors. Sandia has an ongoing program to transfer its technology to U.S. companies, helping improve manufacturing productivity and the nation's international competitiveness at the same time it protects the environment.

Waste minimization makes both environmental and economic sense. Corporations are responsible for maximizing the investment of their shareholders. Therefore, it is incumbent on them to reduce

Figure 1

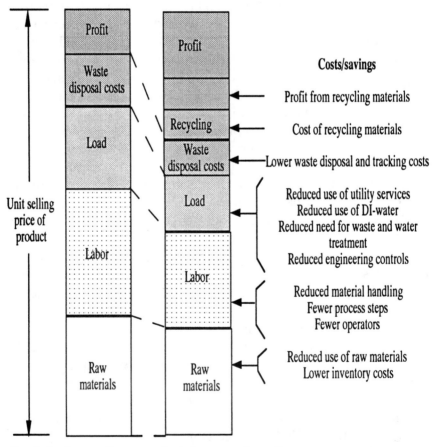

Economic Benefit of Waste Minimization in Manufacturing

Goal: Savings - Costs => 0 → Increased profit

operating costs (**Figure 1**). Waste minimization will lower today's disposal costs and reduce future potential liability costs. Corporations can gain marketing advantages by reducing waste. A national survey conducted by the Gallup organization indicated that about 90 percent of those surveyed would be willing to pay a premium for green products or packaging.[1]

Figure 2

Schematic Representation of Environmentally Conscious Manufacturing

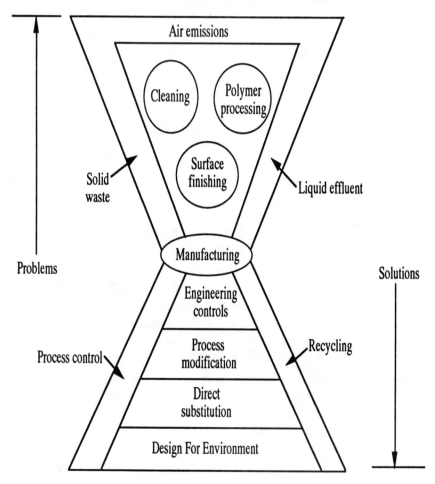

Problems currently being studied at Sandia and AT&T are represented by circles at top of figure. Solutions are represented at the bottom of the figure.

ECM TECHNOLOGY

The problems and solutions addressed by environmentally conscious manufacturing are depicted in **Figure 2**. ECM solutions that can be applied incrementally are shown as bars: The length of the bar represents the difficulty and time required for implementation. Those solutions that can be applied with current or advanced technologies are represented by diagonal supports. Engineering controls, such as the addition of barriers to confine a hazardous chemical, can be used as a short-term ECM solution. Process modifications, such as decreasing the volume of cleaning solvents used, can also be used in the short term. Forward-looking, longer-term solutions include direct substitution of nontoxic for toxic materials (e.g., changing a cleaning solvent from trichloroethylene to isopropyl alcohol). Alternatively, a new process that omits hazardous chemicals can be used. For example, fluxless soldering eliminates the need for cleaning solvents to remove excess solder flux. A combination of ECM approaches is necessary for short- and long-term success in waste reduction.

The most forward-looking scenario goes as far as designing products to minimize waste during item production, use, and disposal. This approach is known as design for environment (DFE). Sandia and AT&T have many programs involving ECM. Representative examples from several areas are discussed in the following sections.

CLEANING/SOLVENT SUBSTITUTION

Because cleanliness is a critical parameter in electronics manufacture, cleaning processes must insure quality and functionality. However, they are non-value-added processes that produce waste. It is important to eliminate or reduce as many of these manufacturing operations as possible. Sandia and AT&T both have active programs in minimizing cleaning waste.

Sandia is coordinating the Department of Energy's (DOE) effort to eliminate the use of halogenated solvents in cleaning. The program is being carried out jointly with the DOE production agencies. Traditionally, cleaning mechanical and electrical components has required halogenated solvents, particularly CFCs and CHCs. Sandia and AT&T have conducted tests to study the cleaning ability of non-halogenated, environmentally safe solvents. One Sandia study involved high-reliability printed wiring board (PWB) assemblies. PWBs require cleaning to remove process residues that can lead to corrosion or degrade their electrical performance.

Four alternative commercially available cleaners were studied. The major active ingredient of each was: terpenes (naturally derived organic compounds), N,N-dimethylacetamide, decyl acetate, and isopropyl alcohol (IPA). The first part of a three-step program evaluated the cleaning efficiency of these solvents to remove oils, greases, and mold release agent from PWB coupons. (Coupons are test strips or pieces.) Weight loss data for soiled coupons showed the terpene-based and decyl acetate-based cleaners effectively remove the three contaminants. The dimethylacetamide cleaner and IPA were ineffective in removing the grease. A second step measured the fraction of a volatile radioactive compound (labeled-tetrabromoethane dissolved in cyclohexane) removed from a coupon. (Labeling indicates to researchers that a radioactive isotope has been incorporated into the compound.) This technique is effective to monitor the degree of surface cleanliness. Again, the terpene-based and the decyl acetate-based cleaners were effective cleaning agents, but the dimethyl-acetamide-based cleaner and IPA were not. A commercially available water-soluble hand cream was also used as a stand-in for body oils, and only the decyl acetate-based cleaner effectively removed these oils from test coupons. Overall, both the terpene- and the decyl acetate-based cleaners showed a broad range of cleaning capabilities. Because cleaning equipment is commercially available for use with the terpene-based cleaner, and not for the decyl acetate-based cleaner, the former cleaning solvent was chosen to clean PWBs.

Another approach to eliminating halogenated solvents is to use a solventless cleaning process. One such process uses a hydrogen plasma for cleaning. Heavily oxidized copper surfaces can be cleaned effectively with hydrogen plasma (or hydrogen-argon) and subsequently soldered without fluxing. Hydrogen plasma reduces copper oxide more effectively than molecular hydrogen would.

Because cleaning is a non-value-added process, the best solution is to eliminate it. AT&T and Sandia are pursuing this approach by developing low solids flux (LSF) technology. LSF has a solids content in the range of 2 to 5 weight percent, compared to the usual 15 to 35 weight percent. LSF leaves little or no post-solder residue and eliminates the need for subsequent cleaning processes. It eliminates not only cleaning agent waste, but also cleaning machine capital, operating, and maintenance costs. It also reduces material costs. Because surface insulation resistance tests have shown that the quantity of applied LSF is critical, development of LSF technology has focused on strictly controlling the quantity of LSF applied to circuit packs.[2]

We are investigating the fundamentals of surface contaminant-cleaning agent interactions to develop environmentally sound cleaning processes, to minimize cleaning agent waste, and to minimize cleaning processes. Our goals are to understand, at the molecular level, interactions between surfaces, contaminants, and cleaning agents; how contaminants bond to surfaces; what is required of a cleaning agent, or what energy is required of a mechanical or combined chemical and mechanical cleaning process. For example, supercritical carbon dioxide (CO_2) is emerging as a potential cleaning solvent. CO_2, when compressed at a temperature slightly above its critical temperature (T_c) (the liquefication temperature), is converted to a supercritical state in which it has singular properties. For example, a supercritical fluid is almost as dense as a liquid but retains gas-like properties such as low viscosity and high diffusivity. Supercritical CO_2 shows promise as a safe alternative to halocarbon cleaning solvents: It can dissolve many organic materials, especially organic species without hydrogen bonding capability. It is nontoxic, nonflammable, and environmentally safe. It contains neither hydrogen nor halogen and will not corrode metal parts. It evaporates rapidly and does not leave any residues on the cleaning surface.

Problems with producibility, materials compatibility, and long-term reliability may arise when replacing hazardous materials or processes with environmentally safer ones. These problems can be especially severe in enclosed systems or those designed for long lifetimes. In making any material or process change, it is important to consider the compatibility of a material such as a cleaning solvent with other materials it might contact or which are in the vicinity. For example, halogenated solvents replaced aqueous-based solvents for cleaning because of corrosion problems associated with the latter. But aqueous-based solvents are now replacing halogenated solvents. Corrosion problems may recur unless the process changes are carefully conducted to avoid moisture accumulating in recesses or holes. Often a design change, such as adding a hermetic seal, another barrier, a scavenger, or changing the size of holes, is needed to ensure compatibility.

PLASTICS AND POLYMERS

Several hazardous materials are used to produce plastics and polymers. These include methylene dianiline (MDA) and toluene diisocyanate (TDI), both of which are suspected (or listed) carcinogens; TDI is also a respiratory sensitizer. Though these materials have not been banned, they are being more strictly regulated, and Sandia is evaluating replacements. MDA is a major constituent of a widely used polymer curing agent. Sandia has been evaluating materials as drop-in replacements for this curing agent. (Drop-ins can be substituted without any other process changes.) One is a commercially available aromatic amine. However, this material has a slower cure rate than the original material. To increase the cure rate, salicylic acid was added as a catalyst. Tests have shown that the new material is an acceptable replacement for MDA.

Plastics can be a major proportion of a factory's waste stream as a result of manufacturing processes such as extrusion or injection molding. These wastes result from purging equipment to change plastic type or color, in the case of extrusion, and from mold sprues and runners, and defective parts, in the case of injection molding. (A sprue is an extra piece of hardened plastic created during injection molding.) These materials can be granulated and reused. More thermoplastic wastes are being recycled this way within manufacturing plants.

ELECTROPLATING, SURFACE FINISHING, AND RINSING

Metal finishing processes are commonly used to inhibit corrosion and to make surfaces suitable for painting. Metal finishing processes also provide functionality, reliability, and long life to electrical components. Unfortunately, many of these processes use hazardous materials (e.g., hexavalent chromium (Cr^{6+}), cadmium, cyanide, and formaldehyde) or produce hazardous chemical waste, such as volatile organic compounds. One example of an improved electroplating process uses a non-cyanide bath for gold plating. Most of today's gold plating solutions are based on cyanide salts and are considered acutely hazardous. Sandia is evaluating a gold sulfite complex for microelectronic manufacturing applications.[3] The gold sulfite is in an alkaline solution with a pH between 8.5 and 11. Positive photoresists typically used in commercial microelectronic production facilities are sensitive to alkaline solutions; this sensitivity could present a problem with the new gold bath. We have shown that under controlled electroplating conditions, the standard positive photoresist can be used under normal processing conditions using a photoresist postbake temperature as low as 90°C.

Wet processes such as electroplating and surface finishing involve spraying or immersing parts in aqueous solution. After processing, the parts retain a film of the process solution (dragout) that is removed by a rinsing process. Rinsing processes are needed to produce clean parts but, by their nature, create a waste stream. Indeed, the volume of waste from rinsing is significantly higher than from electroplating. One effective way to handle this type of waste is recuperative rinsing. In this process, rinsewater from the first rinse, containing process chemicals, replenishes the process tank, which loses fluid through evaporation. This effectively recycles some or all process chemicals, thereby minimizing waste. AT&T has developed a recuperative rinsing process model that ensures adequate rinsing but minimizes process chemicals and water losses. The recuperative rinsing program analyzes several plating and rinse processes to ensure water conservation and minimal process chemical discharges to waste streams, while not compromising product quality.

PROCESS MONITORING AND CONTROL

Process monitoring can automatically obtain and report the information on chemical usage, process quality, and emission levels required by the Environmental Protection Agency (EPA) and other governmental agencies. Process control can minimize waste, reduce production costs, and improve product quality by detecting and correcting problems early. **Figure 3** represents the four steps involved in process monitoring and control. Initially, a chemical sensor or

Figure 3

Schematic Representation of Steps Involved in Process Monitoring and Control

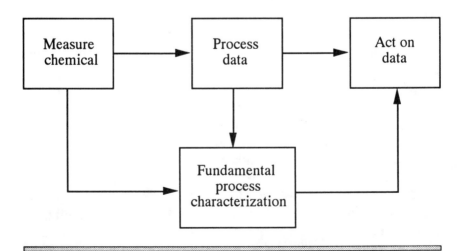

automated analyzer measures the concentration of the chemical (or a physical parameter, such as temperature). Next, the data are analyzed using chemometrics, signal processing techniques, or neural networks. (Chemometrics are advanced statistical techniques used to process chemical data.) Sandia has pioneered work in this area, especially in applying multivariate calibration methods to quantitative Fourier transform-infrared (FT-IR) analyses.[4-6] Neural networks are another approach under study.

After the data have been processed, some action is required. This may simply be an alarm or recording the data for internal use or for reporting to EPA. A more advanced option is to control the process. This may require regenerating chemicals, changing temperature, pressure, or time. To control a process, one must characterize and model the process, and understand the controlling parameters.

We are developing and applying process monitor and control systems to several manufacturing processes. For example, Sandia is developing an integrated on-line monitoring and control system for electroless copper plating. The electroless copper process is used to plate through-holes in printed circuit board manufacturing. Through-holes provide electrical connections between circuits in separate layers of a laminated multilayer circuit board. The holes are subsequently plated with tin-lead for making solder connections. Typically, electroless copper baths are controlled by monitoring copper, pH, and formaldehyde; the baths may be replenished manually or automatically. Copper layer thickness is controlled by plating for a specific time. Our monitoring system includes Sandia-developed and commercially available sensors. The Sandia sensors include a fiber optic sensor to measure deposit strain and a quartz crystal microbalance to measure simultaneously the plating thickness and solution properties. Commercially available probes monitor pH, copper concentration, and temperature.

Sandia has developed FT-IR spectroscopy coupled with chemometrics for process monitoring and control. FT-IR and chemometrics have been used for in-situ monitoring of polymer encapsulant mixing. They are also being developed to monitor process chemicals and decomposition products in electroless copper baths.

DESIGN FOR ENVIRONMENT

To focus on pollution prevention, it is essential to address environmental concerns in the product and process design phase. Decisions made during the design phase have a profound impact on the entire life cycle of the product, from design through manufacturing, distribution, installation, servicing, and disposal. It has been estimated that from 80 to 90 percent of the total life cycle costs of a product are determined in the design phase.[7] Integrating the design process with environmental engineering concerns will avoid environmental problems after the design phase. Thus, overall costs associated with process wastes will be reduced.

AT&T has worked to integrate the design process with other functions, using the concept of DFX, where DF stands for design for, and X stands for manufacturability, installability, reliability, safety and other considerations beyond performance and functionality. DFE (design for environment) will integrate design and environmental engineering to minimize the environmental impact of product manufacture as well as other downstream considerations (see Figure 2).

There are several waste streams associated with a product life cycle, starting with manufacturing, and DFE approaches to these are being investigated. For example, process design guidelines would help process designers assess the environmental soundness of a new manufacturing process or new equipment. DFE helps process designers to analyze the environmental ramifications of a new process before developing and installing it. By doing a material flow balance or waste audit on a process *before* it is implemented, designers can prevent expensive, intrusive fixes later on.

DFE is a means to an end bigger than reducing factory waste streams. During the design stage, environmental concerns associated with the front end (of the supply chain) and the after-sale phase of the product life cycle can also be addressed. It is this idea of influencing the entire product life cycle that makes DFE a potent concept and more than just a waste minimization approach. For example, energy efficiency and final product disposal can be taken into account. Design for recyclability is a concept that illustrates this. A complex product can be designed so it is easy to disassemble into various components and material types for ease of recycling.

DFE is a concept in its infancy that has the potential to significantly affect types and quantities of waste. If done properly, it also has the potential to minimize the environmental impact associated with a product's use and eventual disposal. It is a paradigm shift in managing waste by preventing pollution in the design phase.

CONCLUSION

Environmentally conscious manufacturing reduces the environmental impact of manufacturing operations. It involves a paradigm shift from end-of-pipe control to meet environmental regulations, to avoiding pollution in the first place (see **Figure 4**). There are many approaches a company can take, some of which have been summarized here. But the critical point is that ECM is the responsible and economically sound thing to do. It decreases costs and future liability, and often improves the quality of the end product because of more efficient processes that generate less waste. It is a technology for the '90s.

Figure 4

ECM Involves a Paradigm Shift from the Operating Practices of the Factory of Today to the Factory of the Future Where Waste Minimization Is an Operating Philosophy

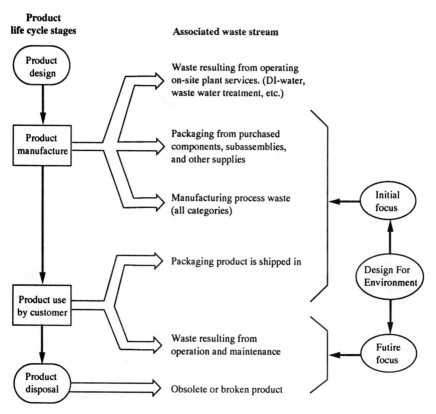

ACKNOWLEDGMENTS

This work was supported by the United States Department of Energy under Contract No. DE-AC04-76DP00789. The concepts and results presented in this paper are based on the work of many people. Those involved in this effort at Sandia include Kathy Alam, Jim Arzigian, Adra Baca, Barry Granoff, Vicki Granstaff, Dave Haaland, Mike Hosking, Paul Nigrey, Mike Oborny, Henry Peebles, Dennis Rieger, John Sayre, Mark Smith, Ron Stoltz, Ken Wischmann, and Walter Worobey. Among those involved in the work at AT&T Bell Laboratories are Iris Artaki, John Fisher, Bill Gillum, Werner Glantschnig, Leslie Guth, Jim Lloyd, John Piazza, Urmi Ray, M. Saminathan, Geoff Scott, George Williams, Gary Wolk, and Yulia Zaks.

Notes

1.   Denis Hayes, "Harnessing Market Forces to Protect the Earth," *Issues In Science And Technology*, Winter 1990-1991, p. 46.

2.   L.A. Guth, "Applicability of Low Solids Flux," *Proceedings of U.S.-Singapore Conference Cum Exhibition on CFC Alternatives*, September 1990, Singapore.

3.   J. Horkans and L.T. Romankiw, *Journal of the Electrochemical Society*, Vol. 124, No. 10, 1977, p. 1499.

4.   D.M. Haaland, "Multivariate Calibration Methods Applied to Quantitative FT-IR Analyses," *Practical Fourier Transform Infrared Spectroscopy*, Academic Press, New York 1990, pp. 395-468.

5.   D.M. Haaland and R.L. Barbour, "Quantitative IR Analysis of PCBs in Transformer Oil," *American Laboratory*, Vol. 17, No. 7, July 1985, pp. 14-19.

6.   D. M. Haaland, "Partial Least-Squares Calibration Diagnostics Applied to the FT-IR Analysis of Borophosphosilicate Glass (BPSG) Thin Films," *Fourier Transform Spectroscopy (1989)*, 7th International Conference on Fourier Transform Spectroscopy, June 19-23, 1989, Society of Photo-Optical Instrumentation Engineers (SPIE), Bellingham, Washington, Vol. 1145, 1989, pp. 425-426.

7.   D.A. Gatenby and G. Foo, "Design for X: Key to Competitive, Profitable Markets," *AT&T Technical Journal*, Vol. 69, No. 3, May/June 1990, pp. 2-13.

24

REDUCING LIFE-CYCLE ENVIRONMENTAL IMPACTS: AN INDUSTRY SURVEY OF EMERGING TOOLS AND PROGRAMS

Michael S. Sullivan and John R. Ehrenfeld

Corporate environmental practices have been evolving quite rapidly in recent years, as consumers express their preferences for environmentally friendly products and practices, as manufacturers look "upstream" and inquire into their suppliers' environmental practices due to liability and marketing concerns, and as company operating costs increase as a result of new environmental regulations. New corporate efforts are made to anticipate (rather than respond to) outside environmental pressures, to internalize costs, and to find strategic opportunities or competitive advantages based on company or product environmental performance. This article describes a survey and research project designed to explore one aspect of these evolving corporate practices—the use of analytical tools and associated programs, such as life-cycle assessment and design-for-environment—by companies to account for impacts throughout a product's life cycle.

Exhibit 1 shows a schematic diagram of the product life cycle. This figure demonstrates the potential cyclical nature of material flows,

Michael S. Sullivan is a recent graduate of the Technology and Policy Program at the Massachusetts Institute of Technology. He is currently an independent consultant researching recycling and take-back environmental regulations worldwide, as well as "green product" and "design-for-environment" research and development programs conducted by industry, governments, and other researchers. John R. Ehrenfeld is director of M.I.T.'s Technology, Business & Environment Program.

Exhibit 1

Product Life Cycle

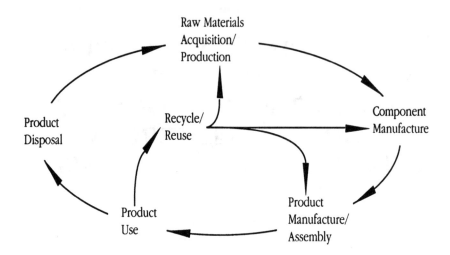

- Impacts from distribution and transportation of materials and products may also be significant and can occur in association with many life-cycle stages (manufacture, use, etc.). These impacts should be considered, even if distribution/transport is not considered a separate stage in the life cycle, as shown here.
- Numerous paths for reuse and recycling exist for different products, components, and materials. Only a few of these potential paths are shown.

and the complexity of trying to trace and calculate those flows objectively. This research project was designed to characterize the nature, extent, and effects of current industry efforts to adopt life-cycle frameworks, including product life-cycle assessment, design for environment, and any similar or related frameworks.

The analytical tools and company programs of interest in this survey reflect *not only increasing environmental concerns but also extended life-cycle concerns,* as they address environmental problems beyond, as well as at, the production facility. Industry has traditionally been concerned with reducing environmental impacts at the production phase of the product life cycle. Although this type of work is necessary, in many cases it may be short-sighted and miss some fundamental, multimedia, geographically dispersed, and/or intertemporal problems and solutions. Product life-cycle assessments and several other frameworks are increasingly mentioned as promising tools for comparing the relative merits of products along environmental dimensions. By taking a systems view of products and their life cycles, these frameworks and programs are designed, among other things, to prevent the transfer of environmental problems from one location to another, from one time period to another, or from one medium to another (e.g., from water to air). Many who have looked at these frameworks expect they will also aid in pollution prevention efforts by encouraging product and process innovation in the private sector.

Because a whole range of analytical tools and programs—including product life-cycle assessments, life-cycle inventories, life-cycle analysis (which appears to be one of the least specific terms in this field), eco-balances (as product life-cycle assessments are commonly known in Europe), and design-for-environment—address life-cycle environmental impacts, we have coined a new term, life-cycle frameworks, to describe the whole set. The term "life-cycle framework" is used broadly to refer to any and all of these tools and programs that provide insights into and to some extent quantify a company's *extended environmental concerns.* Extended environmental concerns are associated with activities beyond as well as at the company's own production facilities, from raw material acquisition, to component production, to recycling or disposition of a product. The term "life-cycle work" is also used in this article to refer to any work or action by companies in which they use, are developing, or are considering the use of life-cycle frameworks. It is essentially shorthand for the longer expression, "company work on or within life-cycle frameworks."

THE SURVEY

In the course of characterizing industry life-cycle efforts, the following questions were addressed:

1. Why are companies interested in and working on life-cycle frameworks, and where do these motivations seem to be leading them?

2. How do life-cycle frameworks serve to guide action?

a. In what specific ways are companies using life-cycle frameworks?

b. What are the constraints or limits on the impact of life-cycle frameworks in some companies?

c. What other practices are missing and must be incorporated in company decision making to achieve pollution prevention through innovation?

3. Which industry efforts to use and develop life-cycle frameworks have been and will continue to be most effective in stimulating product improvements and changing company procedures, while satisfying other corporate constraints?

By answering these questions, the project has identified a set of organizational and management practices and complementary analytical tools that have enabled and will continue to enable companies to make product changes that reduce environmental impacts.

Research Methods

A mail survey was sent to forty-nine individuals at forty-six large industrial companies, each with sales over $1.5 billion a year. All but two of the companies contacted are in the following five industry sectors:

- Chemicals/plastics
- Paper
- Computers
- Other electronics
- Consumer products (personal care or household cleaning products)

The two additional firms produce a broad range of materials and manufactured products, and were not classified by sector. Questionnaires were sent to seven or more companies in each industry sector. As summarized in **Exhibit 2**, responses were received from twenty-eight persons at twenty-six different companies.

To facilitate interpretation of the survey results, the survey respondents have been split into two groups:

- Group I—those companies actively developing or using life-cycle frameworks. Group I companies are also referred to as "active" companies in this analysis.
- Group II—those considering (or who previously considered) use of life-cycle frameworks, or who have no activity with respect to life-cycle frameworks. Group II companies are referred to as "less active" companies.

Exhibit 2

Participation in the Survey

	Plastics and Chemicals	Paper Products	Consumer Products	Computers	Other Electronics	Misc.	Total
Surveys Sent	12	8	8	10	9	2	49
# of Companies Surveyed	12	7	7	10	8	2	46
Total # of Responses	6	3	6	4	7	2	28
Total # of Companies Responding	6	3	5	4	6	2	26

Twenty-two survey respondents indicated their departmental affiliations within these companies, as summarized in **Exhibit 3**.

The profile of respondents in Exhibit 3 raises the issue of respondent bias in the survey, particularly with respect to conclusions about company motivations for doing life-cycle work. The difference between Groups I and II with respect to respondent affiliations (i.e., are they in technology or nontechnology departments) is statistically significant at the $p \leq 0.1$ level using a chi-square significance test. The potential for respondent bias in the survey does not, however, significantly affect conclusions about organizational integration, the use of life-cycle study results, and effects on product and product development. These are relatively objective measures of company activity. Evaluating company motivations and intentions is more subjective, and it should be recognized that the opinions expressed in the survey responses belong to individuals who are most involved in life-cycle work at these companies.

Exhibit 3

Respondent Departmental Affiliations

Functional department	Group I	Group II
Environment (business or corporate)	5	7
Human resources or public affairs	1	1
Regulatory affairs	0	1
Research or technology	4	0
Manufacturing	1	0
Product development	0	1
Quality assurance	0	1

Findings

The remainder of this article provides a summary of our principal findings and conclusions in the following areas:

- Prevalence and nature of life-cycle frameworks in industry
- Managing and using life-cycle work
- Motivations for life-cycle work and its effects on products and companies
- Integration with complementary practices

The data presented below for each topic will in most cases be from fewer than all twenty-six companies, because all companies did not respond to every question in the survey.

PREVALENCE AND NATURE OF LIFE-CYCLE FRAMEWORKS IN INDUSTRY

Responses to the mail survey demonstrate companies are now using, developing, and considering life-cycle frameworks. Twenty-six responses were received from different companies and within this set of companies the levels of activity were

- 23 percent using a life-cycle framework
- 23 percent actively developing a life-cycle framework
- 27 percent considering use of a life-cycle framework
- 23 percent with no activity on life-cycle frameworks
- 4 percent previously considered using them

Duration and Status of Industry Efforts on Life-Cycle Frameworks

As shown in **Exhibit 4**, work on life-cycle frameworks in companies is a relatively recent phenomenon. No company responding to the survey started working on life-cycle frameworks before 1989. Most companies that have started working on life-cycle frameworks at some level in the past three years continue to do so.

Despite the fact that formal work on life-cycle frameworks and methods is such a recent phenomenon, our first finding shows nearly half of the companies who responded to this survey (12 of 26) have

Exhibit 4

Starting Years for Company Work on Life-Cycle Frameworks

Year Work Started	Group I		Group II	
	# of Companies	Status of Work	# of Companies	Status of Work
pre-1989	0	ongoing	0	N/A
1989	3	ongoing	1	discontinued
1990	1	as-needed	1	ongoing
1991	8	ongoing	1	as-needed
1992	0	N/A	1	ongoing

either conducted life-cycle studies or are now actively developing a life-cycle framework.

Future Use of Life-Cycle Frameworks

A majority of companies that are active in using or developing life-cycle frameworks, and many that are considering such use, expect to use those frameworks in the future to evaluate new and existing products. A much smaller number of firms do not expect to use life-cycle frameworks in the future.

Exhibit 5 summarizes the responses about future use of life-cycle

Exhibit 5

Anticipated Future Use of
Life-Cycle Frameworks

	Group I			Group II		
	New Product	Existing Product	Product of Strategic Importance	New Product	Existing Product	Product of Strategic Importance
Sample size	11	11	11	12	8	10
Once, before market introduction	10	N/A	N/A	5	N/A	N/A
Once	N/A	3	2	N/A	0	1
Periodically	1	7	7	2	3	5
Never	0	1	0	3	3	2
Additional Responses Not Included in Survey List but Supplied by Respondents						
Upon customer request	0	0	0	0	1	1
Unknown	0	0	0	1	1	1
Case-by-case determination	1	1	1	0	0	0
Rarely	0	0	0	1	0	0

frameworks for Groups I and II. Respondents were asked when they anticipated a life-cycle framework would be used by their companies in the future for (1) a new product, (2) an existing product, and (3) specific products with strategic importance.

Active Industries

Different industry sectors appear to use and implement life-cycle frameworks in different ways, adopting those frameworks to suit their specific needs. As anticipated, the survey responses of firms producing commodities are different from the responses of firms producing more complex or highly-engineered products.

The consumer products and electronics sectors (including computers) appear to be more active than other sectors (chemicals, paper companies) in using or developing workable life-cycle frameworks. Companies in the electronics and computer sectors are principally researching and developing design-for-environment and recycling frameworks. Consumer products companies (which include those making personal care and home cleaning products) are very active in using product life-cycle assessments. Chemical companies are less active in developing the new life-cycle and design-for-environment frameworks described here, but are active in monitoring life-cycle methodologies and have demonstrated significant life-cycle thinking through the Responsible Care program of the Chemical Manufacturers' Association. Paper companies are also using life-cycle assessments.

Types of Frameworks and Their Components

Frameworks

Ten of twelve Group I companies have developed frameworks for considering the extended environmental impacts of products. The names of the frameworks used or being developed by Group I companies include

- Life-cycle inventory (1 company)
- Design for environment (3 companies)
- Product life-cycle assessment (4 companies)
- Life-cycle analysis (2 companies)
- Product stewardship (1 company)
- [Company] product life-cycle (1 company)
- Environmental quality (1 company)

Some companies use more than one framework, whereas others did not indicate the framework they use by name.

The two most common names for life-cycle frameworks in industry appear to be (1) product life-cycle assessment (and its variants, life-cycle inventory and life-cycle analysis) and (2) design-for-environment. Frameworks focused on environmental quality, product stewardship, and recycling have all been adopted by at least one company in the survey. Exploring the differences among these life-cycle frameworks was not a principal objective of this study. In some cases, the different framework names used by companies may be only differences in terminology, whereas in other cases, the differences in frameworks may be significant.

Common elements

Even though many of the frameworks are used for different purposes, they often include common elements that demonstrate life-cycle thinking and management. These common framework elements were explored in the next three questions from the survey.

Environmental Impacts and Life-Cycle Stages Addressed by Frameworks

The types of environmental impacts and life-cycle stages addressed by company life-cycle work appear to be fairly standard. Air, water, and soil emissions and solid waste generation are addressed by all company life-cycle frameworks from the survey, and natural resource and energy use are addressed by eight of ten frameworks. Habitat alteration is addressed by four of ten frameworks, but biodiversity is rarely addressed. These last two impacts are the most difficult to quantify, and the farthest removed from the company's direct experience.

All major stages of the product life-cycle shown in Exhibit 1, except distribution/transport and raw materials acquisition, are addressed to some degree by all company frameworks. Distribution/transport and raw materials acquisition are not addressed by two of the ten companies. Although the environmental impacts and life-cycle stages addressed by companies are fairly standard, not all impacts and stages are addressed in every study by a particular company. In at least two and probably many more companies, the impacts and stages included in a study change depending on the study objectives.

Impact Assessment Methods

Impact assessments were not standardized across companies as of early 1992. They range from quantitative assessment techniques, like indexing the importance of various impacts, to more subjective techniques, like consensus building and professional judgment. This variety of methods reflects the developmental, nonstandardized status of impact assessment methodologies as of early 1992. Use of life-cycle study results in broad advertising claims or even for internal decision making can be expected to lead to great confusion, unless the impact assessment method is fully explained and understood.

Managing Life-Cycle Work

Companies that have changed products and product development procedures appear to

- Use product design/development departments as a source of information more often than companies that have not changed products and product development procedures ($p \leq 0.01$);
- Use the process design department as a source of information more often than companies that have not changed products and product development procedures ($p \leq 0.1$); and
- Have product design/development participate more often on teams responsible for life-cycle work than do companies that have not changed products and product development procedures ($p \leq 0.05$).

The "p values" shown above indicate that these differences were found to be statistically significant, using a chi-square significance test. Sample sizes were small in this survey, so these differences are somewhat suspect. Nevertheless, the survey responses do indicate that leading companies tend to involve product design/development and process design departments most often to conduct their life-cycle work.

Integration of Existing Departments into Life-Cycle Work

The departments most heavily involved in life-cycle work are marketing, product design and development, research, health, safety, and environment (HS&E), and manufacturing. Strategy, process design, product teams, and purchasing are moderately involved. Finance, accounting, and legal departments are absent or barely represented. These trends are consistent for all three measures of departmental integration—departments that are sources of information, departments receiving information, and departments participating on life-cycle teams.

Product design and development, manufacturing, marketing, strategy, and purchasing departments appear to have been affected by work on life-cycle frameworks to date. There is some evidence that research departments may also have been affected. Technology- and market-oriented departments are most heavily integrated into life-cycle work. These integration trends seem to be strongest for companies that have shown environment-oriented product innovation. Technology- and market-oriented departments central to a company's operations may be important for life-cycle work because they have access to large amounts of technical or market information that they can filter and appropriately translate or interpret for a company.

Communication within firms on life-cycle issues appears to have been quite broad to date, increasing the chances that coordination and personal relationships that cross boundaries are established. This coordination and cross-functional communication may facilitate the development of technically realistic, marketable product innovations, and enhance the success of future multidepartment life-cycle efforts.

External Contacts in Life-Cycle Work

The most common external sources of information for survey respondents are consultants, customers, and suppliers. Consultants are very common sources of information because they may have databases of environmental impacts in many industries or stages in a life-cycle and experience in conducting studies. Suppliers and customers are a company's direct contacts with the market, and to upstream and downstream impacts, so they are also common sources of information for predetermined study parameters.

Regulatory and nonregulatory government agencies were sources of information for only three of the ten most active (Group I) companies in the survey, whereas environmental interest groups were not cited by any companies as a source of information for company life-cycle work. These results seem to indicate that most detailed life-cycle work occurs within and between firms, and not with public agencies or citizen organizations. However, information from the survey and other sources indicates that is an incomplete picture. Group I companies participate in development of life-cycle framework methodologies with other organizations:

- Nine of ten Group I companies do so through industry associations.
- Seven of ten participate in multi-interest forums/workshops

with government and environmental advocacy groups.
- Seven of ten participate in both industry associations and multi-interest forums/workshops.

It appears that companies participate in outside forums not to gather specific environmental impact information, but rather to learn about methodologies and public concerns. All parties would probably agree that the most important, detailed, technical information for specific product life-cycle evaluations currently resides in the private sector, but public opinion and regulatory context provide important signals as well to the firm. For instance, governments have assumed and will continue to assume an increasing role in regulating life-cycle or other environmental marketing claims.

Integration with Other Programs
The survey responses show integration of life-cycle work and other company programs to date has been minimal. **Exhibit 6** summarizes the survey responses to questions about integrating life-cycle and quality programs. Only moderate levels of integration between quality programs and life-cycle frameworks in just a few companies have been achieved, but most respondents believe these efforts should be highly integrated.

Parallels between quality and life-cycle programs (customer focus,

Exhibit 6 ▬▬▬▬▬▬▬▬▬▬▬▬▬▬▬▬▬▬▬▬▬▬▬▬▬▬▬▬

Integration of Quality and Life-Cycle Programs

	Current Integration Status			Future Integration?		
	Highly Integrated (6–7)	Moderately Integrated (3–5)	Not at All or Slightly Integrated (1–2)	Should be Highly Integrated (1–2)	Should be Moderately Integrated (3–5)	Should Not Be Integrated (6–7)
Group I	1	4	7	7	2	2
Group II	0	3	9	9	0	5

need for continuous improvement) and opportunities for cooperative research on market demand and product improvements have been recognized by some companies. In one company, the quality program is viewed as ineffective by the respondent (and perhaps by other company personnel). In such a case, integration may be detrimental to long-term environmental life-cycle improvements. However, in the majority of companies, where quality improvement programs are permanent and moderately or highly successful, integration would probably confer legitimacy to life-cycle efforts.

Economic evaluation systems have been, and continue to be, poorly integrated with life-cycle work; there are only indirect signs of integration in a few survey responses. Development and integration of these programs seems advisable in the long run, however, because economic realities will continue to drive company decision making in many cases.

Uses for Life-Cycle Survey Information and Results

As expected, companies often use life-cycle frameworks to compare products and materials, but two other important uses for life-cycle frameworks in companies appear to be "to stimulate product innovations through alternative design" and "to influence company research priorities." Some companies do use life-cycle studies for marketing purposes ("to provide information useful in marketing," "to determine how to respond to market opportunities," and "to back-up product labeling claims"). However, it appears many other companies that are market- and customer-oriented have refrained from using life-cycle studies for product marketing, or are doing so in a cautious manner. Companies also appear to use life-cycle work to educate themselves about environmental issues.

Obstacles to Conducting Life-Cycle Work

Inadequate information or data is the most common obstacle to conducting life-cycle work, but costs of startup and staff time are also significant obstacles. A lack of support from senior management appears to be a significant obstacle in several firms, and may be related to cost and profitability concerns. The management obstacle to life-cycle work in some companies provides evidence that a power promoter or sponsor for life-cycle work is needed in upper-level management, just as others have found such sponsors essential for other projects.

Support from senior managers for environment-oriented change and life-cycle work appears to be a precursor to significant amounts of that work, but senior management support may also be the deciding factor in determining the effects such work has on products, as routine economic assessment tools are not available at this time. Long-term senior management support itself may depend on the establishment of new systems that can justify management decisions in economic terms.

Just as total quality management (TQM) requires a commitment by senior management to the idea of quality and an understanding of the potential returns from improved quality, proactive environmental management requires a commitment to and an understanding of the potential returns from actually building environment into design and other company operations. The impetus for making such a commitment may come with the realization that product environmental impacts and perceived environmental quality have implications for competitiveness similar to price, durability, and other elements of quality. Some companies, in and outside of the United States, are moving to establish better product performance along environmental dimensions. There may be negative consequences for companies that fall behind on product environmental performance, just as there are consequences when a company falls behind on other quality criteria.

MOTIVATIONS FOR LIFE-CYCLE WORK AND ITS EFFECTS ON PRODUCTS AND COMPANIES

Based on survey data, the primary motivations for life-cycle work in companies appear to be desires to capitalize on strategic opportunities and to provide customer satisfaction through product improvements. At the same time, company responses seem to indicate a motivational difference between Groups I and II. The most active companies (Group I) appear to be motivated primarily by market/strategy considerations. Group II companies appear to be equally motivated by market/strategy and regulatory considerations. Thus, Group I companies appear to have a more positive vision for life-cycle work, as opposed to the more negative vision (avoiding something undesirable, like regulation) of Group II companies.

Effects of Life-Cycle Work

Changes in Product and Product Development Procedures

Five companies indicated that as a result of their life-cycle work, at least one of the following product characteristics changed for one or more products:

- Product packaging (5 companies)
- Product material content (4 companies)
- Physical configuration of the product (3 companies)
- Product labels (1 company)

Though only five companies noted specific product changes, eight of the thirteen Group I companies indicated their product design/development process had been affected by their life-cycle work in one of the following ways:

- Seven indicated the materials selection process had been affected, often through the addition of new criteria for materials selection.
- Four companies indicated additional issues had been added to their design checklists.
- Two companies indicated they had established incentives for designers to minimize extended environmental impacts.

Other Departments Affected by Life-Cycle Work

Four companies indicated that both manufacturing and process design have also been affected by their life-cycle work. These four companies are among the most active in terms of life-cycle work and the development of technical and managerial support systems for that work. They also span the range of industrial sectors covered by this study from complex products to materials manufacturers.

The effects on manufacturing listed by companies were

- Establishment of emission reduction goals
- Establishment of toxic use reduction goals
- Better modeling, system tracking, and information systems
- Increased source reduction work

Product changes that have been documented through the survey are an indirect indication that manufacturing and marketing have been affected by life-cycle work.

Effects on Materials Handling and Recycling

Evidence from conversations with survey respondents indicates some companies are adopting programs, based at least in part on life-cycle frameworks, that will achieve higher rates of recycling for materials or product components as well as improved financial performance for the companies themselves. These efforts may have significant impacts on materials handling and recycling infrastructures, as well as impacts on individual products. Life-cycle assessments and similar analyses are product-oriented, but they also track impacts of products throughout larger systems. Impacts are (perceived to be) problems, and problem alleviation can come from (1) product change or (2) system change. The former is really only a subset of the latter. Life-cycle analysis or other life-cycle frameworks tend to focus attention on product change solutions, but they can also facilitate and focus efforts on infrastructure or system change strategies. Recycling infrastructures are of interest for many products, and are demonstrated by specific examples noted in company interviews from this study:

- One electronics firm has started investigating refurbishment/recycling of parts and has reported increased asset utilization rates for the company.
- Another electronics firm has reported cost savings and/or increased profits in its service operations as a result of pilot take-back programs for its products.

By conducting systemic product evaluations with a life-cycle framework, relevant infrastructures and recycling opportunities such as these may be identified.

INTEGRATION WITH COMPLEMENTARY PRACTICES

Because life-cycle frameworks explicitly outline the connections of a company to outsiders, particularly to its customers, externally-oriented departments, such as marketing, might be expected to become involved in life-cycle work.

Environmental Marketing

Consumer surveys indicate increasing demands for "green" products and green behavior.[1] Our survey shows that marketing is heavily involved in life-cycle work in active companies in at least two areas: (1) as life-cycle team participants, and (2) as sources and recipients of life-cycle study results. In addition, the survey provides some evidence that two parts of a product strongly associated with marketing practices, namely packaging and labeling, have changed as a result of life-cycle work. Packaging and/or labeling changes were identified through the survey in five active (Group I) companies.

The fact that marketing has been affected by life-cycle work in some companies is an important development. Because labeling and packaging design are often driven by marketing considerations, change in these areas probably indicates that marketing has been, at least, flexible and willing to accommodate life-cycle thinking and environment-oriented change, and perhaps is interested in and supportive of such change. Even though marketing seems to be involved in life-cycle work, the links between marketing and life-cycle work may need to be strengthened, as the survey indicates many companies do not yet use information from life-cycle studies for marketing purposes. Although marketing claims of "environmental friendliness" or "life-cycle soundness" are not justifiable at this time, many useful marketing ideas may be identified through a life-cycle system. In many cases, marketing efforts that outline specific favorable features of the product seem to be practical and advisable, given the number of firms with competitive/marketing orientations and the need to make a return on investments in environmental performance. To foster innovation, life-cycle work should be integrated with marketing practices like market research.

Market Research

To justify many product changes in a company, it will not be enough to conduct an environmental life-cycle assessment, particularly when cost is a concern. Life-cycle assessment will have to be supplemented with other existing practices, including market research. Market researchers, in turn, can probably use the information and insights from a life-cycle study to ask customers more informed questions about environmental impacts and product performance.

Without market research, the potential payoffs to a firm from product environmental change may not be realized, because firms will not know which environmental issues customers find most important and for which they are willing to pay more money. One total quality management and market research technique, Quality Function Deployment, seems particularly well-suited to integration with life-cycle frameworks because it identifies specific characteristics of a product that the firm can change to satisfy customers and to enhance the firm's competitiveness.[2] In many cases, companies simply would like to be able to sell more products based on their environmentally-friendly attributes. Companies and marketing departments may be able to identify, through a life-cycle framework, what some of those positive characteristics are.

Economic Evaluation of Investments and Products

Routine economic evaluation of product changes and investments in new environmentally friendly products appears to be very rare, and an area that needs much more development. Company economic evaluations of environmental projects have historically been limited to *process* modifications. Examples of economic evaluations for environment-oriented *product* changes have not been found in the literature. This begs the question of how nonenvironmental product innovations are normally assessed. Logically, one would expect to compare all the costs of designing and producing an improved product against sales projections for the product before and after a specific change is made. In this manner, one could determine whether the change would be sufficiently profitable before proceeding. However, in practice, traditional cost accounting has not allocated costs and benefits of redesign or even original product development to products in this manner.

In the case of environment-oriented product change suggested by life-cycle studies, the data on departmental involvement appear to indicate that accounting and financial evaluations are divorced from decision making about product innovation because accounting and finance departments are uninvolved in and uninformed about life-cycle studies. There is also no evidence that others have taken up these functions as part of life-cycle work. Furthermore, the value of environmental innovation and life-cycle work itself is not generally accepted, and there is only a short (but growing) list of success stories in which product environmental investments have improved financial performance. Two firms we spoke with said that they have realized financial benefits from their life-cycle work, but we did not try to systematically identify such cases. Financial success stories from investments in process environmental improvements are much more common. Financial successes from product environmental innovation need to be documented if this type of innovation and life-cycle work are to expand. Full costs and benefits that accrue to the firm need to be assigned to products, not just to industrial processes, through accounting and financial systems. Based on the survey responses and our conversations with industry, life-cycle work and economic evaluations seem divorced from one another. They should be increasingly integrated.

Environmental Strategies

The survey has provided data showing that at least a few firms have developed product and environmental strategies based in part on life-cycle frameworks. These firms appear to

- Have a strong desire and willingness to compete based on product environmental performance;
- Be changing products for environmental reasons;
- Be developing procedures to ensure that future products have less environmental impact; and
- Be integrating environmental life-cycle work into quality programs that confer legitimacy on that work and perhaps facilitate product change along environmental dimensions.

These firms also appear be at the leading edge of a new era of environmental competition and product improvement. If such an era takes hold, as many people believe it will, given increasing market and regulatory demands on companies, firms that have adopted such strategies early are likely to benefit.

SUMMARY

Survey responses demonstrate that companies are now using, developing, or considering use of life-cycle frameworks. The consumer products (personal care and household cleaning products in particular) and electronics sectors seem most active in developing workable frameworks, but many industrial sectors, including paper and chemicals, are using them and/or monitoring their development. These life-cycle frameworks, which account for the environmental impacts of a product from raw materials or component production through recycling or disposal, have only been recently used or developed by many companies. Most recent users continue to work on the frameworks and expect to use them in the future to evaluate new and existing products.

The two most common life-cycle frameworks appear to be product life-cycle assessment (and its variants) and design-for-environment. Although the life-cycle stages and impacts addressed by these frameworks are fairly standard, impact assessment methodologies are in a developmental, nonstandardized state.

Product design and development and other technical departments are highly involved in life-cycle work. Product design and development procedures have been significantly affected by that life-cycle work. To a lesser extent, manufacturing and research departments appear to have been affected. Marketing and HS&E departments are also heavily involved in life-cycle work, but finance, accounting, and legal departments are absent from life-cycle work in almost all firms. Strategy and purchasing departments are involved in life-cycle work in fewer companies. Only moderate levels of integration between life-cycle work and quality programs have been achieved in a few companies, but most survey respondents believe they should be integrated. Very low levels of integration were found in this study between product change efforts based on life-cycle work and financial or accounting practices.

The primary company motivations for life-cycle work appear to be desires to capitalize on strategic and market opportunities and to gather information on customer environmental concerns. Regulatory concerns do not appear to be driving the most active companies as much as strategic and competitive concerns.

Product changes and departmental procedure changes show that future product innovations and reduced environmental impacts can be anticipated as product designers focus on an additional set of issues. Although learning and integration are occurring in technical areas of companies, the absence of finance and accounting departments and new methods or tools for economic evaluation of product changes are identified as shortcomings in industry practice. In addition, the survey has apparently identified a reluctance on the part of companies to compete or market their products based on environmental performance.

Current practice may change as additional companies eventually adopt more comprehensive and environmentally driven strategies based to a large degree on life-cycle concerns. Only two firms from the survey appear to have comprehensive strategies informed by life-cycle frameworks, but the intentions and actions of survey respondents seem to point them toward greater levels of program, department, and strategy integration with life-cycle work. Integration of technical, marketing, and economic assessments (and corresponding departments) into a comprehensive program may ensure that product innovations will benefit both the firm and the environment.

Notes

1. See, for example, a recent survey of public attitudes toward the environment conducted by the Roper Organization: "The Environment: Public Attitudes And Individual Behavior," The Roper Organization Inc., July 1990.

2. John R. Hauser and Don Clausing, "The House of Quality," *Harvard Business Review* 66 (May-June 1988), 63-73.

25

TOTAL QUALITY PRODUCT DESIGN— HOW TO INTEGRATE ENVIRONMENTAL CRITERIA INTO THE PRODUCT REALIZATION PROCESS

Brian T. Oakley

Recent case studies on the financial benefits of pollution prevention programs well attest to the notion that a commitment to the environment can help profitability not only by avoiding costs and potential liabilities, but also by generating environmentally-based opportunities for competitive advantage. Achieving these benefits, however, represents a complex management challenge that requires embedding environmental concerns in the day-to-day decisions and actions of a company's employees. This article shows how the marriage of corporate environmental stewardship and TQM, better known as TQEM, is particularly well suited to the area of product design, and why environmental health and safety experts can improve a product's environmental performance.

A total quality approach requires that companies look beyond the environmental impacts of their production processes and address the environmental consequences associated with the

Brian T. Oakley *is a senior consultant with Ernst & Young's National Environmental Consulting Practice, located in Washington, DC.*

consumption and retirement of the products they produce. But changing the attributes of existing products introduces a number of complexities into the manufacturing process and often proves costly. The only practical alternative is to design environmental compatibility into the product. A number of companies, including AT&T, General Electric, IBM, Procter & Gamble, Whirlpool, and Xerox, are finding that designing "greenness" into a product offers unique opportunities for improving their performance in environmental management as well as in the marketplace. BMW and Volkswagen are environmental pioneers in the auto industry (see **Appendix**).

DESIGN FOR THE ENVIRONMENT

Product design is the single most important aspect of the product realization process, dictating (among other things) manufacturing cost, product quality, and environmental compatibility. Yet, until recently, its role in determining the competitive position of a product has been undervalued, and its importance in effecting environmental improvements has been all but ignored. Design improvements can enhance all aspects of product performance, because a product's design has a "ripple effect" that affects every function of a company. For example, although the design phase of the product realization process accounts for only 5 percent of the product's cost, between 70 percent and 80 percent of the product's life-cycle cost (materials, manufacturing, distribution, servicing) is in fact determined by its design. Moreover, product design drives product quality. Genichi Taguchi, the design engineer well known for the success of his "Taguchi Methods" in quality improvement, maintains that effective design is essential for producing high-quality products. If the design is poor, he maintains, there is little point in trying to produce a high-quality product from it.[1] In the same way, a green product cannot be produced if environmental considerations were neglected during the design phase.

Green Engineering

Increasingly, design engineers are promoting the concept of *green engineering*. More commonly called Design for the Environment (DFE), this discipline maintains that not only recyclability, but also overall greenness, can be designed into the product without compromising the product's function or integrity.[2] Thus, a green product can be both environmentally compatible and commercially viable.

Consider, for example, laundry detergent. In the 1970s, this product came under heavy scrutiny for its role in the eutrophication of lakes and rivers. In response, manufacturers reformulated detergents to contain less phosphorus. More recently, Procter & Gamble (P&G) reformulated its detergents into more concentrated powders and packaged them in small recycled paperboard boxes. Since P&G first introduced this change in 1990, the new formulation and its characteristic small box have become the industry standard. Consumers get the same product with less waste, and retailers are able to stock the same inventory of detergent using less shelf space. This example of DFE in practice shows how a change in a product's design can bring environmental improvements, while maintaining (and in some cases enhancing) the commercial viability of the product.

A Life-Cycle Approach

DFE is an umbrella term, encompassing a number of environmentally-based design initiatives. All of these strategies strive to design environmental improvements into each stage of the product's life cycle. It is important to note that the environmental impacts occurring in each life-cycle stage should not be considered in isolation. Focusing solely on one stage threatens the product's environmental compatibility because benefits achieved in one life-cycle stage may come with the price of greater environmental costs at another stage. Focusing on the total life cycle will not alleviate the need for making tradeoffs in environmental benefits, but it will ensure a net reduction in a product's environmental impacts over the product life cycle.

As indicated by **Exhibit 1**, four stages are associated with a product and its packaging. By systematically considering each of the following stages in the design process, environmental compatibility can be designed into the product and its packaging.

Exhibit 1

The Product Life Cycle

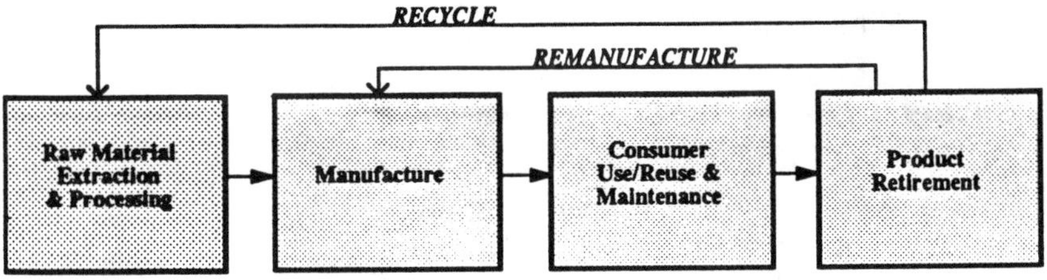

Raw Material Extraction and Processing

The environmental impacts of extracting and processing raw materials needed for the product should be considered during this stage. Simply using renewable resources or substituting recycled materials in the product for virgin material can measurably decrease the environmental cost of this stage. Consider, for example, the use of recycled aluminum. One pound of recycled aluminum saves up to four pounds of bauxite and 95 percent of the energy used in making one ton of virgin aluminum, while producing 95 percent less air pollution and 97 percent less water pollution during the process. The main challenge of this stage is to identify and specify material that can minimize environmental costs, while satisfying the product's performance and cost requirements.

Manufacture

In recent years much attention has been focused on minimizing the environmental costs associated with the manufacturing process. Although most of this attention has been concentrated on end-of-pipe controls, such as electrostatic precipitators or industrial wastewater treatment facilities, waste-minimizing manufacturing techniques have also received considerable attention recently as a method for reducing the generation of pollutants at their source. Product design initiatives offer a sophisticated approach to waste minimization. By considering the manufacturing process during the design stage, processes and materials that may be harmful to the environment can be avoided. Selected examples of this approach include the commitment to

- Design products for easy assembling to help reduce defects and rework;
- Use "molded-in" finishes on plastic surfaces to avoid the environmental effects of paint operations; or
- Specify materials that are compatible with more environmentally benign cleaners, such as water-based solvents or d-limonene.

Consumer Use/Reuse & Maintenance

Because of the magnitude of the environmental costs associated with product consumption, much attention, particularly in the regulatory environment, has been focused on this stage. Over the past twenty years, for example, automobile manufacturers have been challenged by federally mandated fuel efficiency and exhaust emissions standards.

In addition, EPA's Green Lights program has recently been working with manufacturers to develop highly energy-efficient computers and refrigerators. These design-based initiatives reduce the environmental impacts associated with a product during its use.

Product Retirement

Until recently, both product design literature and the environmental movement have focused little attention on this stage of the product life cycle. But with waste disposal problems generating pressure for waste reduction through reuse and recycling, as well as safe waste disposal through toxics-use reduction, companies are being encouraged to design their products with this stage in mind. Moreover, modern products are now composed of a variety of materials, some of them recyclable and some not. Consequently, it is essential that components be separated by material type. This is economically unfeasible, however, unless the design addresses this stage of the product life cycle. Designing for product retirement involves the consideration of the following three criteria:

- *Design for Recyclability (DFR):* DFR focuses on reducing the product's impact on the environment when it reaches the end of its useful life. DFR involves two approaches. First, an attempt is made to facilitate more complete separation of product components, so that the recovered components are purer and therefore more valuable. The second approach to DFR involves making separation easier and therefore cheaper. This is sometimes referred to as Design for Disassembly (DFD). This method builds on the first set of DFR techniques by arranging product components to foster quick and easy removal.

- *Design for Remanufacture:* Parts in a product usually wear out at different rates, making some discarded products very valuable for remanufacture. Designing for remanufacture involves the same techniques as design for recycling. Historically, remanufacturing has been viewed as applicable for products that have mature designs (i.e., they are unlikely to change significantly). However, products often have certain components that experience rapid design change, whereas other components change very little over time. Thus, the challenge for designers is to create products that lend themselves to design upgrades and remanufacturing.

- *Design for Disposal:* Although it may seem strange to consider at the outset how a product is to be disposed of after it has reached the end of its useful life, it is an important issue to consider in the design process. After all, a product containing hazardous materials could create serious environmental problems if it is improperly disposed of. Thus, design considerations for this stage should focus on ways to ensure that the product can be disposed of safely. If, for example, the product has to be constructed of nonrecyclable thermoset plastic, it should be compatible with incineration and other disposal practices.

Measuring Improvement: Life-Cycle Analysis

Balancing the numerous and often competing product requirements is a fundamental challenge of product design. DFE often requires making tradeoffs between various environmental improvements over the product life cycle. Thus, measuring the effect of design changes on environmental compatibility represents an important component of the DFE process. Life-cycle analysis, although much maligned because of its abuse in marketing efforts, provides an excellent framework in which environmental tradeoffs can be considered.

Life-cycle analysis is an objective analytical tool with which companies can quantify the environmental impacts of their products at each life-cycle stage. Few standards, however, exist for comparing the environmental risks and impacts created in the manufacture of different products, and data requirements for accurate measuring can be overwhelming. These concerns notwithstanding, life-cycle analysis can provide valuable feedback if the following data can be determined. First, an inventory of the product's resource inputs and waste outputs in each life-cycle stage is required; and second, weights need to be established to reflect the relative environmental harm posed by the quantities determined in the inventory. Based on these data, a model can be developed for analyzing different design scenarios. Life-cycle analysis then can help product planners measure the effects of trading off one environmental improvement for another.

DFE AND THE PRODUCT REALIZATION PROCESS

Despite the potential benefits of DFE, it would be naive to suggest that these techniques can be easily applied under traditional design procedures and systems. Like other design initiatives, DFE principles have to be integrated into every facet of the design process. Unfortunately, traditional approaches to product design tend to restrict themselves solely to economic and performance requirements. Moreover, the traditional design systems employed by U.S. companies provide neither the incentives nor the organizational structure to support progressive techniques like DFE. There is ample evidence, however, that a new product design paradigm is emerging that stresses above all else the need to incorporate "downstream" product requirements.

Traditional Approach: Linear Design Systems

U.S. companies tend to use a linear approach to new product development. Linear design systems incorporate the major functions of the product realization process in a sequential fashion.[3] A product concept passes through research, development, design, manufacturing, marketing, sales, and service in discrete stages, affording little overlap between each function. For example, when the design process has been completed, the design gets passed or "tossed over the wall" to the manufacturing engineers, who then determine the processes needed for assembling the product (see **Exhibit 2**). Because there is little interaction between design and manufacturing, a product's compatibility with existing production processes is often not considered in the design phase.[4] In addition, each area usually operates under a separate budget, so requests for design changes that may help downstream activities like manufacturing may be neglected because of resource constraints.[5] This lack of integration often generates friction between functional areas. Also, prevailing corporate structures, reward

Exhibit 2

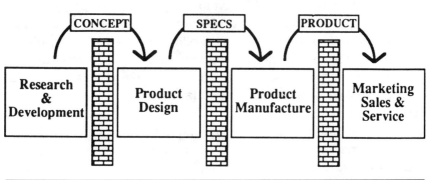

**The Product Development Process
Linear Design System**

systems, and cultures have institutionalized the traditional approach, making the transition to new design systems difficult and slow.

The competitive environment has changed, however, and many U.S. companies have lost market share, because their foreign competitors have proved themselves able to bring high-quality products to market more rapidly than they can. And in spite of this lackluster performance, recent studies indicate that many companies have yet to recognize that their product realization systems have become outdated.[6]

Design for 'X'

Although advanced design techniques like DFE have yet to be widely adopted, anecdotal accounts of their benefits abound, and companies are slowly recognizing that market responsiveness and manufacturing flexibility require improvements to their product realization systems. Given the growing recognition of the impact of design decisions on a product's cost, quality, and overall performance, engineers are beginning to embrace the notion of designing for the product life cycle as a source of competitive advantage. Often dubbed "concurrent design" because it embodies simultaneous product and process design, this approach emphasizes that downstream product criteria should be integrated into the design process (see **Exhibit 3**). Perhaps the most important component of this new design paradigm is that all people involved in the product realization process work together as an integrated team. Unlike the traditional linear approach, this design process seeks to facilitate input from numerous functional areas across the company.

Downstream product criteria can include virtually anything that the product's design can influence. Much of the current design literature focuses on designing products that are easy to manufacture, assemble, and maintain. But these criteria work hand-in-hand and often overlap with DFE and a variety of other downstream considerations. Consequently, researchers at AT&T developed the term Design for "X," or DFX. "X" represents a number of downstream product criteria. These subsets of DFX include manufacturability, ease of assembly, installability, reliability, serviceability, and responsiveness to environmental, health, and safety considerations. Under linear design systems, downstream considerations tended to get neglected in the design process, resulting in products that were difficult to manufacture, install, service, and maintain. Moreover, the incorporation of environmental, health, and safety regulations required costly redesigns that further delayed the product realization process.[7]

Exhibit 3

The Product Development Process
Incorporating "Downstream" Criteria

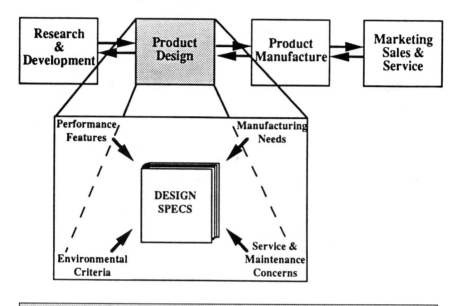

DFX can help integrate and optimize the product realization process. Under DFX, all personnel involved in a new product's development are part of a multifunctional, integrated team. As a result, they provide input up front—before the design has been finalized. For example, manufacturing engineers work with design engineers and suggest ways to make the product easier to assemble. In the same way, environmental, health, and safety experts make suggestions for improving the product's environmental performance. Under a DFX approach, important product factors like quality, life-cycle cost, and environmental compatibility can be designed into the product. Moreover, the successful employment of DFX techniques can help compress the product delivery process into a shorter period, as it reduces the number of design iterations.

By any account, better quality, reduced cost, and quicker time to market are essential ingredients for enhanced competitiveness. Yet few companies have fully adopted progressive design techniques such as DFX. Revamping traditional design systems requires significant change throughout an organization; simply communicating the new ideas is not enough. Personnel at all levels need to be made to understand the new concepts and their importance in successful products. This requires education and training as well as changes to the corporate organizational structure and reward systems.[8] Given that it has taken pioneering companies five to eight years to change over their practices, the adoption of advanced design techniques like DFX clearly requires a fundamental shift in corporate strategy.[9] The experience of the Xerox Corporation illustrates just how far-reaching a change is required.

XEROX CORPORATION'S ASSET MANAGEMENT PROGRAM

In the 1980s, the Xerox Corporation commenced its Leadership Through Quality (LTQ) program in an effort to regain its strength in the copier market. Two products of this initiative were a standardized product realization process that employed advanced design techniques and a new corporate culture that focused on the single objective of "meeting customer requirements." The combination of these changes has made incorporating environmental criteria into the design process an achievable task for Xerox. For both environmental and competitive reasons, Xerox launched the Asset Management Program as part of its environmental leadership initiative. The purpose of this program was to design all elements of environmental quality into Xerox products. Ideally, future product designs would reflect a total life-cycle strategy for the product, including not only form, fit, and function but also disassembly, remanufacturing, and final disposition.[10] Thus, the Asset Management Program required that the environmental implications posed by each stage of the product life cycle be addressed during the design process. Xerox's current effort to redesign copy cartridges for lower environmental costs provides a good illustration of the challenges and opportunities presented by the Asset Management Program.

Customer Replaceable Units

When first developed, customer replaceable units (CRUs), perhaps more widely known as copy cartridges, represented a significant innovation in the design of copiers. Basically, the CRU contains a photoreceptor that is similar in function to film in a camera and toner (dry ink). Both toner and photoreceptors are consumables. By combining these two consumables into an easy-to-install cartridge, manufacturers were able to reduce the number of customer visits required for servicing machines. Not only did this minimize copier downtime, but it also reduced the costs associated with machine maintenance.

Unfortunately, the disposable nature of CRUs has presented

manufacturers with a number of challenges over the years. The development of the CRU consolidated a number of key functions of the copying process into one unit, and as a result, its life cycle is dictated by the part or supply item with the shortest life span. In most cases, the toner runs out before any other parts fail. In fact, the photoreceptor can last up to three times as long as the toner supply. But without toner, the unit cannot function, making it something the customer has to throw away. Some CRUs have even been equipped with a "kill switch" that shuts down the unit after a specified number of copies. Although this ensures that copy quality is never hindered because of CRU failure, it has the effect of forcing customers to throw away a fully functional unit. The copy cartridge recharger industry emerged to offer customers a money-saving alternative to disposal. Soon after the introduction of the CRU, "rechargers" recognized that only toner was needed to make the cartridge fully functional. As a result, rechargers offered refurbished cartridges for prices significantly lower than those the manufacturers were charging for new cartridges.

For Xerox, revenues from consumables like CRUs contribute to a large portion of the company's profits. Like other manufacturers, Xerox has defended its market share from the recharging industry by designing cartridges to make nondestructive separation virtually impossible. In recent years, however, concerns over the designed-in disposability of CRUs have been raised by customers. After all, sending cartridges to rechargers reduces the environmental costs associated with copying, and it is cheaper for customers too. In response, as part of its Asset Management Program, Xerox is now identifying and implementing design enhancements that reduce the disposal problem created by CRUs.

Integrating environmental objectives into CRU production should be a manageable task, because the design and manufacture of CRUs at Xerox has already been influenced heavily by the LTQ program. Most recently, a cross-functional team approach was used to develop a new CRU for the company's 5018 and 5028 copiers. The team, consisting of design engineers, manufacturing engineers, and even assembly line workers, successfully delivered the product to market in less than a year.

Because CRUs are a high-volume product, the team concentrated on making the CRU easy to manufacture. The use of snap fits was maximized, and the use of components that would inhibit the assembly process, such as adhesives, tapes, springs, and foam gaskets, was minimized. In addition, quality was ensured by "designing out" opportunities for failure. For example, the design of some parts guaranteed that they could not be put together backward in the assembly process. Thus, the team approach used in the CRU design process effectively integrated the downstream requirements of assembly and product quality.[11]

Given the historical success achieved in using advanced design techniques in the development of the CRU, integrating environmental product criteria should smoothly dovetail with current practices. The specific environmental principles guiding CRU redesign include designing the unit and its packaging to minimize waste and maximize the reuse of parts and the recycling of materials. Toward this end, CRUs will be designed to be both refurbishable and recyclable. For example, the unit will be designed for easy tear-down and cleaning, and materials selected will be resistant to potential damage caused in the cleaning process. In addition, these materials will be recyclable, and inseparable assemblies will not be constructed of dissimilar materials.

Xerox has already implemented some of its CRU design improvements and is currently enrolling customers in a CRU return program. Customers that enroll in the program receive a discount on new CRUs with the understanding that used units will be returned to Xerox. Although units are not yet being remanufactured, collection from participating customers has already begun. In time, Xerox will refurbish returned units a specified number of times, based on the life of the photoreceptor. At the end of the useful life of the unit, it will be disassembled and the materials will be recycled.

The same approach used to redesign CRUs is also being applied to all Xerox products. Even though these initiatives represent a huge investment for Xerox, the potential payoff is dramatic. James MacKenzie, director of corporate environmental, health, and safety, estimates that the annual value of what was once considered Xerox waste could reach more than $250 million.

SUMMARY

Improving the environmental performance of a product or portfolio of products requires a holistic approach that recognizes the relationship between a product's design and its environmental cost. Spending money on greening a product after it has been designed is often too costly to be worthwhile. By designing environmental compatibility into a product, a corporation can create benefits for the environment without sacrificing competitiveness. But DFE cannot be viewed in isolation. It is part of a systematic approach to product design that puts heavy emphasis on downstream product criteria. Advanced design techniques like DFE are difficult to implement, requiring significant management resources and commitment. Companies that can successfully incorporate new design strategies like DFE into their organizations will be better prepared to meet the future challenges posed by the environment. These companies will also be best positioned to benefit from the competitive opportunities afforded by the environmental movement.

APPENDIX

Environmental Considerations in Automobile Design

The evolution of automobile design over the past twenty years illustrates how design changes in one life-cycle stage can generate environmental cost in another stage. Yet the fact remains that environmental design criteria have influenced few industries as much as the car industry. After all, it was the tough standards of the 1970 Clean Air Act that provided the Honda Motor Company with an opportunity to establish itself in the U.S. automobile market.

Having developed its compound vortex controlled combustion (CVCC) engine in the mid-1960s, Honda was well positioned to take advantage of the demand for clean-burning engines. By combining the CVCC engine with a small and lightweight chassis, Honda engineers designed the highly fuel-efficient Honda Civic that met tough emissions standards without a catalytic converter. The successful Civic set the design standard for front-wheel-drive small cars, and launched Honda on its way to becoming number three in U.S. car sales in just twenty-one years.

Unfortunately, the focus of carmakers on reducing the tailpipe emissions and fuel consumption came at the expense of other environmental design criteria like recyclability. Although the car is arguably one of the most recycled products manufactured today, the increased use of plastics and composite materials in automobile manufacture is threatening to make junked cars a serious waste problem. At the same time, however, plastics are energy conscious both in their manufacture and in their reduction of vehicle weight, making them a good substitute in applications previously reserved for steel. During the 1980s, in their attempt to improve fuel economy, automakers doubled the amount of plastic used in automobiles. Today, plastics constitute 10 percent to 12 percent of the weight of a typical automobile, and experts maintain that this percentage could double again during the 1990s. Based on these projections, it may soon be uneconomical for scrap metal operators to recycle cars.

Despite the increased use of plastics, automobiles still represent a rich source of secondary materials, consuming roughly two-thirds of the iron, half of the rubber, and one-fifth of the aluminum produced in the United States each year. Thus, rather than being a potential waste problem, retired automobiles should still represent a significant resource for secondary material applications. Although the use of plastics has increased, this should not preclude automobile recycling. It is technically feasible to recycle most of the plastics used in cars. The problem resides in the fact that during the design process, little thought is given to the post-consumption phases of the vehicle's life cycle. For example, up to twenty different types of plastics are used in a vehicle's construction. Because it is nearly impossible to identify and separate efficiently the 250 pounds of plastic found in a retired car, this material loses its value as scrap, becoming waste and therefore adding to the cost of recovering other materials like steel and aluminum.

Further exacerbating this problem are the recent efforts to make cars safer through the installation of driver-side and passenger-side air bags. This significant advance in driver safety appears to be coming at the expense of scrap processors. The powering agent of the air bag is sodium azide, a hazardous material and an effective explosive. Because no standards exist for the design removal of air bag systems, the scrap industry has become very concerned over the possible environmental and safety threats posed by undetonated sodium azide canisters in retired automobiles. In a car shredder, the canister could explode or begin to leak. The potential liabilities of either scenario threaten to make automobile scrap recovery an increasingly risky venture.

Given the diminishing profitability and higher risk associated with recycling automobiles, it is clear that the nine million automobiles scrapped in the United States each year may present a serious waste disposal problem in the near future. This is also true in some European countries, where strict inspection laws lead to earlier car retirement rates than in the United States. In anticipation of future regulation, some manufacturers have taken steps to make their cars more recyclable. German carmakers, for example, have developed a "recycling concept" that is now in the implementation stage. The first component of this initiative incorporates DFR techniques. For example, both BMW and Volkswagen have instituted plastic coding programs and have mandated that parts and components be easy to disassemble or be made of similar material when inseparable. The second component of the program involves developing recycling techniques and infrastructure. BMW and VW have set up pilot recycling plants, where research is conducted on the dismantling and recovering of materials from junked cars. This process helps engineers determine the optimal disassembly process and identify design alternatives that will improve recyclability. Volkswagen recently announced that it will deploy a network of as many as forty recycling facilities in Germany over the next decade. The plants will be designed to disassemble re-tired VW Golfs and to recover steel, aluminum, glass, foams, and plastics.

In all likelihood, the German initiatives will generate significant improvements in the recyclability of automobiles. By taking responsibility for their retired cars, these companies will internalize the waste disposal costs of their products. As a result, they will face compelling incentives to design cars that lend themselves to efficient and profitable recycling.

Notes

1.   Charles Overby, "Design for the Entire Life Cycle: A New Paradigm?," ASEE Annual Conference Proceedings, 1990, p. 554.

2.   D. Navinchandra, "Design for Environmentability," *Conference Proceedings: American Society of Mechanical Engineers*, 1991, p. 1.

3.   Hirotaka Takeuchi and Ikujiro Nanaka, "The New New Product Development Game," *Harvard Business Review*, Jan.-Feb. 1986, p. 137.

4.   David A. Gatenby and George Foo, "Design for X: Key to Competitive Profitable Markets," *AT&T Technical Journal*, May/June 1990, p. 5.

5.   Seldon W. McKnight and Jerry M. Jackson, "Simultaneous Engineering Saves Manufacturers Lead Time, Costs and Frustration," *IE*, Aug. 1989, p. 26.

6.   Committee on Engineering Design Theory and Methodology, et al., "Improving Engineering Design: Designing for Competitive Advantage." Washington, DC: National Academy Press, 1990, p. 10.

7.   Gatenby and Foo (cited in note 4), p. 3.

8.   Id., p. 8.

9.   "Designing for Competitive Advantage" (cited in note 6), p. 10.

10. James C. MacKenzie, "Environmental Leadership Through Quality," unpublished paper, Xerox Corporation, 1991, p. 44.

11. John M. Martin, "A Team Approach to Success," *Manufacturing Engineering*, Aug. 1989, p. 77.

26

CUSTOMER-DRIVEN ENVIRONMENTAL MANAGEMENT INFORMATION SYSTEMS

Chris FitzGerald

The most successful corporate environmental programs regard environmental compliance as an opportunity to improve productivity and profits and seek to integrate environmental management information systems (EMIS) into line information functions. Integrated EMIS should provide timely, accurate data to support all three types of environmental management responsibilities: results and comparison reports for source management; material and waste transaction and emission reports for materials management; and compliance, summary, exception, and trend data for risk managers at every level.

Most large American companies now recognize the need to provide information management tools to support their environmental management goals and are undertaking efforts to provide them. The information environment for the environmental professional has expanded exponentially in the past two decades due to the proliferation of regulations and rules and to a shift in emphasis from single-pollutant monitoring to across-the-board materials and emissions management. It is no longer feasible for an environmental manager to track all his or her shifting responsibilities manually, much less meet reporting and management requirements. Managers need access to automation tools and, more importantly, to

Chris FitzGerald *is the editor-in-chief of the quarterly journal,* Total Quality Environmental Management, *and president of Environmental Management Information Systems in Oakland, California.*

existing company and contractor data resources that already store needed information.

Businesses have committed hundreds of millions of dollars to develop and provide environmental information through a combination of internal and contractor products and services. But often these efforts are undermined by the status of environmental compliance in the company as an external process, that is, add-on tasks not related to the company's productive goals.

The most successful corporate environmental programs regard environmental compliance as an opportunity to improve productivity and profits and seek to integrate environmental management information systems (EMIS) into line information functions. To do this, information providers must look beyond the regulators to identify their other "customers" for environmental data.

Motorola, a 1988 winner of the Malcolm Baldrige Award, is currently implementing an environmental information system as a tool in its overall Six Sigma quality systems. "The Environmental Management Information System at Motorola will provide a mechanism for measuring our environmental performance," says Tom Ott, manager of the project. "Continuous improvement in our environmental activities begins by developing an associated sigma metric for the environmental process. Metrics can target emissions, waste reduction, or even recycling efforts. The role of information systems is to support performance metrics as data gathering tools or reporting mechanisms."

ENVIRONMENTAL INFORMATION SERVICES AND CUSTOMERS

Rethinking the role of environmental information is an essential step for companies seeking to integrate environmental practices into overall quality practices. The evolution of environmental management systems has resulted in the required regulatory report being regarded as the ultimate product of the information system. This approach results in special task project efforts to produce monthly (DMR) or annual (Tier I/II) reports.

In a quality context, these reports measure the admitted levels against regulatory standards to show a process in or out of control. Their parallel in auto manufacturing is the postproduction inspections that report defects per unit as a measure of "quality."

"While timely and accurate production of required regulatory reports is essential, companies who have adopted total quality management (TQM) recognize that the report is the product, not the process," says Doug Matkins of the Clorox Company. "TQM attempts to improve the overall process, which will inevitably produce a better product, in this case taking us beyond mere regulatory compliance."

At the Clorox Company, there are three "absolute" Quality Leadership principles:

1. Meet the customer's requirements;
2. Strive to do error-free work; and
3. Manage by prevention.

After thirteen years as a quality improvement specialist, Matkins is now bringing Clorox's Quality Leadership principles to company environmental practices. "Quality Leadership attempts to break out of the mold that quality is solely a product attribute," he says. "Our goal is to have our employees deliver error-free products and services internally and externally. This standard of excellence will exceed external standards set by the regulators."

In this context the regulatory report is just one after-process indicator and does little to support continuous improvement toward pollution prevention. Environmental quality is the ultimate product; environmental data is an intermediate product or tool to achieve it.

Application guidelines for the Baldrige Awards offer some criteria that can help guide design of corporate environmental information tools. Four of the criteria cite information management requirements for award applicants:

- The use of data in spotting and analyzing potential problems and opportunities for improvement and a consistent data management system to ensure that accurate process information is available on a timely basis;
- Extensive employee involvement in the quality improvement process;
- A system for auditing internal quality management processes; and
- A method for measuring customer needs and expectations and a process for developing new or improved products that meet those requirements.[1]

THE ENVIRONMENTAL INFORMATION CUSTOMER

Who are the customers for environmental information? The traditional response—regulators—is clearly not enough. In order to mainstream environmental information practices, designers of corporate

EMIS need to identify internal information customers. A high-level model that classifies information customers into three broad groups based on their environmental responsibilities is recommended: (1) source monitoring, (2) materials management, and (3) compliance/risk management.

Source Monitoring

Source monitoring is the broadest-based, oldest, and probably best understood type of environmental information. The original Clean Air Act and Clean Water Act created the need to record thousands of observations from monitoring equipment and/or laboratory reports and periodically report them against standards or permit levels. Hundreds of subsequent federal, state, and regional regulatory programs have dictated similar reporting requirements for PCBs, underground storage tanks, fugitive emissions, groundwater monitoring wells, and other emission sources.

Most companies have a handle on meeting these requirements at the plant level. Usually each facility assigns one or more engineers to collect the data and produce required reports for each source type. The data collection procedures, software, and database reliability usually vary from plant to plant, however, and are based on the experience and innovations of the individual responsible for the reporting task. This variation makes it difficult to compile and compare data across the corporation or business unit and leaves the company vulnerable to compliance failure when an individual leaves the company or plant.

Standardization, integration, and feedback are the principal ben-

---

Figure 1

Customer Profile: Source Monitoring

Typical Client:	Engineers	
Orientation:	Tasks	
Typical Needs:	Water Treatment	Tank Testing
	Groundwater	PCBs
	Fugitive Emissions	Asbestos
	Stack Emissions	Soil
	Air Emissions	Exposure Monitoring
Integration:	Low	
Data Types & Volumes:	Results by Source	
	High Volume	

efits that corporatewide EMIS charged with source monitoring responsibilities can provide:

- Standardized tools and procedures reduce variation in the data management process, are more cost-effective than dozens of individually designed procedures, and reduce the company's vulnerability when engineers change jobs or companies.
- Integration of data into corporate data systems can reduce the time and cost of data capture and make source data available to other environmental and process information systems.
- Feedback of results to engineers and other workers managing processes and procedures is an essential aspect of the quality cycle.

Materials Management

Materials management is emerging as the most complex and costly field in environmental information management. Waste management requirements originally mandated by RCRA and the inventory accounting requirements originating with SARA have been amended and supplemented by state and regional requirements to create the need for "cradle to grave" tracking of hazardous materials, wastes, and waste containers. Originally these data procedures had the character of exception reporting, in which the storing or disposal of hazardous materials was estimated for listed substances. Now they are beginning to resemble financial accounting, as each hazardous material's life cycle on a property must be recorded as purchases; shipments;

Figure 2

Customer Profile: Materials Management

Typical Client:	Plant or Process Manager
Orientation:	Processes
Typical Needs:	Chemical Inventory
	Waste Management
	Container Tracking
	Emissions Balances (313, AB 2588, etc.)
Integration:	High
Data Types & Volumes:	Calculations and Reports
	Moderate Volume, High Complexity

inventory; transfers; transformations; manifests; and releases to the air, water, groundwater, and other media.

Materials management professionals have complex information requirements that need to draw on virtually every aspect of plant information, but several factors have kept their information tool kit at a primitive level:

1. Material Safety Data Sheets (MSDS), the basic source of hazardous component information for products, are nonstandard, change continuously, and vary tremendously in quality. Most plants and firms expend a tremendous effort just to store the physical sheets according to HAZCOM requirements. Capturing the sheet information as data for materials management is an expensive task that accounts for a large share of most firms' environmental information management budget.

2. Although many plants producing similar product lines may use many of the same chemicals, the decentralization of environmental data management responsibilities has meant that data capture of hazardous materials must be repeated at each plant.

3. Corporate environmental, health, and safety functions all require access to accurate MSDS data. However, the evolution of these corporate functions has usually isolated information into at least two separate departments. Without a centralized database, both departments must capture and manage data on the same sheets.

Individual plants typically develop or contract with consultants to provide chemical life-cycle reports (Form R) on a project basis, using the best available data and professional judgments. Now overlapping regulations are beginning to highlight the lack of replicability of many current emission estimating procedures. California's Air Toxic Hot Spots program (AB 2588) requires reporting on many of the same chemicals covered by SARA 313 (Form R). In the first cycle of 2588 reports, some plants' emissions reports varied by order of magnitude due to differences in data sources and estimation techniques.

The magnitude of the materials management data tasks has largely kept managers busy with the work of data capture and accounting, with little time to analyze the data products for use in source reduction or other pollution prevention efforts. Integrating these procedures into corporate quality data systems will have several key benefits:

1. As in source reporting, corporatewide automation tools will

reduce variation and costs for materials management. And although transaction data are specific to plants, corporate chemical libraries can reduce the enormous efforts required in plant-by-plant MSDS capture.

2. Much of the data required for environmental materials management are currently tracked in other data streams. Competitive pressures are forcing companies to develop integrated MRP systems for materials management functions such as purchases, shipments, and inventory. These data streams can be accessed to create reliable, replicable transaction sets for environmental materials management.

3. The close vendor relationships mandated by quality systems can be an opportunity for electronic data sharing. Electronic Data Interchange (EDI) standards for transactions such as purchase orders and transmittal of test results have already led to great efficiencies in vendor-customer transactions. In July 1990, the EPA approved the ANSI X12 committee to set standards for environmental EDI. The ANSI X12 standard for Material Safety Data Sheets has been approved and is undergoing pilot implementation. EDI standards for other key environmental data transactions are expected to follow in the early 1990s.

Environmental Quality Management

The corporate environmental manager has the responsibility of identifying corporate environmental responsibilities and developing programs to meet them. This role was once seen as "compliance

Figure 3

Customer Profile:
Environmental Quality Management

Typical Client:	Corporate Environmental Managers
Orientation:	Programs
Typical Needs:	Compliance Tracking
	Auditing
	Prioritization
	Crisis Management
	Program Development
	Permitting
Integration:	Highest
Data Types & Volumes:	Summaries and Exceptions
	Low Volume

management," but most companies now realize that mere regulatory compliance is inadequate. Corporate exposure to liabilities and risks based on their property holdings and operations extends far beyond that defined by current rules and regulations.

The risk manager needs to see a relatively low volume of highly integrated information. He or she must track rules, requirements, and liabilities across multiple plants and states and provide guidance and critical information to "nonenvironmental" decision makers in real estate, insurance, and financial departments as well as operations. It is impossible for corporate managers to review all these data in a meaningful way, so they rely on plant and division environmental managers to fulfill program requirements and provide environmental data on a summary and exception basis.

Although risk management is a top level responsibility, the corporate manager typically must rely on qualitative information that varies in quality and completeness. Without centralized, standardized information tools, the compliance audit is the key tool for assuring that corporate guidelines are being followed. The best corporate audit protocols attempt to provide a standardized system of reviewing and scoring environmental performance. They are typically conducted only annually, however, due to the expense involved in these "postprocess" inspection procedures. True quality environmental management systems require continuous quantitative measurement tools to support continuous improvement.

INTEGRATED ENVIRONMENTAL INFORMATION MANAGEMENT SYSTEMS

Integrated EMIS should provide timely, accurate data to support all three types of environmental management responsibilities: results and comparison reports for source management; material and waste transaction and emission reports for materials management; and compliance, summary, exception, and trend data for risk managers at every level.

Environmental managers at Florida Power & Light (FP&L), the first American company to win the prestigious Deming Prize for quality, recognized these needs early on due to the exacting data requirements of the award application process. FP&L's Deming quest, which began in 1985, focused on the principle of "policy deployment."

Policy deployment requires implementation of corporatewide information systems to analyze problems and structure solutions for which progress against goals can be measured continuously. FP&L

adopted a Quality Improvement Program (QIP) story format that requires program managers to answer a series of process-related questions in recognizing planning, implementing, and tracking improvement opportunities.

Joe Sicbaldi of FP&L's Environmental Affairs Department was involved from the beginning in developing corporate information tools to support quality improvements in company environmental practices. "The QIP story doesn't let you get away with broad 'motherhood' programs," he says. "The analytical requirements are rigorous and force you to identify and verify root causes for problems and specific, achievable, measurable actions to correct them."

FP&L implemented integrated corporatewide environmental information tools to support specific needs at all three EMIS functions: air, asbestos, and water reporting tools for source management; chemical inventory and manifest tracking for materials management; and an environmental events module to record occurrence and resolution of any violation or noncompliance. Much of the system was available off the shelf from a commercial vendor, and FP&L worked with its vendor to develop additional functions and customizations. Through this process and using EMIS, Florida Power & Light reduced total environmental nonconformance by 45 percent and the submittal of environmental reports by more than 85 percent.

CONCLUDING THOUGHTS

The challenge of Total Quality Environmental Management is more managerial than technical. The technological advances in pollution prevention have far outstripped industry's ability to implement them, and in fact many environmental "fixes" are procedural rather than technological. By implementing consistent, corporatewide tools for all three EMIS functions, managers will be able to shift their sights from the clerical burden of compliance reporting to continuous improvement toward pollution prevention.

Note
1.   A. Gabor, *The Man Who Discovered Quality*, pp. 270-271 (Times Books, a division of Random House, New York, 1990).

27

THE POWER OF *IT*: HOW CAN INFORMATION TECHNOLOGY SUPPORT TQEM?

Lynn Johannson

Business is undergoing unprecedented changes. With the globalization of markets, the opening of international trade borders, growing customer demands for environmentally friendly products, and spiraling government controls, competition is taking on a whole new meaning. Organizations must make evolutionary changes at revolutionary rates to play in this market. It is fast becoming a truly international market—even from the comfort of your own home office.

To be able to compete in this aggressive climate, one must, as Campbell's Soup (and others) affirm, "do the right things right." This approach is not based on good luck. It is the result of planning, doing, checking, and acting on information focused on improving your product, process, and service to meet customer needs. As any quality manager knows, customer needs have a habit of changing. The speed of these changes can be frightening to those who are not trained or who lack the appropriate tools. It is less of a barrier to those who are familiar and comfortable with constant change. For those with the right tools and knowledge base, change is not only accepted, but also sought with the same enthusiasm as skiing on fresh powder, teeing off on a new course, or riding the curl of a wave.

In this column we are going to explore how the power of information technology (IT) can reinforce your effectiveness in

---

Lynn Johannson is the director of E2 Management Corporation in Georgetown, Ontario.

applying quality management to ecological (environmental) issues. Information technology is one of the fastest growing industries, and has, in fact, been described by Nuala Beck, a well-known Canadian business consultant, as one of the engines that is driving the new economic era. Businesses are realizing that environmental management is among the highest corporate priorities. In fact, IT provided us with the evidence of mankind's impact on the environment when space exploration gave us our first truly global perspective.

Supporters of this global perspective include such groups as the International Chamber of Commerce (ICC), Canada's National Round Table on the Environment and the Economy (NTREE), and the U.S.-based Global Environmental Management Initiative (GEMI). But many organizations remain in a quandary as to how to effectively use this knowledge and rise to meet the challenges of this new global economy.

As shown in **Exhibit 1**, *Ecology*, the science of the structure and function of nature, and *quality*, the management science of human values in qualitative and quantitative forms, share common elements with *information technology*. IT provides a skill base and a systems perspective that enhance the two sciences, forming an important triad.

Exhibit 1

The Ecology, Quality, and Information Technology Triad

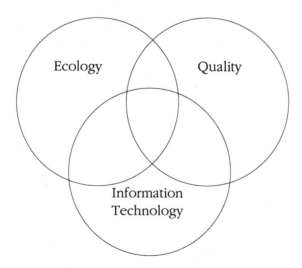

To best understand how ecology, quality and information technology interrelate, a brief explanation is in order. Ecology refers to the structure and function of nature of whatever system you are a part of.

Quality, in its broadest sense, is anything that can be improved. In the TQEM context, quality is not only associated with products and services; but it also includes the way people work, the way machines are operated, the way systems and procedures are dealt with, *and the ecological systems involved in the creation of the product, process, and service.* It includes all aspects of human behavior. Frequently the term *kaizen* (meaning improvement) is used. *Kaizen* assumes that our way of life—be it working, in a social context, our home life—deserves to be constantly and forever improved.

Information technology is not just data. It encompasses computer and telecommunication products and services that allow access to data, with the means of access and options that are astounding.

At the risk of beating a dead horse, remember that once the philosophical acceptance of quality is achieved, the act of improvement requires an ongoing assessment of customer needs. Why? *The basis for making decisions founded on quality, environmental quality, is improved information.* Hence information technology, the use of computer and telecommunication products and services, forms a crucial link in meeting the goals of this new economic era. IT will be instrumental in the development of sustainable products, processes, and services that will allow your organization to thrive in the new economy. (See **Appendix** for an outline of general benefits.)

To assist your understanding of how IT can make your total quality environmental management process more effective, I contacted a number of experts whose services, products, or experience demonstrate the power of IT.

RICHARD UNDERWOOD, NASA

Our first respondent is Richard Underwood, now retired, who served as the technical assistant to the director of photography and television technology for the National Aeronautic and Space Agency (NASA). He lectures around the world using an incredible collection of slides to show the rate and extent of environmental changes that have occurred over the last three decades. I have started the responses with Richard Underwood's, as it provides us with an understanding of how IT and space exploration initiated the environmental movement by giving us a truly global perspective, and reinforces the need to make TQEM a global process.

"For more than thirty years space photographs have captured on film the Third Planet," Underwood says. "One may well ask, 'What was the value of those NASA trips to the moon more than twenty years ago?' I believe that the greatest value, by far, was the fact that they went translunar 'blunt end forward.' That is, they never saw the moon until they were in orbit about it. The window always looked back to planet Earth getting smaller and smaller each passing minute. It gave them their psychological connection to the home planet.

"Christmas in 1968, Frank Borman said it best as he was about to make the first lunar orbit. *'Planet Earth, I can hold out my thumb and block it out.'* It is truly a minor planet going around a minor star near the edge of a minor galaxy. Not very important in the great celestial scheme, but it is the only planet we have and we must take better care of it, or we may very well lose it.

"Being in the space photo business since it began, I feel that those photos of a small disk (Earth) against the pitch blackness of space have changed the world. I had the great fortune to be the first person to see them and they changed the world. Photos like AS-17-148.22727, a fully-lit earth disk, brought about the birth of the environmental movement on a worldwide basis. People saw a finite Earth for the first time. More people have seen it than any other photo in human history, and it was taken en route to the moon.

"The space photos of Earth cover large areas for a synoptic view. One can cross North America in nine minutes; thus they show the exact environmental status of vast areas with no respect for political, geographical, geomorphic, or any other type of boundary.

"For instance, over thirty years of space photos have shown the rapid growth of African deserts due to imprudent land use procedures of primitive people. It has determined why it happened, recorded by the destruction of vast areas, and clearly shows what will happen: the destruction of many tens of millions of people in the next two decades. What we predicted twenty (and more) years ago is now headlines from the Somali situation. The power of customs and religion will destroy everything. Somalia, unfortunately, is but the tip of the iceberg. It may well develop into the human equivalent of a 'feedlot' mentality. The predictable cause and effect have been clearly seen in space photographs for a quarter century, but, alas, nobody would listen. And, of course, today we clearly see the destruction of worldwide rain forests (and other forests); the polluting of oceans, rivers, lakes, etc; industrial environmental problems, the destruction of arable lands, acid rains, etc., all clearly seen worldwide in the space photography. The space photos of the former Soviet Union showed unbelievable environmental disaster and were dismissed as merely anti-Soviet propaganda from the United States. Then the great wall was knocked down in Berlin and the light of reason crossed Eastern Europe and beyond the Urals toward the Pacific. The horrors seen from space are in no way propaganda.

"The potential use of the Space Station for understanding the worldwide environmental situation and then having the knowledge to take proactive action is unlimited. But, alas, nobody listens."

DAVID OLSON, GEOMATICS INTERNATIONAL

Our second respondent is David Olson, U.S. operations manager for Geomatics International, who shares information on a specific information tool and its applications. Geomatics International is an environmental consulting firm specializing in the use of Geographic Information System (GIS) and remote sensing technologies for mapping, analysis, and management of environmental and natural resources.

"For those readers who have not had exposure to GIS technology previously, it should be thought of as an information integration and analysis tool. GIS is a computer database that stores information in a form that relates data attributes or conditions to spatial locations—i.e., a line that represents a road being identified by type, traffic volume, bearing capacity, construction material, or other criteria. Any information that can be tied to a geographic location can be sorted, displayed, analyzed, and reported. Almost any function that can be done in more familiar types of databases can be done with GIS, in addition to many types of spatial and temporal analysis that standard databases cannot do.

"GIS has evolved over the last thirty years, beginning primarily as a mapping tool and more recently as a practical, powerful, and flexible analysis tool. Many societies, such as the American Society of Cartographers and Surveyors, American Society of Photogrammetric Engineering and Remote Sensing; periodicals, such as GIS World and Geo Info Systems; as well as many symposiums and conferences coordinate, report, and track developments in GIS technology for many different application areas, including environmental management. GIS is a rapidly maturing technology that has just recently made the transition from dedicated mainframe computers and complex software with large learning curves to a flexible, easily upgradable and intuitive graphical user interface analytical tool accessible to PCs and nondedicated users. This reduction in complexity and cost, coupled with greater analytical capability, has opened many new areas of economically attractive applications for this technology.

"Some examples of applications which directly relate to environmental management include

Network Analysis—Use road information to select the shortest path for hazardous material transportation routes that represent logistical or operating constraints, such as maximum load-bearing capacity, avoidance of schools or high population density areas and sensitive resources, scheduling to avoid heavy traffic volumes, or other criteria that would result in reduced risk and optimized efficiency.

Emergency Response—Use selected routes and transfer schedules to track transport of materials so that in the event of an incident or problem the shipment can be quickly located and all of the appropriate agencies and authorities notified, as well as potential environmental impact pre-evaluated. This application can also be used to analyze the placement of rapid response equipment and materials to be able to respond with the appropriate resources within designated performance objectives.

Visual Impact Assessment—Generate perspective views of planned projects to determine visual impacts of facilities before they are built for the permit and public review process. This application can also identify locations that an object can be seen from—e.g., from what locations would you be able to see an exhaust stack that is one hundred feet tall in this location and how will it look from those perspectives.

Point Source Dispersion Models—Almost any mathematical model that has been developed, from atmospheric to wind tunnel, can be applied to GIS. Many models significantly improve from incorporating spatial and temporal elements that can be integrated in GIS modelling—e.g., running a model of dispersion of exhaust from a smoke stack using wind speed, direction, temperature, and humidity information for an entire year from a data recorder on the stack to estimate the average deliveries to the surrounding areas. These data can be used for reporting or controlling emissions during certain weather conditions to reduce impacts on high population areas or sensitive resources.

Non-Point Source Pollution Modeling—This type of application is even more dependent on GIS technology, because much of this type of analysis becomes complex with multivariate factors to the extent that the relationships are not 'humanly graspable' in their entirety. An example that we recently finished was to calculate the amount of fertilizer nutrients that can be transported into Lake Erie. This analysis takes into account the type of crop grown, the fertilizer treatment, the soil type, the drainage, the tillage practices, proximity to the lake, and interactions of the fertilizer with sediment and aquatic plants. Imagine all of these variables over a hundred square miles and you have a task that is not humanly graspable, but is relatively easy for GIS once the scientific relationships of the variables have been defined and the database of the conditions has been mapped.

"In addition to improvements in the quality and timeliness of analyses, the analysis of processes, too complex and variable to be accomplished otherwise, GIS also improves communication through geographical representation of information. Some government agencies, like the Washington State Department of Natural Resources, are already requiring that regulation compliance reporting to their agency is in GIS-compatible formats. It should be expected that as this tool continues to grow in usage, the trend for agencies to require reporting in their specifications for compliance and monitoring will grow as well.

"As with any tool, if GIS is diligently applied to the appropriate types of tasks, it can make significant qualitative improvements to and impacts on operations and provide a good return on your investment. The best advice is while looking for ways to continuously improve products, services and efficiency, make a serious evaluation of this tool, learn where it can work for you, and begin to take advantage of a technology that has an incredible amount to offer for total quality efforts in environmental or natural resource management."

DOUG ARCHIBALD, SESI

Our last respondent is Doug Archibald, president of SESI, a firm that markets software technology developed to assist organizations in the management of hazardous materials.

"In this age of high technology the emphasis has been on *technology* and how technology can be utilized to improve quality of life, corporate results, health care, etc.

"At SESI our emphasis is on *information* and how technology can be used to provide more timely, accurate, and current information. Information is the lifeblood of industry and commerce and must be available instantly to all levels of management to facilitate the decision-making process.

"As we march toward the next century, all sectors of the global economy are coming under intense pressure from the citizenry (through all levels of government) to become more and more environmentally and ecologically conscious of their effects on our globe.

"These same sectors are also under intense economic pressure from shareholders to continually provide maximum return on investment. These demands are, to a certain extent, mutually exclusive; however, this will not be the first time that business and industry have addressed and overcome this conundrum. The key to decreasing or negating these pressures is the prudent and strategic use of information in a timely manner.

"The original principles of data processing have not changed dramatically in the past forty years—the technology that allows us to enter, store, update, manipulate, access, display, transmit, and secure data has changed dramatically over the past forty years—indeed, over the past ten years.

"There is absolutely no excuse for corporations of all sizes not to have access to information that is necessary to ensure successful and profitable operations. The software currently available and under development at SESI is designed to ensure that data, once entered, can be used, reused, processed, and reprocessed to provide the information necessary to support the complete function of management, which demands timely decision making based on accurate and current information.

"The starting point for all information systems is the establishment of accurate and comprehensive databases. Data entry technology is becoming available that is lessening this onerous task—e.g., scanners.

"These databases, once established, must be kept current by the daily transactions of the business—e.g., wastes produced (by type and quantity), at which processes, exactly where the wastes are stored and exactly how much is stored there, wastes shipped (again by type and quantity), sites to where the wastes are shipped, which company transported which wastes, etc.

"It is apparent that the information available in the database can be used to produce (virtually at the push of a button) regulatory documentation—e.g., manifests, NPRI reports, environmental ministries reports and summaries, TRI reports, storage facility information, and transportation information. These data are also available for the provision of information to management at all levels to make decisions relative to operations, storage, treatment, transportation, and disposition of toxic wastes and hazardous materials produced and used during the production process.

"Timely use of the available information also ensures that the corporate executives, officers, and directors are informed as to the corporation's adherence to EPA/CEPA regulations."

SUMMARY

The power of IT therefore can be summarized as follows:

Technology provides the tool, information provides knowledge, and knowledge is power.

The age-old expression "a picture is worth a thousand words" comes to mind when sitting through one of Dick Underwood's presentations. It would be hard to imagine how someone could not grasp the need to change when exposed to pictorial proof of our impacts on this planet.

David Olson's explanation of GIS and its applications and Doug Archibald's description of the power that good software provides its users are intended to expand your TQEM toolbox and assist you in the implementation of your TQEM goals. As change is a constant, these tools will allow managers to be more effective with stewardship and efficient in the use of resources, leading to greater competencies in the TQEM process. We all share the responsibility for the rate of change that the globe is experiencing. We are fast being held accountable for the results of these changes. A focus on compliance is not the answer. Define who your customers are in the context of TQEM and determine what their needs are. The faster we can input and synthesize data leading to better decision making, the sooner we will be able to achieve sustainable development using these new tools as part of our TQEM toolbox.

Thank you to David, Richard, and Doug for sharing these tools with us. Thanks also goes to Nuala Beck's "Shifting Gears," ITAC's Barry Gander, and Rosemary Walsh from Stentor Telecom Policy Inc. for assisting in the research of the power of IT.

Appendix

The benefits of IT are described by the Information Technology Association of Canada (ITAC) in a five-level process referred to as the "Enabling Effect" (see "Things Change," ITAC, September 1992).

Level 1—Cost Reduction
Dramatic reductions in costs—direct and indirect—for such things as energy, materials, labor, and transportation, typically soon after implementation.

Level 2—Quality Enhancement
Minimize breakdowns, shorten delivery delays, eliminate product defects and close client-product expectation gaps, typically early in the implementation.

Level 3—New Products and Services
Launch an organization into new, IT-dependent product areas.

Level 4—Enhanced Strategic Management
More productive use of management time and better information to see where to focus, deploy resources, set standards, uncover deficiencies, forecast, plan, and analyze.

Level 5—New Concepts and Models
Some applications are new concepts themselves; some are so influential that the workplace of five years ago is unrecognizable.

John T. Willig is the editor of the quarterly journal *Total Quality Environmental Management*, published by Executive Enterprises. A long-time expert in the field, he is based in Norwood, New Jersey.

Executive Enterprises Publications Co., Inc. (New York, New York) is a professional management education organization whose activities include the development and presentation of business-related conferences, books, and periodicals.